PRAISE FOR *THE VINYL DIARIES*

"[*The Vinyl Diaries*] is a music book unlike any you've ever read, filled with the soundtrack of a city—apartment to apartment, bedroom to bedroom—and fizzing with torrid and emotional sex. Lots of sex. A thrilling read."
—Dave Bidini, singer, songwriter, newspaper publisher and bestselling author of *On a Cold Road* and *Midnight Light*

"A delightful, funny, moving and insightful account of one listener's love affair with music and his burgeoning queerness."
—Torquil Campbell of Stars

"Pete Crighton writes of music, lust and love like a journal of historic hookups amongst the backdrop of yesterday's songs. [*The Vinyl Diaries*] is funny, sexy and truthfully dirty with a hurt we all need to feel when sharing a stereo next to someone's heartbeat."
—Kevin Drew of Broken Social Scene

"In *The Vinyl Diaries* Pete Crighton took me on a mind-blowing tour of his epic record collection AND let me ride shotgun on his even more epic sexcapades. Now it's your turn—lucky you."
—Elvira Kurt, comedian and writer for *Canada's Drag Race*

"Pete Crighton's *The Vinyl Diaries* is a thrill ride! Filled with hook-ups, queer connections and a one-of-a-kind playlist, this sexy page turner will warm your heart."
—Mae Martin, writer, performer and creator of *Feel Good*

"*The Vinyl Diaries* is a coming-of-middle-age story about confronting fear and daring to live your best queer life."
—Rachel Matlow, author of *Dead Mom Walking*

"A queer *High Fidelity*. Totally engrossing . . . Pete Crighton is a modern-day Pan: horny, bearded, with a highball glass in one hand and an LP in the other. His story is told without an ounce of cynicism, just the voice of a true lover of music and men."
—Marcus McCann, author of *Park Cruising*

"The core of Pete Crighton's *The Vinyl Diaries* is passion: a palpable and intense passion for art and music that bleeds into his journey through love, sex, fear, aging, and pandemics . . . *The Vinyl Diaries* is not only a fully entertaining, relatable, funny, sexy page turner, it inspired me to search beyond my rather limited musical tastes to an appreciation of all things Yoko Ono. This memoir sings."
—David Pevsner, author of *Damn Shame*

"*The Vinyl Diaries* is a life-affirming journey through music and queerness. Like the greatest pop songs, it speaks directly and personally of love, longing, and belonging."
—Jordan Tannahill, author of *The Listeners*

"A triumph . . . When you ask your music/sex-loving queer bestie to tell you everything—and he tells you everything. Like everything. Prepare to blush, gasp and pump your fist in the air with pure queer joy."
—Carolyn Taylor, *Baroness von Sketch Show* and *I Have Nothing*

THE VINYL DIARIES

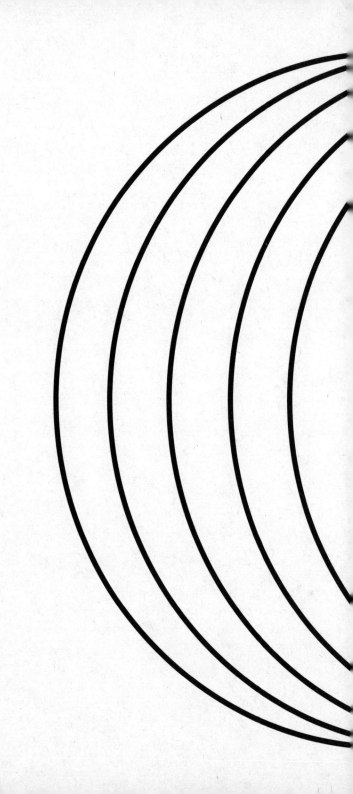

THE VINYL DIARIES

SEX, DEEP CUTS AND
MY SOUNDTRACK TO QUEER JOY

PETE CRIGHTON

RANDOM
HOUSE
CANADA

PUBLISHED BY RANDOM HOUSE CANADA

Copyright © 2025 Peter Crighton

Random House Canada, an imprint of Penguin Random House Canada Limited
320 Front Street West, Suite 1400
Toronto, Ontario, M5V 3B6, Canada
penguinrandomhouse.ca

The authorized representative in the EU for product safety and compliance is Penguin Random House Ireland, Morrison Chambers, 32 Nassau Street, Dublin D02 YH68, Ireland. https://eu-contact.penguin.ie

Some names and identifying characteristics have been changed to protect the privacy of individuals.

LIBRARY AND ARCHIVES CANADA CATALOGUING IN PUBLICATION
Title: The vinyl diaries : sex, deep cuts, and my soundtrack to queer joy / Pete Crighton.
Names: Crighton, Pete, author.
Description: Includes bibliographical references and index.
Identifiers: Canadiana (print) 20240447999 | Canadiana (ebook) 20240452526 |
    ISBN 9781039011076 (softcover) | ISBN 9781039011083 (EPUB)
Subjects: LCSH: Crighton, Pete. | LCSH: Crighton, Pete—Sexual behavior. | LCSH:
    Gay men—Ontario—Toronto—Biography. | LCSH: Gay men—Sexual behavior—
    Ontario—Toronto. | LCSH: Self-acceptance. | LCGFT: Autobiographies.
Classification: LCC HQ75.8.C75 A3 2025 | DDC 306.76/62092—dc23

Cover design: Lisa Jager
Text design: Lisa Jager
Typesetting: Erin Cooper
Image credits: (vinyl) sponge_Po, (couple) Louis-Photo / both Adobe Stock

Printed in Canada

9 8 7 6 5 4 3 2 1

Penguin
Random House
RANDOM HOUSE CANADA

This book is dedicated to my dear friend Carolyn.

Thank you for constantly telling me to "write it down."
This book would not have been made without your support,
your belief in me and your gentle bullying.

PRELUDE

It was a beautiful March day, the first of its kind when you think winter is almost over. I was in the window seat of one of my favourite queer bars, Lipstick & Dynamite (RIP), on Toronto's Queen Street West, with a handful of close friends, a sextet of gay men ranging from their thirties into their sixties. The sun shone through the window and refracted through the many pints of beer littered around the table—a literal gay rainbow spread across the detritus of our drinking.

My boyfriend Christopher and I were still in the flush of a relationship newly started; we had only been dating five or six months by then and were still figuring out how we fit into each other's lives. He was very physically demonstrative in front of his friends, constantly touching my arm, rubbing my back, placing his hand on my inner thigh and holding my hand. I felt so comforted by his love, by his attentions. I wasn't used to this kind of affection, especially in public.

We drank, we laughed, we listened to music, but the mood was heavy.

It was March 15, 2020, and we all knew we likely shouldn't be gathered together. COVID-19 was a virus we'd been hearing about with increasing frequency and there were rumours floating around that a lockdown of schools, workplaces and non-essential retail would be announced the following day. While not much was known about the virus, what was being communicated through the media was that COVID-19 was wildly contagious and potentially deadly.

It was all happening so fast, and my friends and I were making the most of our last taste of freedom.

That afternoon I was putting on a brave face. We all were, I think. We weren't ready to accept the possibility of a plague, but we also knew that one was creeping ever closer to us.

There we were, sun-dappled, beer-buzzed and facing an uncertain future together. We talked about stocking up on booze and edibles; let the straight folks fight it out for toilet paper and canned vegetables. We gays had our priorities. It seemed as if we were heading on a short adventure: separate and apart.

The speculation in the media was that the lockdown would only last for a couple of weeks. We'd all work from home for a short time and then life would go back to normal. Easy peasy.

Turns out we were wrong. Very, very, very wrong.

A group of gay men of different generations sitting around a bar and debating a pandemic: there was something eerily familiar about that scene.

Little did I know I was facing the second plague of my lifetime. This time, hiding was not an option.

SIDE ONE

AQUARIUS/LET THE SUNSHINE IN (THE FLESH FAILURES)

I was born on April 5, 1969, in Toronto and immediately my life kind of went on pause. My birth mother put me up for adoption and those first few months of my life are a bit of a mystery. *Que sera*, who remembers their first few months anyway? But this is not that story.

The number one record at the time was "Aquarius/Let the Sunshine In (The Flesh Failures)" by the 5th Dimension—an appropriate, or perhaps fitting, record to see me into this world.

It was a song celebrating the hippie movement that was nearing its end and would be decidedly over by December 1969, when four rock 'n' roll fans were killed at Altamont, a music festival headlined by the Rolling Stones with security provided by the Hells Angels (who ever thought that would end well?).

June 5, 1969, is a sort of second birthday for me; when my life really started, as I know it, anyway. I was adopted by a "typical" middle-class family, back when there still was a middle class. My mom and dad had had a son almost five years earlier and decided it was time to add one more to the family. Lucky me, I got plucked from who knows what other fate might have been waiting for me.

When I say lucky, I mean it. My parents took great care of me and provided me with countless opportunities to better myself in this world. Most of those I would fuck up.

Our nuclear family of four lived in a tiny two-bedroom bungalow on a quiet street in the east end of Toronto. It felt like the suburbs to me, but in fact was only a twenty-minute drive to downtown.

Artist and writer Douglas Coupland inadvertently named my generation when he published his debut novel *Generation X: Tales for an Accelerated Culture* in 1991, even though the term existed before his book did. A lot of my peers in Generation X who had been adopted really struggled with it. There was still an air of scandal and secrecy around adoption in the 1970s; most adoptions were brokered by religious organizations, who shamed the often unwed mothers. We were bastard children born out of wedlock! Being adopted truly never bothered me, though. I think in the back of my mind I always knew I had a bigger war to wage.

The number one song those short two months later was the Beatles' "Get Back," from their final album, *Let It Be*. The end of the hippies, the end of the Beatles. The sixties were truly over. I am definitively a child of the seventies.

The seventies were almost too crazy to be true, and music was everywhere. Variety shows ruled the TV airwaves and I watched the collective acid trip that was *The Sonny & Cher Show*, *The Captain and Tennille*, *Donny & Marie* and *The Muppet Show*, to name only a few. Fever dreams all. We also had *Soul Train* and *Dance Fever* on the air; these two shows introduced me to a world of disco, R & B and soul music. AM radio played the hits of the day and FM radio played pretty much anything at all. My dad listened to his Shirley Bassey and Ella Fitzgerald records sporadically while my mom spun Barbra Streisand and Neil Diamond.

My musical influences were vast, and I was taking them all in.

The first 45 rpm single record I can recall having was "Puppy Love" by Donny Osmond. It was the number one song in Canada in 1972, three years after my two birthdays. I'm not exactly sure how it found its way into our home, but I wore the damn thing out. Even at three years of age, I swooned for Donny. I played the song so often I barely took it off the turntable. My brother and I shared a shitty little portable plastic record player, and one day I left it near the window in the sun with my favourite record still on it. The next morning I found the red Polydor label had bled onto the plastic turntable and the disc itself was warped. There were tears. Many tears. (Donny was never quite the same.)

An important lesson was learned that day: don't leave your records in the sun.

While it seems incredible that I was listening to records at that age, the family lore supports it. My mom tells me that whenever I heard music I liked, I would dance and move to the beat with my eyes closed, as though I was in a different world. I was.

At the age of three I could barely talk, but my love of music was clear.

I started asking for music to be played more and more around the house. The radio, my parents' old records, my brother's few albums, the family eight-track player—it didn't matter, I wanted sound. I wanted to move.

The first full-length LP that my mom bought for me was the Jackson 5's *Goin' Back to Indiana*. This was not planned. I desperately wanted a copy of the Bay City Rollers' new album, but it was sold out at the local record store in a strip mall near our house. The Scottish lads were riding high on their hit song "Saturday Night" in 1975 and had released a compilation record in North America I was hot for.

The Jacksons' record had been released in 1971 (following a television special, naturally), so it's curious that the record store clerk steered me towards it in the rack of "best sellers." Maybe they were getting rid of excess inventory? Who knows, but with songs by the Jacksons, Sly Stone and Isaac Hayes, plus a strange appearance by Bill Cosby (eww), maybe it was meant to be? The Jacksons were sure funkier than the Bay City Rollers.

I was disappointed with the makeshift purchase, but I soon learned to love my new record. It was mine and I invested in it by playing the album again and again until I found my groove with it. Eventually, I fell in love with *Goin' Back to Indiana*. My brother would marvel that I could drop the needle on the exact spot of my favourite piano run on "I Want You Back." A budding DJ and lifetime fan of Motown records was born.

I was only in grade one or two at the time but had already started to notice that there were things boys weren't supposed to like. The Bay City Rollers definitely fell into that camp, alongside playing with dolls, skipping rope, jumpsies and other activities only girls were allowed to engage in. If a boy showed any affinity for these things, as I did, they were scorned. Outcast. Maybe the record store clerk was looking out for me. I definitely had feelings for those Scottish lads that I didn't understand.

I hid my fandom for a lot of things I loved during those years, keeping my desires to myself. No more disco for me. No more playing *Grease* and *Saturday Night Fever* soundtracks on loop, at least not when other friends or classmates were within earshot. And let's not even talk about the Village People. These were things that only girls were supposed to like. And boys who liked things that girls liked were fags. Plain and simple.

I started to learn how to keep secrets.

Even though I was learning to hide things about myself, the other boys at school still seemed to have me figured out. I got picked last for sports teams, was ostracized from schoolyard games and didn't get invited to other boys' homes (save one, thanks Mike!), and when they started to call me fag in the schoolyard, circa grade two, that was it. The girls at school became my solace; they weren't threatened by whatever I was. And to be clear, I had no idea what I was.

Another important lesson was learned from that period. Sometimes it's the records we have to put the most work into, by listening to them repeatedly with focus, like that Jackson 5 album, that turn out to be our favourites, that have lasting power, and not the ones that we are immediately drawn to. This is true for so many other things in life: relationships, books, friendships, art. I'm glad I learned that lesson early.

I was eleven years old by the time I bought my first record with my own allowance money, and I had only one target in my sights. Thankfully, it wasn't sold out this time. The B-52s' eponymously titled first record came out in 1979, and when I first heard "Rock Lobster" on the radio, I needed to have it. It was the wildest and craziest thing I had ever heard in my life up to that point, and I loved it. Deeply.

My choice of the B-52s was an interesting one. The band was not a schoolyard favourite. Maybe a college crowd favourite, but not many eleven-year-olds were freaking out to "Dance This Mess Around." Their music sent me down a path of exploring what was new, what was different. I decided then and there that the mainstream wasn't for me.

Lucky for me, as the mainstream didn't want much to do with me, either.

I learned another important lesson from that seminal B-52s record: weird can be good.

The B-52s was the start of a vinyl avalanche. Every spare penny I had went towards buying new records. When I got my first part-time job, at a curling rink, cleaning the ice and clearing empty beer bottles and full ashtrays from tables, I started to make what felt like real money! I tracked my pay by how many records I could buy per hour, per shift. For birthdays and Christmas, the only thing I asked for was new vinyl. I would make lists and hope and pray. Those wishes were mostly granted.

My album collection grew rapidly, and I cherished it like nothing else in my life. Music was my pride and joy. It is still my pride and joy.

I demonstrated some musical ability in grade school on the recorder, but the idea of learning an instrument was never a path offered, nor one I asked to take. It's something I have always regretted.

In high school I had countless crushes on straight guys, oftentimes the ones who shunned me and called me a fag. This was very confusing to my developing brain. Why do I want to touch these bullies? My solution? I'll date girls, that'll fool them! In grades nine and ten I dated two different young women, Lisa and Jackie (sorry to you both). The first was a classic grade nine romance that mainly involved passing notes in class and telling people we were a "thing" while we mostly avoided spending time together. I wonder, was she hiding something too? As for my grade ten girlfriend, we made some overtures at a physical connection with messy, but chaste, teenage make out sessions, but I think it was our shared love of Canada's Spoons (who released one of the best synth/new wave albums, *Arias & Symphonies*, in 1982) that really brought us together. Neither "romance" lasted long. My next move was a classic: pretend to be in love with a girl who was completely unattainable. By professing my love for Nancy, I was able to demonstrate an interest in girls to my friends, all the while aware that there would be no consequences of my stated devotion to her. I probably wasn't kidding anyone, but at the time I thought I had it all figured out.

That was pretty much the entirety of my experience with girls. I became everyone's favourite clown instead, a role I guess I was suited to. I wore stupid clothes, went to school barefoot, skipped classes and sassed teachers—all for laughs or attention. But like Smokey Robinson's classic "The Tears of a Clown," if you looked a little closer, it was clear I wasn't having that much fun.

It took me a very long time to admit that I wanted to date a boy, let alone act on it.

When I look back at those years now, my entire youth, my entire life actually, is defined by what records I was listening to at that time. When I hear them now, it's as though I'm transported to the moment when I first heard each song, each album. I know I'm not alone in feeling this way.

That is the story of this book. My record collection. My memories. My desire. All of it soundtracked to a playlist only I could create.

The twelve-inch vinyl disc, my true love. From day one.

ANTMUSIC

My love for live music followed my passion for vinyl pretty quickly.

The very first concert I ever saw was on February 13, 1983: Adam Ant at Toronto's historic Massey Hall. Massey Hall opened its doors in 1894 and is renowned for its design and acoustics; it is a favourite stop for many touring musicians and bands. I was a thirteen-year-old kid in grade eight, headed downtown with his best friend to see his very first rock 'n' roll show. It was at Adam's peak in popularity on this side of the Atlantic; his highest-charting single, "Goody Two Shoes," had hit number twelve on the Billboard Hot 100 the day before. Adam and I were both celebrating that night, I guess!

I had come to Adam Ant several years before, when he was the front man of Adam and the Ants. I spent summers in Ontario cottage country with a friend who lived most of the year in Los Angeles. He was a devoted listener to the incredibly influential local radio station KROQ and every summer brought albums and cassettes that no one outside California, let alone north of the border, had ever heard of. The summer of 1981 he brought a vinyl copy of Adam and the Ants' *Kings of the Wild Frontier*, which was the first album he demanded I listen to that year. I was an instant fan—the drums, the call and response, the drums . . . damn those drums. Percussion was always a big part of Adam's sound, so much so that he had two drummers in the band—not a drummer and a percussionist, but two guys with full drum kits pounding out complementary rhythms.

Adam had been a student of punk and alternative music in the late seventies in London. As a young man he was hanging out at Vivienne Westwood's fetish and leather shop SEX, and was friends with and mentored by a young Malcolm McLaren (in fact Malcolm stole the original Ants collective to create Bow Wow Wow, leaving Adam without a band for a time). He was influenced by all these things: sex, leather, bondage, music, friendship, the queer community—and all of that came through in his early work and early iconography.

Adam was always true to the music, but he was equally devoted to his image and that of Adam and the Ants. The album that brought me to the band would be much maligned today. Cries of appropriation would be justifiably rampant. But in the very early days of the eighties it was perfectly okay for a white pop star to pound out tribal rhythms, mimic traditional chanting and go so far as to wear war paint on his face. Okay then, not okay today.

If you look into Adam's early work before *Kings*, as I did when I was a twelve-year-old, you'll find a wealth of sexual imagery. Album covers, pins, promotional posters—all featuring whips, leather pants, skirts and kilts with clasps and ties, absurdly high heels, individuals tied and bound, and song titles like "Whip in My Valise" and "Beat Me." I didn't really understand it, but had a sense that the imagery was connected to sex somehow, a sexual expression that wasn't part of the mainstream. Even if I didn't completely understand it, I was more than a little intrigued.

Fast-forward thirty-five years and Adam announced he would be doing a North American tour in 2016/17 to celebrate the thirty-fifth anniversary of the formative *Kings of the Wild Frontier* album. There was no chance in hell I was missing it. To be able to bring along a sexy, tattooed, alternative boy as my date was only icing on the cake.

I had met Dustin about six months before the concert. We had chatted for a while on Scruff, a dating and hookup site for men seeking men, and I followed him on Instagram, where he had a massive following. When we first connected online, he was a twenty-two-year-old student and live-music fan who posted scantily clad pictures of himself with hashtags like #gaysofyyz and #inkedboys, as well as an equal number of photos at concerts totally unbefitting his age: Pixies, Modest Mouse, Arcade Fire, the Kills. Our exchanges were always pretty brief, and each time I received a reply I was flabbergasted. Oftentimes his replies were only a couple of words or a short sentence, but still—this beauty was chatting with me? I was forty-six at the time! Surely this gorgeous boy less than half my age wasn't actually interested, was he?

It wasn't until a year after those initial texts, when we realized we had both been at the same James Blake concert, that our online conversation got a bit deeper. With the shared experience of a fantastic show at Massey Hall, we now had a bit more in common to explore; he was almost as big a music nerd as I was! After a few attempts on my end, Dustin finally acquiesced and agreed to meet me for a beer.

It was one of those dates that surprised the shit out of me. I'd imagined a somewhat self-absorbed boy obsessed with looks, style and status, but was presented with so much more. We met at Lipstick & Dynamite (RIP) on a Sunday night and it was obvious right from the start we had great chemistry. By this point Dustin was twenty-three, totally out of my league. He walked into the bar a few minutes late with tattered jeans,

Blundstones, a leather jacket circa 1980 (think Ramones), trendy haircut, ear gauges and a big grin on his face.

"How does this keep happening to me?" I thought to myself. Dustin was gorgeous, more so than the many photos of him I had seen online, and within minutes I discovered he was a sweet and articulate man. The world of casual dating and casual sex was still quite new to me at this point, but I was starting to discover it was a hell of a lot of fun; and much to my surprise, in my mid-forties, there were a lot more young men who were interested in me than I had ever imagined.

I am attracted to men of all ages but have built a bit of a code of ethics for myself. While there is an implied power dynamic between older men and younger ones, most people get it wrong. It is almost always the younger man who holds the power in these pairings, youth and beauty trumping almost everything else in gay culture. Even with the reverse power dynamic at play, on a date with a man as young as Dustin, I'm often reluctant to make the first move. I don't want to seem like a lecherous old creep, and in Dustin's case I was more than twice his age . . . and then some. Halfway through our first beer, though, I felt his hand on my knee under the table and thought, "Great, it's on."

We chatted effortlessly about music and our respective lives—his experience as a student at York University and mine as a marketing executive for an animation company. When the waitress came over to see if we wanted another beer, it was obvious to her that something was happening. As Dustin and I smiled and gushed, holding hands across the table, she couldn't help herself and asked gleefully, "Are you guys on a first date?" Impossible to deny it, we admitted that yes, we were. I found myself revelling in the fact that this insanely cute punk rock boy was my date.

Dustin and I locked eyes . . . there was no doubt we were having another beer.

The poor guy had a school assignment to finish, so after two beers he suggested we pay up and go for a short walk. We ended up on a bench in nearby Trinity Bellwoods Park overlooking the off-leash dog run and almost instantly our faces and our bodies connected. A couple of hours of pent-up desire led to two horny boys making out on a Sunday night in the park like sex-starved teenagers. We reluctantly pulled apart and agreed to meet the following evening at my place to finish what we had started.

Has a Monday ever felt so long? No. No, it has not. Not ever. We texted each other throughout the entire day and I sensed that he was as anxious for our coupling as I was. Dustin was the kind of guy that every gay man wants to fuck. His body is perfectly proportioned and he goes to the gym daily to shape and maintain what he was born with. This was a man blessed with a cute face, but he had added incredible legs, biceps, chest, abs and ass to boot. Add in a pile of tattoos and a bit of scruff and he was in demand.

I could not believe his anticipation was as strong as mine.

When Dustin arrived, it took no time before we were at it like dogs in heat again. Within minutes we were both stripped down to our underwear, and I took a minute to drink that in. This beautiful man was mine, if only fleetingly, but he was mine. Quickly Dustin suggested we head to my bedroom and it was there that I delighted in fucking him. For an instant, when my dick was inside him, I looked down at his face and for the first time noticed the age difference between us. I closed my eyes and continued the work at hand.

To discover six months later that we were still fucking, still friends, still dating and still going to concerts together was astonishing to me. I was certain he would have found another much younger lover and left me behind.

Leading up to the Adam Ant show, Dustin was a willing student in exploring the back catalogue with me as his teacher. He sat with me patiently as I played him the early records and shared my experiences and feelings about the band. I still have a set of band pins mounted in a frame on the living room wall above my couch, so the iconography was handy as we sat in our underwear, post sex, and spun records I had carried with me for over thirty-five years at that point.

Back in 1983 the shirtless, leather-panted Ant paraded around the Massey Hall stage—horn section blaring, two drummers pounding and a full backup band working overtime. It was the first time that my head, my ears, my eyes and my dick finally worked in tandem. I think the penny dropped that night . . . This was what I wanted. Not just rock 'n' roll, not just the wild abandon, I wanted the man in leather pants.

On January 29, 2017, while my teenaged heart was still in awe of Adam, it was my young date that my heart beat faster for. Dustin had gotten under my skin. Most of the men I had been dating or having sex with at that time in my life were only interested in casual sex, often moving on after only a hookup or two. Dustin stuck around, and my feelings for him grew as the weeks and months passed. Our connection was real; I knew he was a special find.

There were a couple of men my age who had brought their kids to the concert to share a favourite artist from their youth. I was a little nervous that Dustin and I would be mistaken for a father-and-son combo, but if we were, no one gave us a second look. Maybe dating norms had changed? Maybe Ant fans were more open-minded? Or maybe I just didn't give a flying fuck anymore.

During the first song of the night, "Dog Eat Dog," I was a puddle. An emotional storm of nostalgia, mixed with experience and hindsight, hit me like a tidal wave. As we stood to join the crowd and dance, my hand on Dustin's ass, I started to cry, and I barely stopped. I wished I could teleport this image back to the confused and closeted thirteen-year-old at Massey Hall in 1983 and say: *It's gonna be okay, kid. Things are going to work out. And one day, in the faraway future, you're going to have the best-looking date at an Adam Ant concert when you're forty-eight years old.* That poor kid wouldn't believe it, but I would have liked to try to. Hell, the forty-eight-year-old version of me barely believed it, but still, I'd have liked to try.

Adam played the entire *Kings of the Wild Frontier* album from front to back. Admittedly, he could have excised a song or two and been better off, but he was committed to it. The rest of his set was made up of songs taken from the rest of his catalogue, with a strong focus on some of the more punk rock songs from the early days of his career. Both Dustin and I were surprised at the level of effort the sixty-two-year-old Ant put into his show. Adam was not just phoning it in the way so many of his contemporaries on package nostalgia tours do. Adam was giving it all he had. It was nice that those songs, some almost forty years old, were resonating with my young date.

Shortly after Adam peaked in North America in the mid-eighties, and he and I had our first fateful date at Massey Hall, his career took a downward turn. Not off a cliff exactly, but a slow descent from his career highs. I found my own interest waned along with the public's. Adam's songs started to critique fame and the absurd carnival that public notoriety can create. Couple that with his well-documented struggles with mental health, and by the time the nineties rolled around, he had sort of been written off as a crazy old forgotten rock star.

My struggles started around the same time as Adam's. As I became more aware of my sexuality and what that meant in the mid- and late 1980s, I retreated further and further into myself. I denied who I was. I drank too much. I smoked too much dope. I was bullied. I was a failure at school. My struggles were nowhere near Adam's; he was hospitalized several times and infamously arrested for pulling out a firearm in a pub once.

Still, my struggles were real to me.

Somehow, Adam and I both managed to dust ourselves off and find a way forward. Survivors, I guess. Neither one of us did it quickly, but we got there. So it was, with my hand on Dustin's ass, that Adam and I celebrated a reunion that night. Two middle-aged men who had given up caring what people thought and who were focusing on what they loved—music. And sex. Adam was always about the sex. In a special booklet included in the UK pressing of *Kings of the Wild Frontier*, his hard-core fans are referred to as "Sexpeople—People who get off on sexual phenomena; people who like sexual imagery and enjoy being sexual." My people.

Adam moved on to the next night of his tour in Chicago and I headed back home to fuck Dustin. Or him to fuck me. I honestly can't remember. Sharing the concert experience that night meant so much more than sex.

A few weeks later, I got a message from Dustin—*look what I found*—with an accompanying photo of a copy of *Kings of the Wild Frontier* on vinyl. My heart swelled. Not long after, I found a copy of the Ants' first record, *Dirk Wears White Sox*, in a discount bin somewhere for him. I was proud to introduce two post-punk classics into his collection.

I had passed the musical torch to a new generation. Long may "Antmusic for Sexpeople" reign.

The path to Dustin's ass was not an easy one. No yellow brick road for me. I fought hard to get there; against prejudice and ignorance, but mostly against my own lack of self-worth. For most of my life I didn't believe that I deserved much. I was terrified of gay men and gay sex for years, thanks to the cultural baggage associated with HIV/AIDS. I fought against that fear for decades, so the feel of my hand on Dustin's ass that night was all the sweeter because of the preceding struggle. I hoped Adam would be proud.

THAT'S WHAT FRIENDS ARE FOR

When I finally came out in my early twenties, telling a few friends and finally my family that I was gay, I still wasn't ready to act on my sexual desires. I didn't know a single gay person, and instead of spending my twenties with other gay men and figuring myself out, I spent almost all my time with straight folks. They felt so much safer.

AIDS was still rampant at the time, so hiding amongst the comfort and safety of straight people made perfect sense to me. As a result, I spent my twenties mostly celibate. I enjoyed the odd hand job or blow job, but even those encounters scared me. I was terrified of the consequences I was sure I would face for acting on my desire.

I was not embracing my queerness—not sexually or socially.

After stumbling through high school with no academic success, I went into the workforce full-time at the age of nineteen. My first nine-to-five job was doing data entry at the insurance company where my mom worked. After that numbing experience I landed a job working as a bank teller. Those jobs were agony. I was bored, I often overheard homophobic remarks—a personal favourite being when the assistant manager at the bank proclaimed that gay men "deserved" AIDS—and I knew I didn't fit in. I wanted more for my life, but what?

In 1996, months before my twenty-seventh birthday, I pulled the rug out from under that life and ran off to Australia for a year. What a glorious journey. It was a time before the internet, before constant connectivity, and I spent the better part of that year alone, moving from place to place, a bit of a ghost. An observer. At various points I connected with friends from home who were also doing wanderlust tours of Australia, all straight, and even found myself travelling across the country living in the back of a red station wagon with my friend Denise. I even kissed a few boys along the way, but was still afraid of taking things much further than a kiss or a tug.

Back home in Toronto in early 1997, I joined an improv class at Second City with a couple of friends on a bit of a whim. We shared a deep love of *SCTV*, but I didn't have much desire to be an actor or a performer. I was getting enough of that in my day-to-day life, thank you very much—playing a part that I thought made me the most likeable, the most employable and the most respectable to the straight world. By this point I was out of the closet, but still hiding my desires and my as-yet-unexplored identity.

It was here that I met my first queer friend: Carolyn.

Little did I know, the minute Carolyn walked in the door of that improv class on Lombard Street, my life was forever changed. We clicked immediately. I saw in her everything I felt I lacked: exuberance, confidence, *joie de vivre* and a killer sense of humour.

We became fast friends, and within a couple of months of our first meeting we found ourselves living in the same apartment building at 795 College St. (RIP) in Toronto. She was on the top floor in apartment 7; I was one floor below in apartment 6. We each had two women roommates, all straight. Ostensibly, so was Carolyn at the time, but that would soon change.

Carolyn and I spent countless hours together in our respective apartments and in each other's lives. We listened to music together, we dreamt of a future together, we both wondered, "Will I ever get laid?" alongside the ever-present question "What will I be when I grow up?" Those last few years before cellphones and the internet invaded our lives were glorious—we invented word games and drinking games with our friends, wrote inane ditties, got stoned and listened to records on lazy days, threw parties, and man, did we laugh.

One of my favourite memories of that time together was a Saturday afternoon, no doubt hungover. We lay together in my bed, listening to Lauryn Hill's 1998 masterpiece *The Miseducation of Lauryn Hill* (it was playing 24/7 in our apartment building for several years), and as we dreamt and laughed, Carolyn fell asleep and I quickly followed. A friend you can nap with is a true find.

It wasn't long before Carolyn quit her promising job in television advertising sales to take a gig with the Second City touring company, honing her craft in small towns across Ontario and once a week on the mainstage in Toronto. It was a big decision and a big bet, but I would soon learn, when Carolyn makes a big bet, she often wins the jackpot. A promotion to the Second City mainstage cast in Toronto came soon thereafter, and a promising career as a comedian and an actor was born.

When Carolyn did come out of the closet, she came alive. She laughed louder. She loved harder. It was clear, from then on, she was never going to fit into anyone's preconception of who she was "supposed" to be. It was one of the greatest joys in my life, watching her fly. She opened a door to some of the most amazing queer women in Toronto, in the world, in fact, and I would eventually follow her to this promised land. But that was still a few years away.

Carolyn always believed our forties would be our best years . . . and boy, was she right. In her forties she would create and star in two television shows, *Baroness von Sketch Show* and *I Have Nothing*, cementing her status as a Canadian comedy legend. That bet she made in the late nineties paid off big time in the new millennium.

Acting and comedy were always going to be Carolyn's art. What would mine be? I wasn't ever comfortable onstage doing improv, but I always loved writing. As our Second City training continued, we started writing sketches as well as improvising them, and I surprised myself by demonstrating a bit of a knack for it. But more importantly, I liked watching the world and turning those observations into words. Into scenes. Into comedy.

To help my writing practice, I started a weekly written report summarizing each episode of a show my friends and I watched with great glee: *Beverly Hills, 90210*. The *Cheese Critique* was born. After every episode I would write a long-form list of my favourite things about each week's happenings, tongue firmly in cheek, always focused on the most ridiculous and the "cheesiest" moments. On Thursday mornings, when I got to work at a soulless mutual fund company where I was a rep in the call centre, I would type up the *Cheese Critique* and then email it to a few dozen friends. Upon receipt, they would forward it on to dozens of their contacts, and the distribution list would eventually number in the hundreds. The *Cheese Critique* had a certain level of notoriety, and if I didn't get it out by 9:30 a.m. on Thursday mornings, I would hear about it. My newsletter had become part of many recipients' weekly routine, and folks were upset when it didn't arrive on time. It was the kind of thing we all thought email was for in the late nineties. I was a kinder, gentler Perez Hilton, one of the first internet bloggers, before those kinds of things existed.

As with most things at the time, once the spotlight shone on me a little, I shrank away. I didn't like people reading my thoughts or seeing my humour; it was too close to the person I wanted to be. The *Cheese Critique* was not long for this world.

Even if I didn't call myself an artist yet, I sure found inspiration in creating art, along with a best friend, in Carolyn.

As Carolyn predicted, it wasn't until my late forties that I finally felt I truly had something to say. At Carolyn's urging, I had been filling notebook after notebook with reminiscences of dates with men, the records that we listened to and the connection, or lack thereof, that we had. I didn't know what to do with all these notes, but Carolyn kept telling me "just write it down."

When I told my friend Jen, another in Carolyn's close circle, that I had been keeping all these journal entries and was starting to think about how to turn my scribblings into some short stories or essays, she saw it as an opportunity. Jen was starting a small writing group with her friend Hil, did I want to join them?

Jen and Hil were both professional writers and journalists and lived and breathed story creation. When they asked me to join their writing group of two, I felt out of my depth and wondered why they would include me. But I ignored my first impulse to say no and surprised myself by saying, "Let's do it." The path presented itself, so I took it.

Those first few steps were terrifying. Making the connections between men and music came pretty easily, but forming the words on paper, or on screen, not so much. But I forged ahead.

Finding the courage to read my words out loud during our meetings was the toughest thing of all. It took everything I had to do it—my voice often wavering, shaking with fear, even in the comfort of my own home with two women I trusted. I cried often when I read aloud, partly because I was exploring some tough emotional space, but more so because I was finally doing it.

Unplanned and unbeknownst to me, I was finally creating something of my own.

There was no plan. There was no vision. I just started hammering something out. Word by word. Sentence by sentence. Piece by piece. All with the support of two superstar women. They would provide invaluable feedback on structure and content, but most importantly, they provided the emotional space for me to feel safe enough to be vulnerable and write about my experiences honestly.

Those nights with Jen and Hil in each other's homes were so important to me in starting to find my voice. They are two bright lights in this world and I feel so lucky to have them in my corner.

Before I knew exactly what I wanted to write, though, I still had a few more misadventures to experience.

EVERYBODY'S GOT AIDS

I'm not sure when I first heard about AIDS, but it was likely during the mid-eighties, when I was just starting high school. The media was silent. Politicians were silent. But somehow the news started trickling in.

I'd been taunted and bullied with "faggot" and "queer" all my life, but now the bullies had new words and increased vitriol. "AIDS case." "HIV boy." Charming. Teenaged boys are so lovely when left with little to no supervision.

Born in 1969, I was the perfect age to watch from the sidelines as the horror of the plague unfolded. When the news started making its way to me, I was still too young to be having sex at all, let alone with other men. It was bad enough that a whole generation of boys like me were trying to make sense of what was happening to our bodies, our attraction to other boys, in a time when gays were invisible in popular culture. There was virtually no representation of queers in the world. Not on TV. Not in music. Not in the press. Not discussed.

Then, all of a sudden, gay men were everywhere. They were sick. They were gaunt, skeletal. They were dying.

As I tried to come to terms with my desire for other men, one thing became crystal clear: it would kill me. Having sex with other men would kill me. That message was reiterated again and again.

I survived. I cowered, I hid in the closet, I pushed down desire, and I survived.

The news around AIDS was slow to get out, painfully so, and thousands, millions died as a result. My parents never talked about it, and why would they? Even if HIV/AIDS hit their radar, I'm sure they felt safe in the knowledge that neither of their sons was gay . . . Surprise! At school the pathetic sex education we were subjected to completely ignored it. Then, in October 1985, there was a double whammy of deaths that brought the disease a little closer to home for me and resulted in a massive shift in mainstream coverage. Rock & Ricky. Ricky & Rock. One broke my heart, one changed the conversation.

Rock Hudson and Ricky Wilson both died as a result of AIDS complications within weeks of each other, and their deaths also served as their respective coming-out stories. Rock was one of the biggest movie stars Hollywood ever produced. He made over sixty films across three decades, and his iconic films with Doris Day in the fifties and sixties helped cement his public persona as not only a leading man but also a ladies' man. My main knowledge of him was from his guest-starring turn on *Dynasty* in the eighties, but his death on October 2, 1985, was major news. Dead at fifty-nine. He did not look fifty-nine. He looked decades older.

Rock fucking Hudson was gay?

Rock was gay. Then he died.

Ricky Wilson's death hit me much harder. He was the guitarist and some say heart of one of my favourite bands, the B-52s. Sure, I had a crush on drummer Keith Strickland, but still, Ricky was a hero to me. The news coverage was decidedly quieter—I likely read about his death on October 16, 1985, in *Rolling Stone*—but I was shattered. Dead at thirty-two.

Ricky was gay?

Ricky was gay. Then he died.

I was sixteen at this point. My peers were all starting their awkward fumblings with the opposite sex, but I was going deeper into denial. I'd given up my brief foray into dating girls, but there was no way in hell I was going to talk about my desire for other boys. Now, not only was the thing I wanted most going to socially ostracize me, it was going to kill me. I was convinced of these two outcomes.

The news did not get better. Not for a very long time. The lack of public knowledge about AIDS, the misinformation and the rumours, was terrifying. Could you get it from toilet seats?

Anal sex? Definitely anal sex. Oral sex? Probably oral sex. Was kissing safe? Was the virus airborne? Maybe it was in all that fucking Drakkar Noir floating in the air?

No one had any answers.

Wear a condom when giving or receiving oral sex. Wear two condoms for anal. Abstinence. Don't do it. Do it. Don't do it. Do it.

Instead of educating myself or trying to make sense of what was happening around me, I dove into my record collection and barely came up for air. This was a world I could control. A carefully curated collection of vinyl records, my music provided an escape. Alone in my room, without the judgment of peers or my parents, I could be anything.

Finding queer representation in music fandom was a confusing endeavour in the early and mid-1980s, though. There seemed to be gay men breaking through into public consciousness, but were they really? Freddie Mercury, the queen of queens, never came out as queer publicly and only acknowledged he had AIDS the day before he died on November 24, 1991. What a shame. I guess he let his music, his lyrics, his onstage artistry and his wardrobe choices tell the story. But, boy, in 1985, I sure would have loved to hear him say out loud, "I'm queer."

It wasn't just Freddie, though. Almost nobody acknowledged any queerness during that time. Boy George was arguably the biggest pop star in the world at his peak, around 1983/84. He was definitely the world's most popular drag queen, and his band Culture Club sold an estimated 50 million albums in a very short period of time. Surely the drag queen was gay, right?

Alongside Boy George, there was Jimmy Somerville leading Bronski Beat (The Age of Consent, 1984), Holly Johnson with Frankie Goes to Hollywood (*Welcome to the Pleasuredome*, 1984), with its overt and obvious references to queer culture, and George Michael leading Wham! to a couple-gazillion-selling albums in 1983 and 1984. Soft Cell were singing about tawdry sex and dirty alleyways. The Human League kept wondering if I wanted them, and hell yes, I wanted them.

On the alternative scene, Morrissey started popping up in 1983 with coded lyrics alluding to homosexuality with the Smiths' 1983 singles "Hand in Glove" and "This Charming Man." Not to mention all the straight boys like Duran Duran and Spandau Ballet who were playing with makeup and fashion in a way that heterosexual guys had not done so overtly before. And soon we had Pet Shop Boys and Erasure, who both seemed to have a toe poking out of the closet, but still, not all the way out.

With the exception of Jimmy Somerville, none of these performers were really out. Boy George was infamously coy about his sexuality and once told a reporter that he preferred a cup of tea to sex. Amidst all this, Elton John publicly married a woman in 1984, for fuck's sake.

Bronski Beat, on the other hand—pink triangle on the cover of their first album and a video for "Smalltown Boy" that still haunts me to this day—they shouted out loud and proud "we are defiantly gay." Take it or leave it. But they were the only exception.

If Jimmy Somerville could do it, be an out gay pop star, then why couldn't all the rest? Were none of them gay? Queer? I was seriously confused. I know I wasn't the only one.

The conversation around AIDS started shifting away from fear to anger. Activists were fighting back against the indifference of government, health agencies and the general public and the ignorance around the virus, demanding change. Thank the goddesses for those brave men and women.

In the late 1980s and early '90s, while ACT UP (the most visible HIV/AIDS political advocacy group) was fighting alongside so many others for funding, research and dignity for the sick using their slogan "Silence = Death," the only message that hit this confused teenager was "Sex = Death." This message stuck with me for years. And to be honest, it's still kind of stuck on me.

At the onset of the nineties, the conversation shifted again. Straight people started getting the disease in greater numbers and high-profile celebrities started to care. All of a sudden, AIDS mattered.

In November 1991, Freddie Mercury died, but that year a massive shift happened in Toronto. Princess Diana, the most famous human in the world at the time, dropped in on Toronto's Casey House, the first AIDS hospice on the continent, to visit the residents. A picture of her holding the hand of one of Toronto's own was seen everywhere; it was major news and reported globally. Maybe these men and woman deserved some empathy and dignity after all? At the time, I thought Diana was a bit mad to place herself in the centre of the storm.

I was a big anti-royalist as a kid (and still am), but I have to give Princess Di credit. This was not her only effort in the AIDS fight, not by a long shot. She devoted her time and helped to raise funds for various AIDS hospices in the UK, including the Lighthouse and Turning Point, but it was her advocacy and care for the infected that really made an impact. Her contribution to fighting against stigma truly changed the conversation. Princess Diana may have married a fool, but she was a good human.

Princess Diana wasn't the first famous person to champion the cause. Elizabeth Taylor joined the fight in 1985 when her good friend Rock Hudson was dying, fighting against the disease and the stigma. Liz was one of the first to publicly acknowledge the plague, donating time and funds to the fight, but it took on new meaning when Diana spoke up.

The year 1991 also saw Magic Johnson announce that he was HIV positive. That seismic announcement told the world that the disease wasn't just for queers after all.

The year before, in 1990, Ryan White died at eighteen years of age. He had contracted the disease from a blood transfusion, and his life and death became a *cause célèbre*, and a private nightmare. The story was irresistible to the media; Ryan was in the public eye non-stop. He was the focus of news stories and on magazine covers, and ABC even dramatized his life and diagnosis into a TV movie in 1989. Elton John and Michael Jackson were among the many celebrities who dedicated both songs and money to Ryan and the fight against HIV/AIDS.

While the media was mostly sympathetic to their plight, Ryan and his family suffered from the ignorance of their community in small-town Indiana. Ryan was exiled from his school, being allowed to return only after a protracted legal battle. Parents of other students in the school protested his readmittance, some pulling their kids out of classes. He was forced to use a separate washroom from other students, and was bullied by adults and kids alike. The family even had a bullet fired through a window of their home, forcing them to relocate.

And then Ryan died. The public conversation began changing. Still, gay men died. A lot of them. And still, I hid.

When I first started taking tentative steps to find a gay life, a community of peers, all I found were stories about AIDS. Rightfully so. I bought books at Glad Day, Canada's first queer-focused bookstore, on Yonge Street, and their pages were filled with sadness and rage about AIDS. I still have Paul Monette's *Becoming a Man: Half a Life Story*, a tortured elegy to his deceased partner. I was riveted by Monette's story and didn't want to be either the dying partner or the one surviving.

I found films, most notably *Longtime Companion*, and wept as a whole community of men died on screen. I picked up *Xtra!*, Toronto's free gay and lesbian biweekly newspaper, and read the obituaries of men way too young to die. Every two weeks, new names.

In every bar, every store, every bookshop you entered in Toronto's gay village, you were confronted with safe sex posters and handy kits with condoms, lube and safe sex info. I pocketed them, read them and stored them in my bedside table, unused. I even masturbated to safe sex paraphernalia featuring muscled and hairless (subtext: healthy) young men in their underwear in various poses simulating sex and bodily contact. It was safer than the real thing.

In 1991, I was only twenty-one and I watched all of this in horror. My dick, my id, wanted gay sex so badly, but wow, was I scared. It would take me years to find the courage.

There was an entire generation of gay men in Toronto, in Canada and around the world that had been decimated by the disease. Hundreds of thousands of artists, actors, activists, lawyers, dancers, bankers, sons, partners, lovers, fathers, friends— just gone. Wiped away. Thousands of mentors who never had the chance to grow old, to pass on their knowledge, their humour, their wisdom. In their absence, it felt as though there was no one to show me how to be a gay man, how to live a queer life. They died. Like Rock, like Ricky, like Freddie, they died.

The pain of their friends, lovers and families was unfathomable. Those of us left in their wake carried a different kind of pain, though. Fear. Shell shock. Confusion.

No longer did I want to run off to New York City or San Francisco, the gay meccas, and have sex with a million guys. The YMCA could wait. I wanted to get married, just like the straight folks. Good old monogamous married.

Gay and lesbian folks in the 1990s started fighting harder for the right to be legally married, the right to receive partner benefits, the right to hold the hand of their lover while they died. Coupledom. Marriage. Monogamy. These became the new ideal. There was safety in monogamy. I swallowed it wholesale.

Find me a man to marry. That became my mantra. I'd just hold off having sex until then.

THERE'S MORE TO LIFE THAN THIS

Before Dustin with the sweet ass, before Christopher and my friends awaiting the second plague on a sunny March day, and before several Moleskine notebooks filled with dating stories, I was a serial monogamist. My AIDS panic made monogamy seem like the only option available, but it was never a good fit for me.

As a young man, I chased that heteronormative dream of getting married and buying a house like a man possessed. I wanted the Hollywood romantic comedy dream wrapped up in either Brandon Walsh or Dylan McKay from *Beverly Hills, 90210*.

What I got was considerably less.

I turned thirty in 1999 and I desperately wanted to fall in love. I was still too terrified to put myself out there and go to a gay bar or enter a queer space. In my uninformed view of the world, just going to a gay bar felt like playing Russian roulette; I was sure every man I would meet there had HIV/AIDS. It was illogical, but that's what growing up in the eighties and nineties did to a lot of us who were young gay men in that era.

Grindr and other hookup apps were still ten years away from launching, so either you met a potential lover in the real world at a gay bar or bathhouse, or you simply didn't meet anyone at all. There were some nascent hookup sites on the internet like Manhunt and Squirt, but in my mind those sites were way too risky, definitely not for me. Beyond my distaste and fear of these sites, the internet was still a bit of a luxury in 1999; few of us had it in our homes yet.

I pined for the cute boy, Paul, who lived in apartment 5 of my and Carolyn's building, and who, unlike most of my crushes at that time, was actually gay! I couldn't even try to count the number of straight boys I obsessed over in my teens and twenties. As one could easily predict, all those crushes ended in tears and frustration. Despite my sad attempts at flirting in the shared stairwell or my asking breathlessly what he was up to on the weekend, Paul did not take a shine to my advances. No doubt he smelled the desperation. In the face of adversity, Carolyn and I came up with a plan: a reinvention for the new millennium. "Petey 2000." I would pack on some muscle like the men in those safe sex pamphlets, I would ask my friends to set me up with any gay men they knew, and I would land a man somehow.

I finally met a man in the year 2000 in the most predictable way for me at that time: Brad and I were set up by two straight women. It was perfect—I didn't have to enter a gay space, I didn't have to put myself out there, and I didn't have to introduce myself to a stranger. Brad was older than me and had an established career; both of these things were very appealing to me at the time.

I was learning that dreaming and planning with Carolyn often bore fruit.

I didn't have the blinding flash of love I had hoped for, but I did see a lot of myself reflected in Brad. I had a hunch that he was just as scared of his queerness as I was of mine. He wanted to hide in monogamy and "marriage" as much as I did, I think.

So, I took the easy road and locked down Brad. We were an item almost instantly, and in short order we moved in together, later bought a house, and continued to spend most of our lives surrounded by straight people—going to weddings, hosting baby showers, and babysitting our friends' infant children. Whenever I would try to spend time with other gay men, or explore any kind of queer life, it felt to me like Brad would shut down or get jealous; he didn't want anything rocking our straight-acting gay life. It wasn't a good look and only served to alienate me.

This went on for years. Eleven, in fact. I spent the entirety of my thirties in a monogamous relationship with a man who wasn't right for me, nor was I right for him. I settled for something that didn't make me happy because it was safe.

Maybe the writing was on the wall when I saw his reaction to my record collection—he hated it.

When Brad and I moved in together, I took most of my collection to my parents' house at his request. If I ever brought home an album from a used record store to add to the measly collection in my own home, rather than be excited to hear it and share the experience with me, he was convinced it was riddled with bedbugs. I'd have to shake out the sleeves in the backyard or sneak them inside without him noticing.

I finally found the courage to pull the plug on my relationship with Brad after one too many arguments and one too many threats that he would end the relationship. Making the decision to leave Brad was terrifying, but I knew I wanted more from my life, more from a relationship, even if I couldn't define exactly what that was yet.

After the breakup with Brad, the summer of 2011 was my first as a single man in a very long time, and it helped to reignite my life. At the ripe old age of forty-two, I did some couch surfing, found my first apartment of my very own, reconnected with a few friends I'd lost touch with, and even went to a few gay bars and parties. And then I did it again: I locked down another partner as soon as I met him. Everett was younger than me and, just like Brad, steadfastly committed to monogamy. Fine by me. I would just hide again. Safe. Everett was the total opposite of Brad in both looks and attitude. He was taller, skinnier, had fair hair, liked punk rock and didn't demonstrate much interest in material things. That all seemed like the perfect fit for me at the time, and it was, but it would soon become clear that I had let the pendulum swing too far from Brad to the other extreme.

At least Everett and I had more in common than I had with Brad. We had insanely good sexual chemistry and that kept us going for a while. It was like truly discovering sex for the first time in my forties. He was very good with numbers and appreciated simple pleasures in life: beer, video games and playing music. Unlike Brad, he loved my record collection. His love of my music fandom was one of the things I really liked about Everett. We went to see dozens of bands together and spent many afternoons scouring record stores for my next great find. Everett spent a lot of time playing his keyboard with his headphones on and would often be the instigator to see a band that was passing through Toronto. I loved that about him.

The biggest problem with Everett was that I was continuing the pattern I had established with Brad: we were completely monogamous and spent almost all our time with straight folks. It's virtually impossible to build a queer identity or sense of self when you have no role models for what you want in your own life. I ran away from Brad wanting a more authentic life, a queer life, and ended up repeating the same mistakes with another guy who had a very small circle of friends, all of them straight. And, as with Brad, everything went too fast. I moved in with Everett within a year of us meeting and we bought a house soon thereafter. Same patterns. Same mistakes. I didn't know how to talk to him about it because I didn't know what I wanted, I hadn't seen that yet.

I had entered both of those relationships with good intentions and with my heart open, but I think I was fooling myself more than I was fooling anyone else. While I didn't have an exit plan figured out, I was starting to wonder how much longer Everett and I were going to stay together. The end was coming.

Finally, I met a guy who blew it all wide open for me, and at forty-five I was about to have my heart broken for the first time.

LIKE A HURRICANE

Everett was at his office and I was working at home on a November afternoon in 2014 when a friend I hadn't heard from in years sent me a DM on Facebook Messenger, Dave. He was passing through Toronto and making plans to live here. He asked if there was any chance I was free to meet him that night for a drink? Wow. I was shocked, and rather excited. It took me almost no time to reply and agree. We would have years' worth of news to catch up on.

Dave and I had first crossed paths close to a decade earlier while I was in my relationship with Brad. Carolyn and I were celebrating Pride together and unsure of exactly where we fit in the gay community. We found ourselves on the back patio of Crews & Tango, a trashy drag bar in Toronto's gay village, having a few drinks and enjoying the festivities. Across the crowded patio I eyed a very cute, tall bleach-blond guy who seemed to be flirting with me. Our eyes would connect across the bar, he would sheepishly smile and then look down at the floor. Rinse and repeat. I thought, "This can't be happening." It was very rare for other gay men to flirt with me at that time. But with Carolyn's help, I met Dave.

Dave was a young aspiring artist, and was visiting from Montreal with his boyfriend for Pride. It was clear that we had some pretty electric chemistry despite us both having partners, his only a few feet away, mine sitting at home avoiding any Pride festivities, or anything that I considered remotely queer. To each their own.

We talked, we flirted, we laughed, and we drank a ton of beer. After a couple of hours of partying and flirting it was time for us all to go our separate ways. Dave and I traded phone numbers and promised to stay in touch. After he and his friends had started walking down Church Street, he bolted back, kissed me lightly on the mouth and whispered, "I'll be in touch soon."

Dangerous. Forbidden. Totally exciting.

In less than half an hour my phone buzzed in my pocket and I saw a notification I had never seen before in my life. My first text! Ever!

Grt mtg u

Messages were short and sweet before phones had entire keypads built in. It was brief, but it felt powerful. I went home with a secret. And it felt really, really good.

It was a pretty harmless flirtation and we never acted on it apart from that one chaste kiss. I told Brad I'd met a new friend that day, and I hoped to see him again and develop a friendship, a gay friendship, of which I had very few. He replied something along the lines of, "Oh great, you're going to make a new friend and that'll be the end of me, of us." His lack of confidence in our partnership was often demonstrated in responses like that. He could barely stomach the idea of me having any gay friends, let alone a cute, young bleach-blond one. If he only knew the whole story.

A friendship with Dave, just the idea of it, drove a wedge between Brad and me to such an absurd degree that it almost caused us to split up. But this wouldn't turn out to be the relationship Dave was meant to destroy. The eleven-year-long partnership with Brad died a few years after I first met Dave, for a million different reasons, a cute young bleach-blond boy not being one of them.

Now, a few years after the breakup with Brad, and my friendship with Dave about to be rekindled, I remember riding my bike down to Crooked Star (RIP), a down-and-dirty cocktail bar on Ossington Street, and making a deal with myself—or with Satan. Who can be sure? I was allowed to kiss him that night, I told myself, really kiss him, and flirt with him all I liked, but I would draw the line there. This thought surprised me. I had never done anything like this before in my life, and maybe that should have been a clue to my mental state at the time.

Everett and I had been chugging along, and while things were a little stale, the only times I broached the idea of non-monogamy, in an abstract way, the subject was quickly shut down. I would tease the idea by dropping hints about something I had read or couples I had heard about who had open relationships, but he would stop the conversation immediately. It was clear that non-monogamy was not a concept Everett was interested in exploring. Giving myself permission to kiss Dave was subconsciously admitting that my relationship was in trouble. It was pretty presumptuous of me, too. Who knows what was going on in Dave's life? Why assume we would still have the connection we had years earlier?

It turned out my presumption was well-founded. I arrived early to secure a space at the bar and almost instantly after Dave sat down it was clear that the old chemistry was still burning white-hot. He looked incredible. He'd really grown into his looks. When we first met, he was long and gangly like a newborn deer that wasn't sure how to use his body yet—he was tentative, ill at ease in his movements. Dave had filled out in the intervening years, grown some muscle, and he now moved with confidence. At thirty, he was a stone-cold fox. He was breathtaking.

As our first beer turned into a second, we dove deeper into our conversation. He had recently graduated from art school, had just broken up with his boyfriend and was finally leaving Montreal for good—and ready to start a new life in a new city. We talked about music, travelling, making art and living every day to its fullest. We made a pact for ourselves together and apart: to live the fuck out of our lives. No apologies.

As the second beers diminished, the touching started. Furtively at first, with hands lightly "bumping into" each other, but soon those "accidental" touches lingered. This was quickly turning out to be the best date of my entire life. I'd erased my boyfriend entirely from my mind. I was lost in Dave within a couple of beers of our reunion. This was going well. Or it wasn't. I guess it depended on your perspective.

This was what passion, the beginnings of love, was supposed to feel like, I thought. An uncontrollable storm. A desire for another human where nothing else matters. Finally! I had been hit by a hurricane.

Side by side at the bar, our legs were in constant contact, and for the first time Dave's hand found my thigh. Grazing at first, but growing bolder very quickly, making its way upwards and inwards with increasing force. I almost came in my pants. Almost ten years of foreplay was finally resolving itself. My hand found a similar position on his thigh, and I was astounded that this was happening. Astounded that he was allowing it. Dave was a classic "10," and despite our chemistry over the years, I'd always figured guys who looked like him were out of my league. Way beyond my reach.

He walked me to my bike after we left the bar, but we weren't ready to be apart. It was impossible for me to say good-bye, I just couldn't get the word out. We did that awkward dance that two people who don't really want to leave each other do—making the motions to leave but no one actually doing so. As we inched our way along Halton Street, the inevitable finally happened—our first major kiss. The one at Pride all those years ago was quick and clandestine; this one was long and deep, and it felt otherworldly. *Finally*. Years in the making, it was an epic first kiss. Our erections pressed against each other through our jeans, and instead of pulling back, I pushed against him harder. I wanted more.

I walked him to Trinity Bellwoods Park to get out of the harsh street light we were under, to find a bit more privacy. I leaned my bike against a tree and he leaned me up against the other side of its thick trunk. We resumed our kissing as if we'd never broken apart. Our hands pressed against each other through the layers of coats and sweaters and winter fuckery. It was agony. I wanted to be free of our clothes, of everything—especially to be free of my boyfriend, if only for a short while.

Before long, Dave pressed his hand against my cock through my jeans and I started moaning, and pushed against him, my message clear . . . *Don't stop.* He didn't. He slipped his hand under the waistband of my pants and grabbed my cock, flesh to flesh. I almost fainted from desire, or blood loss to my erection. Nothing had ever felt so good. I wasted no time finding my way into the inside of his pants and underwear. The feel of a new cock in my hand was incredible. That it was Dave's was almost beyond belief.

We continued our kissing, stroking, panting—everything else just fell away. It was a fever I had never felt before. I couldn't believe any of it was happening. I was so happy. I was so scared. I was so shocked—at my own behaviour, at his, and that this was taking place in the middle of one of the most public parks in Toronto. We pulled apart finally, both panting, forehead to forehead. Both clearly wishing we could take things further. For better or for worse, we had nowhere to go. He was staying with a friend and, oh right, I had a boyfriend at home. It was time for this temporary break from reality to end and for me to go back to my real life. It wasn't going to be easy. We shared one last kiss on Dundas Street with me astride my bike and Dave about to hop into a taxi he'd hailed.

Riding home, I knew I should feel guilty, knew I had betrayed Everett's trust, but holy shit, that was one of the most fun nights of my life. It felt as though my bike knew the way home; I just sat back and coasted. Some people equate cars with freedom, but for me, it's always been my bike. I'm on it almost every day, rain, snow, sleet, you name it. It pays silent witness to all my highs and lows. In that moment I was sailing on a high and I felt absolutely free.

HOUNDS OF LOVE

Once I had sobered up after my reunion with Dave, I wasn't feeling so great. I had betrayed my boyfriend. I swore to myself that it wouldn't happen again, Dave and I could remain friends, and Everett didn't need to know about my one small transgression. Easy.

The night Dave and I reconnected, I confessed to him my desire to draw and paint and explore that side of my creativity. My job at that time, at Disney's Canadian head office in Toronto, was relatively good, but it wasn't a particularly creative position or outlet. I had always struggled with my own ego and could never summon up the nerve to put pen to paper to sketch, let alone attempt any other creative endeavour, and he promised to help me try to learn. Dave's desire to help me find a creative voice was one of the most attractive things about him.

We started a sketch challenge. Dave would send me a random photo, I had to draw it and send it back to him via text. I would put on a record from my vast collection, sip a beer, try to ignore my self-doubt and give it my best shot. Everett would play video games on his phone, unperturbed by my actions. It was a rich exercise that forced me to dig deep and confront my fear of any kind of artistic failure. I think I surprised both of us by displaying a bit of a knack for it.

These challenges soon evolved into Dave and me sketching together in coffee shops or, most frequently, at the Steady (RIP), a sadly deceased queer space on Bloor Street. We worked quietly, sometimes separately and sometimes together on the same piece.

As we drew on the same page together, our hands would brush against each other, our eyes would connect, and we would marvel at creating something together as a unit. It was almost as good as sex, especially in the absence of sex.

Amidst the sketch challenge texts, we sent each other countless messages and photos, many crossing the line of propriety. Despite my insistence that we were "just friends," Dave was sending me pictures of himself topless to show off his new chest tattoo. He took naked selfies in front of the bathroom mirror with the counter blocking his dick but not his pubic hair. I wasn't quite as bold but would send pictures back, getting dressed to go for a run—topless, or in my underwear.

Friends. Just friends.

Everett finally smelled a rat and one night correctly guessed my phone's PIN. The whole story was there from start to finish, and he read it all. He exploded, and it didn't take me long to realize that's what I had wanted all along. Fireworks. Emotion. Reaction. I was desperately bored.

Everett was pissed but willing to work through it. Now, what did I want?

Trying to make sense of the whole disaster, I headed to a local coffee shop where Dave and I had enjoyed many of our clandestine dates as friends. Being "friends" with Dave was actually the last thing on my mind—who was I trying to kid? When we had our secret meetings, we would gaze across the table at each other swoonily, and as we touched hands or knees, an electric jolt would pass through us both. I felt it in me, I knew that I saw it in him. It was powerful. We wouldn't kiss again, we wouldn't grab each other's dicks again, but the damage was done. We were both hooked.

Drinking my coffee, I stared at my journal and hoped it would give me an answer. The blank page told me nothing. I turned my head up to the sky and implored the goddesses, "Please, send me a sign . . . anything, just send me a sign." Almost instantly the background music gave way to the thumping drumbeat of a song I was all too familiar with: Kate Bush's "Hounds of Love." I was floored. Goddess Kate was clearly listening, and she was not fucking mincing words.

It's one of my favourite songs from one of my favourite albums by one of my all-time favourite artists. Kate Bush is a genius, full stop, and her 1985 album *Hounds of Love* is unquestionably her greatest work. The drum pattern of the titular song is so visceral it hits me right in the gut, every time I hear it.

It took a few bars, but when the driving cello kicked in, I began to cry. I stared at the ceiling, holding my shitty red notebook, and cried. Kate confessed to us all in the coffee shop that she was scared, she didn't know what was good for her, and she needed help. No fucking kidding, Kate. No fucking kidding. I was terrified and, holy hell, I needed some help. Please, Kate, help. Anyone. Help me.

When she sang about just wanting to run and opt out of dealing with her situation, I could relate all too well. I was ashamed. Of my behaviour, of my predicament. And I sure as hell couldn't deal with it. I was the biggest coward of all. I just wanted to run with the hounds.

As the song neared its end, Kate repeated a simple word again and again in the penultimate refrain: *love*. Wow, could the message be any clearer? The push and pull of her use of the word *love* exactly mirrored how my head and my heart felt, a compass that continued to oscillate, not between north and south, but between two men, between two ideas of what my life could be.

In the final moments of the song Kate repeats the word *love* five times for emphasis. We all crave love and whether from a friend or lover, there's nothing better.

Okay, Kate, I hear you. I did want love and I didn't give a shit what the cost would be. It might or might not be Dave, but

I had to give it a try. I think I knew it all along, but I needed Kate to show me the way. A trusted friend always tells it like it is.

I closed my notebook, tossed my empty coffee cup in the overflowing bin, and walked out with a clear head and a clearer sense of purpose. It was time to pull the Band-Aid off. I did need love. Overwhelming, powerful, all-consuming love. I wanted to feel it. I wanted to give it. And I knew I didn't have it.

The "Hounds of Love" were hunting me relentlessly, and it was time for me to surrender.

I WANT YOUR HANDS ON ME

It wasn't pretty, but I ended my second long-term relationship. I felt like an absolute shit for breaking Everett's heart, but if it hadn't been Dave, it would have been something or someone else down the road. Better now than later was my final justification.

The next day, Dave and I met late in the afternoon at his new place when he had the house to himself. I dropped the news: I wanted to start a new life and see what was happening between us. I told him I wanted to "live the fuck out of my life" and finally, just maybe, figure out who I was.

Dave was pleased for me, as he knew the torture I'd been going through; I had shared all my frustrations about my relationship with Everett. Dave knew I wasn't happy.

We proceeded to kiss—a lot. We touched non-stop. But Dave had this romantic notion that our first time having sex should be "special." Despite my pressing erection, I was completely swept away by the idea. It felt like true love—the Hollywood, or the "90210," version of the Pete & Dave story.

The sun was low in the sky and blazing through the back kitchen window and Dave pulled out his camera to photograph me. It felt like the most romantic gesture. I swooned hard. He took several snapshots as I squirmed uncomfortably—I've always hated having my picture taken.

In an attempt to set my mind at ease, Dave told me I had beautiful eyes. Nobody had told me I had beautiful eyes before, and I was flattered, but not convinced. He zoomed in and took a close-up shot of my left eyeball; the lens was so near I could feel it on my eyelashes, even bumping against my cornea a couple of times. I was nervous, but I trusted him.

He shared a few of the shots on the display screen, and I was shocked! My eye sparkled in the late-day sun and I saw colours captured that I had no idea my eyes contained; gold, green and grey all speckled the more prominent brown.

"See, they're beautiful," he told me.

For one of the first times in my life, I felt a little bit attractive. Could it be? It still didn't make sense to me that this gorgeous guy thought I was sexy, but my confidence was boosted, as was my ego. He saw a part of me, an image of me, that I was never able to access for myself. The damage to my self-esteem from hiding in the closet was devastating. I had convinced myself that no one would ever desire me.

Quite honestly, it was nice to see me through his eyes for a change.

We parted ways with a plan to rent a hotel room that coming Saturday and finally surrender to the long-simmering lust we had for each other. Almost ten years in the making, it was going to be out of this world.

The night before the big event, we were texting and both wishing the hours away so we could get to that hotel room. In response to hearing Dave couldn't wait to be with me I wrote:

I can't wait for you to finally fuck me.

Dave had sent me my first text all those years ago, and that night we shared another first—my first dick pic. When I saw that picture of his erection, the head of his penis blocked with his fist, I almost died. It felt like a real moment of intimacy. The morning could not come fast enough.

After a fitful night's sleep, it was time. I trembled at Dave's side while he dealt with check-in at the Le Germain on Mercer Street. I was vibrating with excitement and the thrill of the hotel employee knowing I was about to spend the night with this stone-cold hottie.

But I was also afraid I wouldn't measure up or that my sexual performance would let Dave down. Despite the large age gap between us, he was by far the more experienced sexually and I felt out of my league.

Thank the goddesses for whisky. We'd brought a bottle and quickly poured two small glasses once we got ourselves settled in the room.

That was better.

We kissed. We sucked. We fucked. Finally. We had talked about sex, and sex with each other, for years, and finally the deal was sealed.

It was . . . underwhelming.

One could analyze the reasons why for days. Expectations too high? The forbidden fruit didn't taste so good? Chemistry was off? The whisky was bad? Who fucking knows? But despite the satisfaction and the thrill of having Dave's hands all over my body . . . the sex was not great. And we both knew it.

In preparation for the night, I'd made a playlist of some of my favourite artists old and new: Kate Bush, Grace Jones, David Bowie, Lou Reed, Stevie Nicks, Patti Smith, and so many more. I was excited to share it with him and tell him stories about these incredible artists, about my life and how each of them ended up in my album collection that I would soon introduce him to.

I was certain the night would be saved with music, art and conversation. He was mostly uninterested in the playlist of songs that made me tick, and that reaction was far more telling than the underwhelming sex.

Unsurprisingly, that one fuck was almost the totality of our sexual relationship. The bloom was off that fucking rose, and fast.

A long email came from him in the days that followed, explaining that everything had happened too fast, he was new to Toronto, he was just out of a breakup, he was trying to focus on himself, his career, making new friends and on and on and on. The excuses piled up, and as I read the missive at my desk in my office at work, my heart slowly broke, into one million tiny pieces.

I had risked everything, sacrificed everything, to explore what was happening between us. He couldn't have figured this out before I exploded my entire fucking life? Mother Yoko and Dolly!

This one was gonna hurt, and it was gonna hurt bad. So, so, so bad.

WOMAN POWER

A few weeks after hearing Kate Bush in that coffee shop and having Dave break my heart, I found myself sitting on the hardwood floor of a room in the Gladstone Hotel in Toronto on a cold January afternoon. Room 208.

A white lie had got me out of work after a last-minute call from Carolyn asking if I could escape to attend a spur-of-the-moment performance at 5 p.m. Boys may come and go, but Carolyn was always there for me. She helped me dust myself off after my first long-term relationship fell apart, and now here she was, ready to help me out again.

Carolyn had received a surprise request that day to come and improvise a soundtrack to a puppet show with her band, and she asked me to come. You just don't say no to a call like that. This was the kind of medicine I was desperately in need of. Whenever Carolyn opens the gate to the path less travelled, you are guaranteed to have a fucking blast when you follow her down it.

Thanks to Carolyn, over several years I had been brought into the orbit of the other three women in her band: Christina, Sarena and Celina, known collectively as Mintz. I was in awe of them but had never really established a proper friendship with any of them individually; they seemed way too cool for me. My disastrous self-image extended to friendships as well as boyfriends. Again, we can thank hiding in the closet for that.

The puppet show was part of a larger exhibition that took place annually at the hotel, *Come Up to My Room*. It was the brainchild of one of the ukulele players in Mintz, Christina, the alchemist who dreamt the hotel and its art and culture programs into existence. Different rooms were transformed by a variety of artists into exhibitions and experiences. It was all part of making the Gladstone a home for queers and creatives in the west end of Toronto.

I sat alone and listened to Mintz tune up their instruments and prepare to play while one masked woman "tuned up" her puppets in a room transformed into something out of an Aesop fable, with set direction by a witch. Or several.

Lindsay was the artist who had built the entire room of puppets, sets and decorations. She had big witch energy; she was grounded, oozed creativity and confidence, and likely had a crystal in her pocket. She looked as if she could cast a powerful spell. Lindsay was a genius for bringing Mintz into her performance. Four outrageously talented musicians, artists, feminists and self-proclaimed witches became five that day.

Somchow, I was the lucky audience of one.

Without any fanfare the show started, and I let all my pre-occupations drift away. Almost instantly, I was transported. Music has always done that for me, provided a complete escape from the world and whatever might be troubling me. A place where my brain, my body and my person can just be. Add in a few witches and cat puppets and I was more than ready to take that trip.

For forty-five minutes the band improvised and the puppeteer did her thing as I watched and listened. As much as I tried to ignore my own thoughts, the action of the piece, the imagery and the intense energy made it impossible not to draw parallels with my life. Death and decay were represented by fallen leaves scattered around the room and by the laying down of the beautiful, aged witch puppet. I too was ready to let a few things die. It was time to kill heteronormative Pete. Nice Pete. Just-wants-to-fit-in Pete. Corporate Pete. Bend-over-backwards-to-not-offend Pete.

Was this the birth of something new for me? New friendships? A queer tribe?

There was healing energy in that room that day. Witch vibrations that were working on my broken heart, my broken spirit.

There was power in this collaboration, that much was clear. Within Mintz, each player was necessary and distinct, and it was amazing to watch how the music influenced the puppetry, how the puppets' actions influenced the music, and how the result was so much better for the input of all. It takes a lot of trust in your people to allow that to happen.

During the performance a few random folks popped their heads into the room to see what was happening, but none stayed. I think the energy rejected them. It felt as though it was solely for me. I felt so warm, so taken care of. It was like being inside a womb of sorts—nurtured by these five magical women.

As we walked out of the room at the end of the performance, we all took a collective breath. That was something. Something powerful. It was a transformative experience for me. For them too, I think.

Who knew what would happen next for me, but it felt as if I had stumbled upon a queer path forward. I knew I didn't want to end up in another monogamous relationship playing out heteronormative roles in a partnership that didn't inspire me. In fact I had no interest in being in any kind of relationship. I had tried to find my identity in a few long-term partnerships and that hadn't worked.

It was time to date artists, weirdos and freaks. Men of all ages and all stripes. Men who embraced being queer and weren't afraid of showing it: the men I had always wanted to be near but was afraid to. Maybe the kind of man I wanted to be.

Most of all, I needed each of these women in my life. In a major way. My army of women was growing.

It was time to tear down everything I was taught to believe in and start all over again.

OH! YOU PRETTY THINGS

With Dave out of the picture, it was time to try my hand at the sex apps. If I was going to try new things and meet all sorts of new men, hookup apps seemed like a good place to start. In truth, I was still terrified of anonymous sex and what I perceived to be high risk for HIV transmission. It was time to get over that too.

The whole world of hookup culture facilitated by apps was new to me, and I honestly didn't really understand how these things worked. I wasn't sure of the language, the etiquette (or lack thereof) or whom to trust—I was a total neophyte.

Grindr, Scruff and all the other apps like them forever changed the way men would meet for sex. We now accept hooking up on apps as the norm, but it wasn't so long ago that you had to meet other men in the real world to find a sex partner. Before the ubiquity of apps, I had hooked up the old-fashioned way once or twice. I had met a couple of guys at different times at a gay bar, and had gone home with them. I stumbled onto a cruising beach in Australia by mistake one day while I was travelling and had my dick sucked on one of the trails in the tall grasses. None of those hookups were planned, but desire won the day.

Bathhouses are an age-old tradition enabling men to meet and have sex with other men, but they were vilified during the AIDS epidemic; in some cities during the eighties and nineties there were forced restrictions and closures. Even though bathhouses survived, I was still terrified of setting foot in one. In Toronto there was also the ugly stain of the 1981 police raid Operation Soap. The police raided four local bathhouses, and in the process bullied and beat many of the patrons, destroyed private property by smashing up the businesses, and dragged hundreds of terrified men to jail. For a very long time it was on record as the largest mass arrest in Canadian history. Ugly. I wasn't over any of that. So, onto the apps I went.

My very first app-based hookup was with a young man named Antonio. He was a cute twenty-six-year-old bearded guy from Mexico City studying in Toronto away from his family. I was excited by the idea of a twenty-six-year-old being interested in me. More importantly, after being spurned by Dave, I was looking to get back in the game, and fast.

As a novice to the world of apps, I had assumed there would be a courtship of sorts before connecting, but Antonio wasn't having any of that. The exchange went something like this:

Antonio: *You're hot*
Pete: *Thanks. You look pretty handsome too.*

Antonio: *Are you looking—do you want to come over now?*

It was that quick. To say I was surprised would be the understatement of the century. I had assumed there would be some "getting to know you" texts—some chit-chat about shared interests or whether we liked pina coladas or getting caught in the rain. Antonio went for the jugular.

Antonio did not have much time for our hookup, so he encouraged me to get to his place quickly. He was just across the train tracks on the other side of Dupont Street, and after being sent the address, I brushed my teeth, hopped on my bike and nervously pedalled myself north.

I was terrified. I thought about backing out, but I kept pumping my legs to keep the bike moving. This was exactly the kind of encounter I was convinced would kill me when I was younger—anonymous sex with a stranger. But it was time to put aside my fear and start living my life. Time to start celebrating my sexuality instead of being afraid of it.

The house was a bit sketchy-looking, with an unkempt front yard and window blinds closed, but I swallowed my trepidation and knocked on the door. No answer. I knocked harder. No answer. Great, my first Grindr hookup was going to be a dead end. Is that how these things go?

I walked back to my bike and thought, "I'll try one last time and send him a message."

Wow, that was fast, was his reply, followed by, *I'll be right down*. Gulp. Here we go.

Antonio answered the door wearing nothing but a white towel, which caught me off guard, but I was pleased with what I saw. Trim body, a nice sprinkling of hair across his chest and torso, and an easy-going smile.

"I was just having a shower. You came so fast."

I refrained from reminding him that he had been urging me to hurry up and get there so that I could hurry up and leave.

"Let's get this started," I thought.

Antonio led me through a construction site on the main floor to the stairs leading to his room. He explained that he was renting a room in a family's home and really only had use of his bedroom. "Holy shit," I thought, "if only his landlords knew he was inviting random strangers into their home for sex." I'm sure that wasn't included in the lease agreement.

I sat on the single bed in his small room and wondered, what happens now? I was almost as clueless as I was terrified. Thankfully, Antonio took the lead and kissed me as his hand found its way to my crotch and started fondling me through my jeans. Okay, we get right to it! Great, I can work with that.

Between kisses, Antonio apologized for being rushed, but honestly, I was happy to get the encounter over with as soon as possible. I was surprised by how much more handsome he was in person, but I was still anxious to pop my Grindr cherry and move on.

Antonio's towel fell to the floor to display a pretty impressive uncut erection. "Two can play at that game," I thought as I slid my pants and underwear off onto the floor to join the wet towel lying between us. The absurdity of standing in this tiny room, in this family home, making out in a T-shirt with a complete stranger was not lost on me, and I stifled a laugh.

We sucked each other off in the dead quiet of the empty house and I wondered, doesn't he even have a radio in here? Some music would have helped to break the bloody tension. We continued our sex in silence and quickly helped each other orgasm on the narrow single bed. I hadn't been on a single bed since high school and I'm not sure I really enjoyed the experience.

I got my underwear and pants back on quickly and asked to use the bathroom. As I relieved myself into the bowl, all I could see was evidence of this family he lived with: baby bath toys, his-and-hers toothbrush holder, family pictures on the wall. It was so strange to get this peek into a world so dissimilar to mine.

Back in his bedroom, Antonio had dressed, and now he proceeded to escort me downstairs to the front door again. After an awkward hug, we said goodbye. No plans to meet again, no promises of anything other than what it was: sex. I liked it. Very efficient.

I was back at home within forty-five minutes. I poured myself a beer, put *The Rise and Fall of Ziggy Stardust and the Spiders from Mars* on the turntable and enjoyed the post-sex glow with one of my oldest records.

While listening to David Bowie, I laughed at myself, glad to have the awkward first anonymous hookup out of the way. There was still that nagging voice in the back of my head telling me, "Holy shit, that was risky, that was crazy," but the joy I felt in sharing another body far outweighed my fear. I turned up Mr. Bowie until I couldn't hear the little voice in my head anymore. It was time to try to silence that noise once and for all.

While my meeting with Antonio may not have been the greatest connection or the greatest sex, it was a hell of a good time. Grindr cherry officially popped.

TUSK

It was a chilly April night in 2015 and I should have been heading to bed early in anticipation of my forty-sixth birthday party the next day. Instead of sleeping, though, I found myself awake thinking about a date with Matthew.

I had connected with a few guys after my comical first hookup with Antonio, but nothing too exceptional.

I met Thomas for a few beers and we jerked each other off in the washroom of a shitty pub in the financial district at King and Simcoe.

I met Magnus and made out with him on a street corner in the Annex and sucked his dick on the stairs only a few feet inside my front door.

I met Jose, visiting from El Salvador, who dressed me up in a harness for the first time, to explore a little light S&M play, who then threw me around my bedroom for some amazing sex . . . and then proceeded to fall off the face of the earth.

All these experiences were new to me. Sure, I had enjoyed the odd one-night stand or short-term connection in my lifetime, but for the most part, sex took place in a relationship.

Matthew was one of the more promising fellows I had met on Scruff, and we quickly fell into an easy back-and-forth conversation. Since my hookup with Antonio I had discovered that Scruff was a slightly friendlier version of Grindr. The men were a little older, had a little bit more respect for each other and were a bit more inclined to get to know each other before jumping right into the sex.

Matthew was a thirty-seven-year-old bearded leftie who loved a lot of the same things I did. We bonded quickly over cycling, writing and reading, and I still maintain that ours is the only hookup in gay sex app history fuelled by a debate about the Canadian Margarets, Atwood vs. Laurence. I was firmly in the former camp and he the latter, but we convinced each other to reassess the other's Margaret. Admittedly, I came away the better after reading *The Diviners* as an adult. Clearly, it is a novel that should not be wasted on high school students.

After a week or two of many long text conversations, we decided to have a "Manhattan challenge" and planned for Matthew to come over to my place after he enjoyed a few drinks at a friend's birthday party.

I knew Matthew would be arriving late and with a couple of cocktails in him, so I indulged in a few beers and a crossword puzzle, ever living on the edge. While waiting, I decided to also indulge in a musical guilty pleasure of mine—all four sides of *Tusk*. The album is not for the faint of heart. It takes devotion and a little stubbornness to make it through all four sides, but I am nothing if not stubborn.

Tusk is Fleetwood Mac's deeply flawed 1979 double album named after the male member. The follow-up to their monstrously popular *Rumours* album, it was deemed a massive failure upon release. A failure that still managed to sell five million copies!

I remember Lindsey Buckingham had remarked about the pressure for the band to make *Rumours II: The Sequel*, and his response was something along the lines of "let's not do that." I feel you, Lindsey. After a few failed long-term monogamous relationships, I was thinking the same thing. Let's not do that again. Definitely.

So while I can admire the artistic vision to try to do something completely different, some consensus from Lindsey's bandmates might have helped. It sounds as if Buckingham, Mick Fleetwood, Christine McVie, John McVie and Stevie Nicks are all making a different record.

There are a handful of beautiful songs on *Tusk*, but it boils down to simply too much Mac; it is an enormously over-indulgent record. With a good bit of editing they could have delivered another smash, but, like me, it seems Fleetwood Mac are a stubborn lot. No doubt the mountains of drugs they are rumoured to have consumed while recording and promoting the record didn't help. The super high don't always have the best perspective.

Midway through side four, the worst of the quad, I heard a knock at the front door. Panic. Matthew was early. I had no time to change the record, and having no music on seemed a greater risk, so I took the path of least resistance and answered the door.

Matthew and I had never met in the flesh and had a lot to digest about each other quickly.

Him: He was shorter, smaller than I'd expected. Bow tie—wow, bold choice. Definitely cute.

Me: Who will ever know? I didn't scare him off, that's all I know.

As he was taking his jacket off at the front door, he asked, "Do I hear *Tusk*?", and a new friendship was born. Anyone who can pick out "Beautiful Child" and identify *Tusk* that quickly is someone I need to know better.

As promised, the Manhattan challenge began. Me first. I shook the mix of Crown Royal and sweet vermouth as we made small chat about his night up to that point. He leaned casually against the counter, and while we were close, I didn't feel any sexual charge yet.

Since Matthew was a confirmed *Tusk* fan, rather than trying to pick another record at its conclusion, I decided to start it all over again. On went side one.

I think we were both a bit nervous, and the delicious manhattans went down easy as we moved around the kitchen island and settled into each other's company.

Matthew's turn. As he used the same tools and ingredients to mix our second drink, we started to become closer. My hand on his back as I reached to rinse the glasses. He patted my ass in thanks for passing him the bitters.

I flipped disc one over to the second side and we settled on the couch and talked about how ridiculous we both found *Tusk* but confessed we each had a huge soft spot for it. We were both big Stevie Nicks fans and agreed she was the best thing that ever happened to Fleetwood Mac, and to *Tusk*.

The album had escaped my notice outside of the title track and "Sara," both major hits, until my late twenties. During the late nineties you could find amazing albums for a buck or two in the few record shops still operating, and it was during these glory days that I picked up a copy of *Tusk* for next to nothing. While the album was a slow burn, I learned to love it warts and all.

With my final sip of Matthew's Manhattan, I contested that my drink was the winner and he politely disagreed. Maybe Stevie Nicks was the only thing we saw eye to eye on, and maybe sex?

Hopefully sex?

I still hadn't quite figured out sex and hookup culture, but I needed to get laid. It had been several months since that ill-fated night when Dave fucked me in a hotel room, and I was horny. I hoped, by placing my left hand on his right inner thigh, he'd get the message. He did.

He turned to face me, put his hand under my chin, stroked my beard softly and kissed me. Thank you, Stevie! I was thrilled to forcefully kiss him back.

I unclasped a few of Matthew's shirt buttons and slipped my hand under the fabric to discover a soft, hairy chest. Nice. To get the bow tie off, though, he needed to focus, so we broke apart for only an instant. Our shirts came off with the tie and he lay down on top of me as Lindsey proclaimed, "That's All for Everyone." I hoped that wasn't all for me. I wanted more.

After a good long make-out session, pushing ourselves harder and harder against each other, Matthew asked if I wanted to go to my bedroom. Yes sir, I most certainly did. "Sisters of the Moon" was fading out and it was nice to have Stevie see us off. Surely this was a good omen.

When we got upstairs to my bedroom, I was a bit self-conscious and awkward. I still wasn't used to graduating from shaking hands to sexual contact so quickly. My relief was palpable when he took control and removed the rest of my clothing and his. I started to relax.

Matthew pushed me backwards with some force and took my erection in his mouth. Just as we were establishing a good rhythm in that position, he hopped up on my chest and pushed his dick in my mouth. Admittedly, this turned me on even more than getting my own dick sucked. As he pinned my hands behind my head, Matthew really took control and pushed in and out while I gasped for breath.

I was in total shock that the polite and timid guy sipping Manhattans downstairs turned into a total monster in bed. His epic thighs from constant biking were a nice surprise too. He shifted positions and lay down on top of me—chest to chest, stomach to stomach, dick to dick.

Moving his dick to position it against my asshole, I pushed back against him. With my enthusiastic response, he asked if he could fuck me.

Good question.

It would be the first time I had fucked someone at first meeting, the first time I would let someone put their tusk inside me before I'd established some kind of relationship. I had this insane idea, driven by my AIDS panic, that anal sex was only for men in committed relationships. For men "in love," whatever that meant. I had distorted the idea of anal sex into something twisted and shaped by hetero norms, sort of like the idea of straight folks saving their virginity until marriage. I did not think that anal sex was casual sex.

I reached for the condoms in my bedside table as an answer. Condoms for me were synonymous with sex. Even within the confines of my eleven-year monogamous relationship with Brad, we used condoms when we fucked—that's how freaked out I still was about the risk of HIV contagion from having anal sex. Matthew quickly unrolled a condom on himself and spread lube on his sheathed dick and my ready-and-willing asshole.

I told him to enter slowly since it had been a while since I'd been fucked. He thankfully took heed and was gentle as he pushed his way inside me. A few deep breaths and a nod from me and he started to get a bit more aggressive in his fucking and his control over me. I completely submitted to it.

After a few glorious minutes, he pulled out, ripped the condom off and exploded come all over my stomach and chest. With a quick tug or two, while he was still hovering over me, smiling, my come joined his.

Matthew collapsed on top of me, squishing our ejaculate between our torsos, and we both laughed. We lay naked side by side for a while and talked about growing up, about coming into our queerness. I confessed I was still working on it and still had a long way to go. With a laugh, he agreed it could be a long road.

"Do you ever top?" he asked.

You could probably count the number of times I had topped my two previous boyfriends using one hand, so I told him "not really."

"Well, let's change that next time." I was beginning to like Matthew.

The night was getting late and I really needed to get to sleep in anticipation of my party the following day. There was still time for one more tune, though. We headed back downstairs and enjoyed one last spin of "Sara." The two of us swayed and swooned to the sounds of Stevie while cuddling on the couch in our underwear. When Stevie was done, Matthew picked up each piece of his discarded clothing and finished getting dressed. With his bow tie in his pocket, we kissed good night at the door.

I was certain this would not be the last I saw of Matthew and his tusk. I lay in bed unable to sleep, still buzzed on Manhattans and killer sex. If I had been told even a year prior that a night like this one was in my future, I wouldn't have believed it. The idea of a one-night stand, especially one that included anal sex, was so wrapped up in shame and fear for me that I would never have imagined I could enjoy it. Matthew helped me recognize the beauty of queer connection, even if it was only for a night.

TAKE ME TO THE LAND OF HELL

I was turning forty-six and it was going to be my first birthday as a single man in over a decade. Forty-five had been a hell of a year of upheaval and change after breaking up with Everett and him moving out of the house. It felt right to mark the shift into the latter half of my forties with a party.

I wanted a small gathering but was reluctant to get the ball rolling or make a concrete decision on what to do. With the Gladstone puppet show fresh in my mind, and aided by a bottle of wine with Carolyn, we came up with a crazy plan—a living room show at my house with Mintz improvising a set.

Somehow, Sarena, Christina and Celina were all on board with this insane dream Carolyn and I cooked up. The idea of a sequel to that January evening at the Gladstone puppet show was enticing to everyone—a sequel of sorts to the Audience of One, but with more of my friends.

Now, who to invite? I decided to focus on a few of my closest friends, the people who were there for me the prior couple of months when I needed them most.

Them and Dave.

Unlike my two long-term relationships, which I found easy to walk away from, I couldn't let go of Dave for some reason. I knew he was bad for me and he certainly didn't have my best interests at heart. Even though he had ripped my heart to shreds, I still wanted him at my party. I guess I was trying to resolve my intense feelings for him, and for the way things ended between us.

The band, smartly, didn't want to try to pull everyone's attention later in the evening after too much drink and pot had been consumed, so we planned an early start time for the party, with a posted Mintz set time of seven. Come or don't. Listen or don't. Arrive late and miss the best part of the night.

True to their word, my four musician friends showed up early to load in and set up in my living room. I'd cleared my already sparse furniture to create as much floor space as possible by pushing it all to the walls and corners. The members of the band started to settle in on the floor and created a little nook for themselves under the window facing the street. Carolyn was on a portable keyboard with a built-in "beat box" (kind of like a beat maker your friend's organ had in the seventies), Sarena on electric ukulele, Celina with percussion and guitar, and Christina on ukulele and guitar. We were set.

I posted the handcrafted sign I'd made that day on the front door:

MINTZ
CONCERT
IN PROGRESS
ENTER. ENJOY.
AUDIENCE OF ONE
4.11.15

I had urged Dave to come early and enjoy the music with me so he could be treated to a one-of-a-kind experience, a chance to witness something he would remember for the rest of his life. He passed. If I needed further proof he was an idiot, this was pretty definitive.

No one else who was invited made the same mistake. We all congregated on the hardwood floor, a huddle of ten or twelve of my closest friends sitting cross-legged, sipping wine and cocktails, smoking a joint or two, and watching and waiting for Mintz to start.

Carolyn found a suitable beat on her keyboard, and without any notice the band began to do their thing. It took some time to find the groove—they call it "greasing the chain," getting the energy passing back and forth between musicians and finding a pattern or line that feels cozy. They had been playing together long enough that they intuitively knew when something clicked, a rhythm or a pattern, and they all jumped on it and started to push that idea forward. It just sometimes took time to find it. When they did find the groove, though, there was no turning back.

For an hour and twenty minutes we were treated to an entirely improvised set of continuous music. As one section reached a natural conclusion, someone else found a new pattern or groove that the rest of the band quickly followed. Carolyn improvised some incredible lyrics off the floor—sometimes hilarious, almost always profound and insightful. She has always had her ear open to what's happening in any room, and in the world, and easily integrates that into her art. The rest of the band contributed vocals and chants and repeated key lines and phrases as they played . . . and the audience was encouraged to chime in and contribute. And they did.

I was way too chickenshit to open my mouth or touch any of the instruments scattered on the floor. Much like my AIDS baggage, I was still carrying a lot of fear and self-doubt about my ability to create art, or to contribute to any artistic process. Though my sketch challenge with Dave had opened up my creativity a bit, I wasn't quite ready to join in on a Mintz jam. I was still letting my insecurities and lack of self-esteem get in my way. I was still afraid to be seen and heard.

There were times when the group was so hysterical with laughter it seemed impossible that the music would find a way through, but it did. Similarly, there were times when the band was super-focused and sharp and we were all awed by how talented this four-some was, and how tight an improvised set could sound.

As the groove found its natural conclusion, there was a resounding ovation. We all felt so lucky to have been witness to such creative joy and to have been a part of such a special moment. It will forever go down as one of the best nights of my life—and there were still hours of partying ahead of us!

We all gravitated to the kitchen for more drinks and snacks and, most importantly of all, to gain access to the turntable in the adjoining room. Almost everyone in attendance had great musical taste, and no one was shy about putting on a new record or taking over DJing for a while.

When Dave finally did show up, the post-Mintz party was in full swing. I was a little bit drunk and a whole lot high. Dave was like a wave of energy crashing the party, threatening to over-power me. I wanted to be close to him. I wanted to touch him. He mostly ignored me.

Just when I was about to get pulled out to sea in a state of desire and confusion by riptide Dave, one of my friends would grab me and pull me back to safety. It was unplanned and I'm not sure they knew they were doing it, but with each hug, each hand on my arm, each arm around my shoulder or back, my friends grounded me. It made me realize that my friends' energy was what I needed. I didn't need a thirty-year-old self-absorbed train wreck. I needed my friends. My queer friends. My queer witches.

As the night wore on, the spell Dave had over me started to wane. The other powers in the house were far more forceful than his. Witch energy wins every time.

Dave was one of the first to leave, and then the rest of the crowd started to thin out slowly. Finally, there were me and seven queer women remaining, including all of Mintz. It turned into a dance party to Caribou's *Our Love*, which had never sounded so celebratory before . . . or since. The album would skip intermit-tently, a sound we all knew from our youth, so we grounded our-selves to the floor and rocked out, flat-footed. Only folks of my vintage would understand that need. With our feet firmly planted, we swayed and shimmied like a field of tall grass in the wind.

Joints were passed again and I had a flash of inspiration. Witches need a witch. It was time for Yoko.

I bought Yoko's album *Take Me to the Land of Hell* on a bit of a whim when it was released in 2013. I can't remember what drew me to it exactly—maybe a good review, maybe a good price point, or maybe hearing that it was her fifteenth studio album, released during her eightieth birthday year. Regardless, I'm glad I was compelled to grab it that fateful day at Rotate This on Queen Street. A lot of people have a lot of opinions about Yoko Ono, and I'm here to tell you—almost all of them are wrong.

I grew up buying into the widely accepted notion that Yoko was responsible for breaking up the Beatles. No one wanted to believe the truth, which was likely that John, Paul, George and Ringo got tired of the fame machine, got tired of each other and got tired of the insane responsibility of being in the most famous band that will probably ever play together. Peter Jackson's series *The Beatles: Get Back*, released in November 2021, certainly shows that the boys were pretty tired of each other by the end of their commitment to the band.

Yoko's music was considered unlistenable noise, her artwork completely overlooked, and it was argued she only had a platform because she was John Lennon's wife. Most of that nonsense is racist and misogynistic bullshit. Yoko is a visionary.

Born in Japan in 1933, seven years before John Lennon, she established herself as an important artist and thinker in the late fifties and early sixties in New York City. She lived in a studio apartment that hosted performances and art shows, and she ran around with John Cage, Philip Glass and other incredible creators. She was performing, making art and establishing a vibrant and influential music and creative scene years before the Beatles ever recorded a note.

It was at a 1966 exhibition of Yoko's work in London that Lennon was drawn to her as both an artist and an equal. Their artistic and romantic partnership was born the day they met. Often tumultuous, their relationship still stands as probably the single greatest love story in rock 'n' roll. They will forever be more interesting to me than Courtney & Kurt, Beyoncé & Jay-Z, Stevie & Lindsey, or any other high-wattage coupling in the rock 'n' roll hall of fame.

Together, they were:

- lovers
- collaborators
- shit disturbers
- iconoclasts
- artists
- protesters
- thinkers
- hippies
- musicians
- counterculture heroes
- performance artists
- songwriters
- activists

Their partnership yielded more interesting music, performance art, visual art, thought pieces, writing, drawings and more—both collaborative work and creations inspired by each other—than almost any other partnership in the twentieth century. That they lasted together until Lennon's murder in 1980—only three weeks after their most successful and arguably best album, *Double Fantasy*, was released—is a testament to their incredible partnership.

I adore them both (if that's not clear). There were a million reasons the Beatles broke up and, sure, Yoko may have been one of them, but to blame her for the collapse of a band as popular and under as much pressure as the Beatles is giving her far too much credit. She's a powerful witch, but even Yoko has her limits.

There is, thankfully, a slow but steady re-evaluation of Yoko's work happening in popular culture, finally. Reviews of her albums on Pitchfork.com and other tastemaker sites are recognizing her music and artistry as revolutionary, and as a major influence on many important bands and musicians in her wake. Her music is oftentimes challenging, but to dismiss it as nonsense, talentless or without merit is lazy. Sadly, I suspect it's not until she dies that people will finally wake up and realize, "Whoa, she was major."

Yoko has always been ahead of her time.

When I dropped the needle on side one and "Moonbeams" started, the whole energy in the room shifted. The witches sat up and took notice. The bird calls definitely suggested something new was arriving. A few synths faded in and then Yoko's voice began reciting prose. It was slowly building. Her heart was ruminating. The birds. The high hat dropped in with a tick, tick, tick. A groovy synth line and a beat started to build, and then . . . FREAK OUT! Yoko wailed like a woman possessed and the band kicked in at full tilt.

All the women involuntarily dropped their jaws simultaneously, then got up to dance and move. It was clear in that moment that *Take Me to the Land of Hell* would become canon to this group. It was as though the house lifted off its moorings and we flew off to a magic place with Yoko as our guide. We were with her one hundred percent.

The transition from "Moonbeams" to "Cheshire Cat Cry" was gorgeous, as is every transition on this album. We were led by a sweet funk bass line, and all of us danced to the weird amalgam of funk and rock crafted in Yoko's inimitable way.

I reminded everyone that this was the sound of an eighty-year-old woman. If I sound like this, attract this level of talent and have this creative energy when I'm eighty fucking years old, I will thank the goddesses.

After track four, "Bad Dancer," the dance energy flagged a bit, but we each found ourselves a seat and rode out the rest of the record together. All conversation was completely halted and the only words that passed between us were related to the music, and how much everyone was awed by it.

By the end of side two, "Hawk's Call," it was clear that we were done. Spent. It was time to call it a night and say our goodbyes.

The witches gave me the best gift that night. Art. Freedom. Friendship. I thought I wanted Dave, but was more than happy to be proven wrong. In return, I gave them the gift of Yoko's *Take Me to the Land of Hell*. That's a pretty great trade.

Thank you, witches, for April 11, 2015. Thank you, Yoko, for everything.

GUILTY

My marketing gig at Disney afforded me what in 2015 was a great luxury: the odd day of working at home. How novel that seems now. One of the many advantages of working from home back then, along with the opportunity to do laundry and shop for groceries, was the ability to hop on Grindr and take a break from checking email every ten minutes. Working from home before the COVID pandemic really looked a lot different; it was a far more relaxed experience.

I was still feeling my way on the sex apps but was getting more comfortable with the transactional nature of some of the connections. Many of them were all about sex, nothing more.

I was finally starting to listen to my id, and I liked what it had to say. A lot.

So it was, on a lazy June morning, that I was at home and noticed a cute blue-eyed fellow online fairly close by. Grindr and apps like it are all geo-target based; you see men who are within a certain catchment area close to your location—handy for finding guys who can walk down the block or zip over by bike in a few minutes. Immediate gratification is a beautiful thing. After exchanging a few cursory messages, Ian and I agreed that he would bike over for a short hookup before heading to Canada's Wonderland for the day.

I got out of my track pants and hopped in the shower as Ian rode over. When I answered the door, I was very pleased with what I saw. Ian was slightly taller than me, and his blue eyes were coupled with dark, wavy hair and a scruffy dark beard to match. He was a total babe.

With barely a hello, Ian walked in the door, pushed me up against the wall and started to kiss me; no time for small talk. I had a hard-on instantly. Before we'd even left the entranceway, both of us had our shorts and underwear around our ankles. I kicked mine aside and got down on my knees to start sucking his dick.

From my position on the floor, I pushed Ian upstairs towards my bedroom. Watching his fine ass climb the stairs to my second floor was a beautiful sight. Cyclists for the win yet again. The sex happened quickly, as agreed upon. He had things to do and I was, technically, working. Still, we made time for some naked small chat once our desire was sated.

Ian was thirty-three, had just officially become a lawyer and had secured himself his first job in the field. He was in the sweet spot of knowing he had a job but with a few carefree weeks before his new position started. After only a few minutes of conversation it was clear that we liked each other quite a bit. I was definitely getting better at picking my hookup buddies.

Ian split to go have fun with his pals at the amusement park and I got back on the computer to answer one or two more work emails. Then it was back to the crossword puzzle.

The next day, I sent Ian a Grindr message to say thanks and how great it was to connect. *I'm down to repeat that any time or grab a beer with you.*

No response. Sigh. "Oh well, we had a fun one-off connection," I thought to myself. I hadn't expected such a handsome thirty-three-year-old would be into hooking up with a forty-six-year-old with salt-and-pepper hair and a beard to match. A second date was too much to ask, I figured.

A week later I finally got a reply—*Sorry, I missed the message, haven't been online*, or some other excuse I don't remember—but to my surprise, Ian was keen to connect again too. He gave me his phone number so we could communicate outside the Grindr loop and within a few messages we had a date the following week to reconnect.

Do you have a speedo? Ian asked me via text the afternoon before our date.

I do, I replied.

Wear it tonight. I want to lick your hard dick through it, peel it off you, then fuck you.

I smiled as I sat at my desk at work with my dick stirring in my pants. What's that about fourth-quarter forecast?

When Ian arrived at my place later that night, I answered the door with my Speedo on under a pair of shorts. We were feverish for each other and could not wait to enjoy the act he promised, and soon the shorts were a distant memory. Before long, my dick was licked, my Speedo was tossed aside and Ian fucked me as promised. The chemistry we had enjoyed during our first hookup was clearly no fluke.

Post sex, we were both famished and decided to head out to grab some food and a few drinks.

Date time.

We found a table on the back patio of Bar Neon, a queer-owned and -operated café on Bloor Street West, and ordered beers and a pile of appetizers. We both grooved to the Motown playlist and it served as the perfect background music for us to get to know each other better.

Fresh out of law school, Ian wanted to use his education to help human rights cases and causes. Swoon. I was able to tell him about my time inside abortion rights activist Dr. Henry Morgentaler's legal circle as a fourteen-year-old spectator and fighting for social justice in the early and mid-eighties—a friend's father was part of Morgentaler's legal team. Ian listened raptly, amazed I had this privileged access.

Then he told me he was a huge fan of 1970s Barbra Streisand. Uh-oh.

I am not a Barbra fan. For years it felt like a betrayal of gay male culture to admit my dislike for her or any of the divas who were worshipped when I first dipped my toe into gay-bar waters. Celine. Mariah. Barbra. Whitney. They're still worshipped, and I still can't stand any of their music. I confessed to Ian that the only thing I could stomach in Barbra's catalogue was her epic duet with Barry Gibb, "Guilty," which I love for all its cheesy glory.

"'Guilty'!" he gasped.

It was pure bloody genius, we both agreed.

Released in September 1980, "Guilty" is the title track on Barbra's twenty-second studio album. It was produced by Barry Gibb of the Bee Gees and written by Barry and his brothers Maurice and Robin, alongside Albhy Galuten, a big name in seventies songwriting and production who worked on some of the Bee Gees' biggest hits and co-produced Dolly Parton and Kenny Rogers on "Islands in the Stream."

When I was growing up, it seemed almost mandatory that every household had a copy of that campy, over-the-top classic.

I think I have four copies in my collection now. "Guilty" may have been released in 1980, but the song reeks of 1970s excess, and it is pure magic. Golden cheese.

Okay, back on track.

The conversation thankfully shifted from Barbra, and Ian shared that before law school he had published two volumes of poetry and acted as managing editor for Toronto's gay and lesbian newspaper *Xtra* for a time. A poet! A writer! Double swoon. I had always been told by friends and co-workers that I should write, that I was good at it. But to be fucking an honest-to-goodness published writer, wow.

I've always struggled with poetry as an art form, unless it is set to music. But maybe, just maybe, Ian could be my window into that world. I was definitely getting better at trying new things. Bring on the poets. Bring on the poetry.

Then Ian mentioned baseball. Ugh, pro sports. Yuck. He followed the Toronto Blue Jays almost obsessively, tracking games and statistics, and he casually told me, "Me and my boyfriend try to go as often as we can."

My stomach dropped a little. Boyfriend? What?

"Boyfriend?" I asked, as calmly as I could.

"Did I not mention that I have a boyfriend? Shit, sorry."

Nope. You most certainly did not mention you had a boyfriend. I'd sworn off dating in the traditional sense, but I was really starting to like Ian. Damn.

He went on to explain that he and his partner had an open relationship. They were free to have sex with whomever they liked, as often as they liked, and it was fine to develop friendships and go out on dates with other men, like the one we were currently enjoying.

Okay. This was new for me. I pushed the disappointment aside for a minute and thought, "Maybe this is just what I need?" A great fuck buddy with good chemistry, a new friend but with none of the pressure of trying to figure out what a relationship between us could look like. No drama. Just easy. Fun. Why the fuck not? This was what I had asked for when I decided to embark on this single life—to date all kinds of guys. So why not partnered ones?

We had a couple more beers and spent the warm summer night holding hands and stroking legs under the table. After paying the bill, we headed towards Ian's place side by side on our bikes. I kissed him outside his house as we sat astride our bikes and we agreed to get together again soon.

Back at home, I went upstairs to bed and found my Speedo on the floor in a crumpled pile. What a fantastic fuck. What a fantastic guy. What a fucking drag he had a boyfriend. Or was it? I was taking a shine to this whole hookup culture, but having sex with partnered guys? That was still a bit of a pearl clutch for me and my heteronormative thinking. But with a little help from Ian, maybe I could get past that stale, dated idea too. Perhaps Ian having a boyfriend was not a drag after all.

GRACELAND

I was right about Matthew, his tusk and our mutual love of *Tusk*. Our first night together with Fleetwood Mac and our Manhattan challenge was the beginning of a beautiful friendship.

A week or so after our *Tusk* date we had a plan to meet at my place again. As promised during our first date, it was my turn to fuck him. My experience as a top was pretty limited, but I think that had more to do with my lack of self-confidence than my lack of enjoyment. I was ready to give it another shot.

When Matthew arrived at my house, neither of us exhibited the bashfulness on display during our first date. There was no time for drinks; no time for records; no time for small talk. We both knew sex was on the menu and we wasted no time getting to it. Matthew had barely made it in the door and we were upstairs, naked on my bed. After several minutes of making out and sucking each other off, it was time to do the deed. Gulp.

I was nervous and took a while to find my footing, or more accurately, my positioning, above him with his legs up in the air. It took a few fumbled attempts, but Matthew was patient, helped guide me to the right spot and, bam, I was inside him. Mission accomplished.

Part of my worry when I had fucked guys in the past, my two ex-partners, was that I'd hurt them by somehow not doing it right; confidence in my topping skills, like most things, was not great. Pain during anal sex is really more of a communication problem than anything else, and Matthew was a great communicator, and was turning out to be a great lover.

I fucked him very slowly at first but at his encouragement got a bit more active. Damn it if this wasn't a ton of fun. It felt fucking glorious, and I really took to my task. I was clearly not the only one enjoying it, and Matthew encouraged me to fuck him harder as he moaned and twisted underneath me. Before long he came while I was still pushing inside him and watching his face light up in pleasure. I pulled out, ripped the condom off, threw it on the floor and proceeded to orgasm over his shoulder and onto the pillow behind his head. I hadn't come with that kind of force in ages. Maybe I wasn't just a bottom after all?

Post sex, it was time for a beer, and as I headed to the fridge I told him to pick out a record. He was a bit overwhelmed. The wall of records in my home can be a bit intimidating, but he took to his task as I had done to mine earlier, and dove in headfirst. When he surfaced, Matthew was holding *Graceland*.

Paul Simon released *Graceland* towards the end of the summer of 1986, when I was seventeen. It was one of only a handful of albums that were positively ubiquitous that year, and the next. No matter what generation you belonged to, you could not get away from it. In a pre-internet world there weren't many records that got this much play and attention, and when they found a wide audience, they stuck around. For months.

Matthew would still have been a small child when *Graceland* was released, so I was surprised by the choice. After he dropped the needle on side one, we sat and listened to a record I hadn't heard in years. As the album played, we shared our experiences with *Graceland* and his choice became more clear.

It was decidedly not cool to like Paul Simon amongst my friends at seventeen. I was mostly listening to British imports like the Smiths, Depeche Mode and the Cure, not sixties folk stars. My experience with *Graceland* was a solitary one, spent mostly in my room in the basement, headphones on, escaping the horrors of high school all by myself.

The album is widely considered Mr. Simon's best, but it did not come without a bit of controversy. His solo career was at a bit of a low point and he took a big gamble by infusing his sound with a wide variety of styles and influences—and therein lies the problem. He collaborated with dozens of musicians, including many from South Africa, and while the beats and the sounds of that country are what make this album truly soar, Simon got a lot of criticism for what many perceived as breaking a cultural boycott in place at the time in protest of South Africa's apartheid policies. Simon was not making a political statement, he was simply collaborating with artists who inspired him (not to mention paying them and giving a few songwriting credits to his co-creators). Most of the controversy flew over my head, and it sure didn't stop the album from selling truckloads, but I'm sure it tainted the success for its creator.

Matthew's experience with *Graceland* was very different. He was too young to discover the record on his own; it was his parents who introduced it to him. They loved the album and he shared warm memories of being at home and on road trips listening to it on cassette. Happy memories to a great soundtrack.

I never had these kinds of musical experiences with my parents. On car trips with them I listened to my yellow Sony Sports Walkman as loud as I could to drown out the adult-contemporary "soft sounds" radio, all the while suffocating from cigar smoke. Yes, my father smoked cigars in the car with the windows rolled up tight. Hotboxed by my dad! My parents' record collection of jazz artists, Barbra and popular Broadway musicals mostly sat in a corner, rarely played, and I don't remember them ever coming home with a new album to introduce me to.

It wasn't exactly a generation gap, but it was interesting to hear how we both came to appreciate Mr. Simon's most successful solo record. We also agreed that anyone who was married to Carrie Fisher, even briefly, had to be a bit of a badass. We both loved the original *Star Wars* films and had made many a bad lightsaber joke in reference to our boners over the weeks of our courtship. Sometimes boys just don't grow up.

It was all fun and games until "Under African Skies."

"Listen, listen . . ." he told me, and as the bass drum kicked in and Linda Ronstadt started harmonizing with Simon, Matthew completely disappeared. He was gone for the entire running time of the song and his eyes teared up while he quietly sang along.

Linda's voice is exquisite and pairs perfectly with Simon's. It's not just him, though, she's one of the great vocal collaborators there is. Paul Simon, Neil Young, James Taylor and others all have songs made infinitely better by her voice. The records Linda made with Dolly Parton and Emmylou Harris as Trio are inspired; the three of them harmonizing together is sweet magic.

Not to mention the gazillion records she made and sold as a solo artist in the '70s and '80s. Linda Ronstadt is a talent for the ages.

Matthew and I were discovering that we were pretty good collaborators too. I could get really excited about a fellow who got so worked up about a deep cut on a Paul Simon album.

After that night, Matthew came back to my place again and again. More often than not we listened to Stevie Nicks or *Graceland*, but we played dozens more records and artists during our dates. He came over after yoga, we fucked. He came over for Friday night dinner, we fucked. He was riding by on Sunday afternoon, we fucked. Sometimes him fucking me, sometimes vice versa, and best of all, sometimes both. Matthew has the distinction of introducing me to the flip and fuck, and I am indebted to him for life.

Another thing Matthew and I agreed on was condom use. Matthew and I had talked about how more and more guys were using PrEP (Pre-Exposure Prophylaxis) to protect themselves against contracting HIV, but I wasn't convinced of its efficacy yet and would only fuck while using a condom. A few of my online conversations on the apps would end when I wouldn't agree to have bareback sex with the man on the other end, despite the assurances they were on PrEP. Could I trust them? Most of those men were in their early twenties and what they didn't understand was that for this Generation Xer, I had thirty years of HIV fear to unpack and get over before I could even consider anal sex without a condom, PrEP or not.

One major problem arose after a few weeks of our ongoing dates: I liked Matthew. He was definitely worth dating, but I'd promised myself that I wasn't going to jump into another relationship. Not any time soon, anyway. And this was way too soon. For the first time in my life I had to have the "I'm not looking for a boyfriend" talk. I wasn't even sure how to do it, but Matthew received the news incredibly well—he was happy to stay fuck buddies and friends. Wow. Great.

Maybe there was a whole world of these lovely guys out there who just wanted to have sex and enjoy their lives as single men. To build real friendships and real intimacy but not end up dating.

The concept was something I had never really considered. I'd never been shown any kind of gay relationships growing up, let alone something like this. We were friends, and we were fucking, but we had no romantic commitment. Matthew and I were clear on that—we were not boyfriends. Maybe that's what I had wanted all along: true connection, real friendship and a healthy dose of sex. Was that real grace? Was that me?

Gay Graceland, that's got to be a place I can find.

JOLENE

Pride 2015 was going to be my first one as a single man since the turn of the century, and I was determined to make the most of it.

I had always had a hard time finding my place at the festival, much like finding my place in the gay community overall. The parade was never my cup of tea; it was always too crowded, too hot and way too corporate—I didn't need to see banks and booze companies hire straight models to throw out condoms from floats at the masses. I still don't. Furthermore, most of the Pride events I'd attended in the past felt like an outdoor version of Woody's, one of Toronto's oldest gay bars, rather than anything subversive, political or interesting. Shitty dance music. Boys posing for each other. Very little live music. No mingling outside your clique. Overpriced beer. Just like Woody's.

I felt a little like Peggy Lee after attending my first Pride festival in 1998 with a couple of straight friends. "Is That All There Is?"

Pride is billed as a festival, or a party, to celebrate the great diversity of our community. What I saw the first several years I attended looked more like a spring break party for twenty- and thirty-something white gay men and their straight girlfriends. (Just like Woody's.) There was inherent ageism on display; you really have to search for the older folks, the weirdos, the more diverse communities that make up our beautiful queer landscape. Pride still seems to celebrate the young, but I was starting to discover that if you look hard enough, you can find your people.

What better way to help form a new relationship to Pride than by attending a queer event I'd never been to before—the annual Steers & Queers: Night of 1,000 Dollys party at the Gladstone Hotel? It was the eighth annual Steers & Queers, a dance and performance–based bash where everything is country-and-western themed, with a major dose of Dolly Parton.

I'm not really a country fan, but I love Dolly. I kept my obsession with Dolly Parton private when I was a kid. I was only eleven years old when the film *9 to 5* and its titular (pun intended, sorry) song were released in 1980 and took the world by storm. While I loved everything about the film, the song and most of all Dolly, even at eleven years of age I knew that to admit it would mark me as a faggot. Boys were supposed to like hockey (I didn't) and *The Dukes of Hazzard* (which I liked for all the wrong reasons . . . John Schneider, sigh). Admitting you liked Dolly Parton would have been like flying the Pride flag in the schoolyard. Kids at school had already started calling me fag, so I did what I could to mitigate the bullying. Lying by omission helped. It was impossible to entirely hide my love for Dolly, though.

In the wake of *9 to 5*'s popularity, I was chosen to perform the recorder solo in my class's rendition of the song at a school assembly. My enthusiasm was palpable. I tried to keep my excitement and my preteen Pride quiet, but it was almost impossible. Bullies be damned. You can only really try so hard to keep the lid down on epic faggotry, and prepubescent faggotry is in a class of its own. It can just erupt, unannounced, at the most unexpected times. And when it strode across the Courcelette Public School stage in the early eighties, it was pretty fucking special. My head held high, my chest puffed forward and my fist clutching my recorder like a trumpeter about to announce the cavalry, I was beaming. I wanted to be seen, I wanted to be heard. For a kid who was learning how to hide, it was a beautiful moment of celebration for my otherness.

The Steers & Queers evening started at Carolyn's apartment with some drinks and costume prep. I was told that almost everyone attending the event wore some kind of western theme or Dolly drag, and just like my preteen self with my recorder, I was ready to be seen! After spinning a few albums and enjoying a few beers, we tied red kerchiefs around each other's necks, hopped on our steeds and steered our bikes the few blocks down Queen Street to the party.

We arrived early to check out a queer photography exhibit also taking place at the hotel that night. As we perused some of the portraits on the second floor, I noticed a very good-looking guy taking in the exhibit on his own. My height, he had a lean runner's build with the most incredible head of dark, curly hair with just a hint of grey. I whispered to Carolyn, "Let the games begin," and the dance was on.

I was dressed in Daisy Duke–style cut-offs, rolled up with the pockets hanging below the cuff, workboots, a red-and-white gingham checked shirt with the sleeves cut off, and the previously mentioned red bandana tied jauntily around my neck. All class. I hadn't unbuttoned the shirt to tie it across my stomach just yet. The object of my affections was dressed as a perfectly normal person. Cute running shoes. Nice jeans. A fitted T-shirt. Instead of feeling embarrassed, I was emboldened. The two of us moved around the room slowly and took in the portraits, all the while slyly checking each other out as we did so. Eyes connected. Eyes averted. Eyes connected. A slight smile. Eyes averted. A dance as old as time.

Finally, I approached. "Howdy, partner!"

Forgive me, Dolly, I couldn't help myself in the moment. It was the kind of night where everything was amped up, and I was only too happy to join in.

"Hello there . . ." he replied as he scanned me head to toe. ". . . Great outfit." I could tell he actually meant it.

Immediately I was lassoed and hog-tied. His smile slayed me. We didn't avert our gaze once we were face to face.

The handsome stranger looked vaguely familiar, and it turned out we had chatted on Scruff and had established a few things in common already. We both ran, liked art and seemed to like other fellows with a bit of grey in their hair. I hadn't recognized him because his profile pics did not do him any justice at all. He told me his name was Andy and that he was meeting some friends at the Steers & Queers event later. Perfect! Our paths were destined to cross again at the party downstairs on the main floor.

"Save a dance for me later, cowboy!" With a wink and a spin on my booted heel, I was off to reconnect with Carolyn and hit the party.

And what a party! There was Dolly drag. Burt Reynolds drag. Slutty country drag. Bad wigs. Great wigs. Short-shorts abounded. The main thing I noticed, though, was that everyone was having fun. Laughing. Dancing. Talking to strangers. No one was afraid to look silly or felt they were being judged. I felt at home, and while I had a few friends at the event, I was amazed at how many new ones I met and talked to.

This had never happened to me on Church Street, the main drag of Toronto's gay village, or at Pride. Ever.

When the Dolly Choir, a.k.a. the Tennessee Mountain Homos, hit the stage, the place really took flight! You haven't lived until you've seen several dozen performers with sky-high wigs and matching white robes sway together drunkenly and perform "Two Doors Down." A new life goal crystallized in that moment: to perform with the Dolly Choir. As I listened to their voices raised in queer song, I wondered, had I finally found my queer people? My scene? Had I found my place at Pride?

"Can I get a Dolly-lujah?" the Reverend Fluffy Soufflé, our host for the evening, asked.

Hundreds of voices replied, "DOLLY-LUJAH!"

This place might just be heaven.

Throughout the night, my new friend Andy and I were in constant contact. We had several friends in common and as I chatted and danced with old friends and new, he was never far from my sight. We flirted like mad. We touched—gently on the arm at first, and then more boldly on the back and each other's ass as the night progressed. I bought him a drink. We did a shot. I ran off to dance with other friends and repeated the cycle. Flirt. Touch. Ass. Drink.

"Can I get a gay-men?"

A chorus responded as loudly as we could, "GAY-MEN!"

Around midnight, during a break in the performances, I sensed the time was right and asked Andy for that promised dance. He agreed. I led him by the hand to the centre of the dance floor and turned to face him. I couldn't have timed it better if I had tried. The disco ball clicked on and the opening notes of "Jolene" welcomed us as we stared at each other, face to face on the hardwood floor. Jo-fucking-lene. It was surely a sign that something momentous was happening.

"9 to 5" may be Dolly's biggest hit, but 1973's "Jolene" is the one that really stands the test of time. They are both incredibly well-written songs, but while "9 to 5" is catchy as hell, it's pretty kitschy, a bit of its time. "Jolene," on the other hand, is perfection. It's a gorgeous melody, the guitar line could fit any genre, in any era, and her voice is impeccable. The emotions of the song are so pure, you can't help but feel it. A song about a gorgeous woman, potentially stealing Dolly's man, "Jolene" is timeless.

I listened to Dolly describe an incomparable beauty as I gazed at the beautiful man I was holding in my arms. No, he didn't have red hair like Jolene, but Andy's chestnut curls looked pretty good to me. We slow-danced, old-school-style. I hadn't danced like this since my preteen fumblings with girls at grade eight basement make-out parties, and I had no idea that it felt so fucking good to be dancing so closely with someone you were actually attracted to. Our bodies pressed together, we touched each other all over.

Midway through the song, we started to neck. There is just no other word for it, really. Necking, in the great tradition of high schoolers in heat on the gymnasium floor. We were really going for it. We both had erections that we pressed together on the dance floor, under the flashing lights.

It was a fantasy come to life. In Toronto. On the dance floor. Under the disco ball. At the Gladstone Hotel.

"Can I get a Dolly-lujah?" DOLLY-LUJAH!

"Can I get a gay-men?" GAY-MEN!

As the song played out, Andy and I held on to each other for dear life. The moment seemed almost too good to be true. I gave a silent Dolly-lujah that I had decided to come to the event that night. "Jolene" ended and I reluctantly broke apart from this handsome stranger.

"Thanks for the dance, cowboy," and off Andy went, disappearing into the madness. I would have loved to go home with him that night, to take our flirtation to the next level, but he was gone. Off to another party somewhere, and out of reach.

It was better that way. It had been a perfect moment in time at the perfect party, and that counted for a lot.

As had happened after my recorder performance in grade school, I left the Gladstone that night triumphant. I'm not sure

I had ever enjoyed a night out amongst other gay folks as much in my life. Certainly not on Church Street, certainly not during Pride.

Maybe I'd just been doing Pride wrong all these years. In the Gladstone ballroom I saw a lot more than drunk twenty- and thirty-year-old gay men. I saw dykes, I saw gender diversity, I saw men and women older than me—a beautiful spectrum of queer people in Toronto performing and celebrating. This was what I had been looking for. I think I may have stumbled onto Queer Pride by accident.

Dolly-lujah!

JUST CAN'T GET ENOUGH

When I stopped having contact with Dave, I thought to myself, "Well, that's the last time I'll have sex with anyone that young." I was certain that no one under thirty would be interested in fucking a guy with a salt-and-pepper beard in his late forties. But one week during that summer of my forty-seventh year really helped me to understand that there is a big market for what I have to offer. Whatever that may be.

Rob, twenty-four. Over six feet tall, blond hair and brown eyes, he looked a little like Dave, actually. We met on Grindr and I discovered he was a recent transplant to Toronto, in town to attend theatre school. He was a singer, piano player and aspiring actor, and was looking to make some new connections in Toronto. The sexy kind of connections. He arrived at my place chewing gum, and to my surprise he never took it out when he sipped a beer, or when we started making out, or when he started sucking my dick. I blew a load in his mouth and still, the gum.

Kids these days.

Gordon, twenty-five. He was a cute nerd around my height with glasses and dark hair whom I connected with on Scruff. He worked as a human resources manager and played in a gay sports league for laughs. During our text exchanges he had asked if I would dip my dick into a glass of red wine so he could lick it off me and enjoy the glass with my scent in it. Have you ever tried to stuff a hard-on into a glass of red wine? It's not easy. But where there's a will, there's a way. Dick licked, wine drunk, Gordon was gone.

Derrick, twenty-three. Over six feet tall, with dark features and shortly cropped hair, he could have been a model. He had just finished university and was positively breathtaking. Derrick and I met on Grindr and he was intrigued about my record collection and confessed a thing for older men (hooray!). He came over to share some wine, and before we could finish a glass, we were naked in bed and I'd found a new friend.

I had a fresh perspective on sex and dating by the end of that week. I had started the year certain I was washed up at forty-six. I truly believed my best years were behind me and that my sexual life would be masturbating to porn, dreaming of men out of my reach. It was a revelatory discovery that these young men found me sexy, had desire for me. All three of them born decades after I was. The more men I connected with and had sex with, the more I realized how much I liked both the frequency and the variety of men. I was starting to relax about random hookups that I had perceived as an HIV risk, and began to really enjoy myself during these connections. For so many years sex had always seemed dangerous to me, truly a forbidden fruit, but all these guys were making me realize sex was fun. It was to be celebrated. Cherished. And most importantly of all, age didn't matter.

I wish someone had shared this kind of narrative with me growing up. The gay culture I had been exposed to seemed to focus exclusively on the young. The image of the mid-twenties, gym-fit frat boy was the ideal in the 1990s and 2000s—thanks a lot, Abercrombie & Fitch. There was something about that A&F imagery that made me, as a gay man, feel as though I wasn't living up to the ideal body, wasn't being the ideal gay man, and this further eroded my fragile self-confidence as a sexual being. A lot of men, gay and straight, felt the same way. Not only was I missing gay role models in my own life, there was scant representation of any gay men over thirty in both mainstream and queer media. It sure would have been nice to know that sexual life didn't end at thirty, but I probably wouldn't have believed it anyway.

Some stories you have to write yourself.

WE ARE THE CHAMPIONS

I inadvertently signed myself up for a season of dodgeball when I saw a friend post that he was looking for new queer folks to play in a league. I thought I had agreed to try it out for just one night, but that mistake turned out to be one of the best I ever made.

For an entire season I spent Thursday nights in the Givins/Shaw Junior Public School with an all-queer, mixed-gender team throwing little rubber balls at mostly straight folks on the other side of a gym. Why we all signed up for this grade-school torture exercise only Freud and Yoko know, but regardless, we loved it.

Our team name was ever shifting: the Dark Heathers, the Wanda Sykes and finally . . . the Rosebuds.

It was the kind of sports experience I had always dreamt of. No matter how well or how badly we performed, we cheered each other on as though we'd just made the gold medal–winning play at the Olympics. Despite our spirit, though, we were bad. Disastrously bad. Comically bad. Epically bad. We also had more fun than any other team in the league, by a much wider margin than our losses. Every night, we left the gym feeling like total champions.

Hoping that I might meet some new friends and maybe a cute guy or two, I was delighted when I first spotted Mike on my team. A towering six foot three or four, red hair and beard, with beautiful blue eyes, he was one of the younger members of the team. I wasn't sure how young exactly, but I pegged him around thirty and figured I'd never stand a chance anyway. For months I delighted in watching him bound around the court. Mike was one of the best players on our team. He could leap mountains, it seemed, with his powerful jumps. He had the second-best forehand on the team. He could catch and crouch and dodge and sprint. I assumed that all this evidence pointed to him being a monster in the sack.

I also learned at some point during after-game beers that Mike had a boyfriend. Naturally.

We still eyed each other up between games, on the sidelines or as we all changed into our street clothes in the middle of the grade-school gym. It was an interesting experience, flirting in an environment filled with small-kid things—construction paper art projects on the walls, little shoes in the lost and found, nutrition posters, urinals that were six inches off the ground . . . It all felt a little bit weird, and a little bit wrong. Weird or not, we were not deterred.

Early in the fall, after our summer break, Mike and I were the only Rosebuds who could head out for after-game beers. We had never really connected one-on-one, so I was a little nervous as we walked my bike to a local spot for a beer, a burger and a mutual comedown after our sports adrenalin rush.

We flirted even more aggressively now that we were alone, and in pretty short order I discovered he was now single. Excellent. I also discovered that he was twenty-two. Holy shit. *Twenty-two.* I was still in the closet at twenty-two. I was twenty-five years older than him—more than twice his age. I could actually have been his father. All these thoughts swarmed around in my brain as I looked into Mike's beautiful big blue eyes. He averted his gaze with a smile every time I caught him looking directly at me.

Conversation was flowing very easily until one of us broached the idea of intergenerational dating—in an abstract sense, of course.

"I'm pretty open to dating men of all ages," Mike told me.

"I'm very open to dating younger guys," I told him.

The air hung heavily between us.

Our knees bumped and stayed connected under the table in the silence, but what we didn't say was that we'd be interested in going on a date with each other.

Who knew this young gent would be such a charming guy, let alone that he wasn't ageist? Aren't all young gay men ageist? Despite some of my more recent experiences with a few younger men, I still expected most young guys to be chasing the "golden youth ideal," not a man twice their age. The gay beauty standard of youth is real, but it was nice to find a young hunk to debunk what I thought was a steadfast rule. I guess every rule has its few exceptions.

Finding a connection with Mike was a sweet surprise, and I silently thanked the rest of the team for having other plans that night. We paid our bill and headed back out onto the street. My bike was only a block away, and with it as a silent witness, we embraced awkwardly and said a hasty goodbye. I kicked myself the entire ride home. He was practically putting a date on the table, and I didn't take the bait. Amateur move. I felt like a fool.

Once I was home, I resolved to fix the situation.

ME:

> TEXT 1: *Mike! Great night, thanks for dinner afterwards.*
> TEXT 2: *I totally chickened out. I wanted to ask you out on a date when we said goodbye . . . and maybe wanted to kiss you.*

MIKE:
> TEXT 1: *I agree, great to connect.*
> TEXT 2: *There may have been some mutual chickening out. I thought the same things.*

ME:
> TEXT 1: *Excellent! We can easily rectify this!*
> TEXT 2: *You free next Friday night for a date?*

MIKE:
> TEXT 1: *I am. I'd love to.*

We texted back and forth and agreed that he would come to my place for dinner after he was finished work. I was excited for the date, but still a little annoyed at myself for not stepping up to the plate. Did I really think a hot twenty-two-year-old guy would ask me out? Maybe that was expecting a bit too much.

SET YOURSELF ON FIRE

I was incredibly nervous in the days before my date with dodge-ball Mike. Sure I'd had the odd hookup with men almost as young as him, but this reeked of a real date. It *was* a date, no question. Somehow the idea of having a friend over to share a meal and get the opportunity to know each other better was more nerve-racking than having a complete stranger over to have sex; those random encounters had clear outcomes.

We had talked about my record collection during our post-dodgeball burger semi-date and Mike was most anxious to get to it after he arrived at my house. Like a zombie, he walked straight towards the vinyl and proceeded to go absolutely bonkers for it. A lot of the young guys who visited me displayed a passing interest in my records, but he could hardly believe his eyes. Those big, beautiful blue eyes.

To be clear, and not to brag, my collection is a work of art unto itself, numbering over a thousand records, with at least a third of those purchased between 1975, when I tried to buy the Bay City Rollers' compilation album, and 1988, when I got a CD player for Christmas, sigh. U2's *Rattle and Hum* may have been one of the last vinyl releases I bought before I migrated to buying CDs for several years. Even while I was buying CDs, I was still buying vinyl for a dollar or two in now long-gone record stores around the city, and I have been gifted a few collections over the years from folks who were decluttering their living space and unwisely decided that albums were no longer for them. Now that artists are releasing new music on vinyl again, I buy a number of records each month. It's a big collection.

In between gasps of surprise as Mike found more and more albums he loved, I learned that he was not only an engineer but a musician too. He had played bass and keyboards for most of his life, performed in a couple of bands and knew his way around a tune. Well, well, there was more to Mike than met the eye.

I put on an album by our dodgeball teammate Casey while I made dinner and Mike continued to flip through the records. Casey led the band Ohbijou, who released three fantastic albums between 2006 and 2011. Back in 2009, I remember getting a free download card for Ohbijou's song "New Years" at Starbucks. Those free downloads felt like Christmas morning sometimes. I loved the song but never found the album until I started playing dodgeball with Casey. Ohbijou, comprising Casey along with her sister Jenny and a pile of other talented men and women, created a beautiful hybrid of indie-folk-pop, and Casey's voice was the gorgeous binding agent that held it all together. Mike and I both remarked how insane it was that we played dodgeball with this incredible woman. Not only was she mad talented but she was one of the kindest and sweetest folks I'd ever had the chance to meet. I fell in love with her almost instantly. Casey was a crafty one on the dodgeball court, too.

I served Mike a delicious barbecued steak with roast potatoes and vegetables and discovered how nice it was to court someone with a meal. Mike was very appreciative. It had been a while since I'd made that kind of effort. As much as I was revelling in my many random hookups, a meal and conversation was nice for a change.

With dinner out of the way, I asked Mike which of the dozens of albums he had pulled out he wanted to hear. He surprised me with a left-field choice: Stars' 2004 album *Set Yourself on Fire*. Stars are a five-piece indie rock band with hints of synth pop and electronica composed of members from Toronto and Montreal.

Mike was only an infant in the early 2000s, but it was a glorious time for indie music in Canada in the wake of Broken Social Scene's defining release of *You Forgot It in People* in 2002. Canada was all of a sudden a hot spot for indie rock music.

The year 2004 was a big one for Canadian indie bands. Not only was *Set Yourself on Fire* released, but that same year gave us Arcade Fire's *Funeral* and Feist's *Let It Die*—an indie trifecta that made all us music fans really believe that Canada's time had arrived. I was thirty-four at that time; Mike would have been in grade school. I shook that thought off and returned to the couch with a couple of fresh glasses of wine.

Set Yourself on Fire is a moody, melancholy indie-pop masterpiece. The sound of busted relationships, emotional car crashes and trying to pick yourself back up after a heartbreak, it's a beautiful record. "Your Ex-Lover Is Dead" kicks off side one and establishes the mood. The interplay between the two lead vocalists, Amy Millan and Torquil Campbell, is a big part of what makes Stars so great, and the album's first song sets that dynamic up beautifully. Mike's physical reaction was immediate; he moved and swayed with the rhythms and sounds while tapping out musical patterns on his body. I could tell he experienced music the same way I did—as a transport to another place.

We grew bolder with each passing track by playing different rhythm parts on each other's legs and gradually pulled closer together. As I mimicked the percussion part of "Ageless Beauty" on his leg, he asked if I was a drummer! I wish! I explained that, nope, I just seem to gravitate to rhythm parts. He told me I should be. Dang. I could get to like this one.

As Mike nudged a teeny bit closer to erase the last bit of distance between us, I was desperate for him to push things a little further. I wanted to give him the chance to dictate the action, and while his signs were pretty clear, he wasn't crossing the line that I wanted him to.

Finally, I told him, "I would really like to kiss you," and was answered with a smile and "Go for it." So I did.

We leaned into each other as if we had been waiting to connect our faces since our burger date. A first kiss for the ages. I straddled him on the couch as we continued to kiss—my knees burying themselves into the back of the couch on either side of him. I had never been so happy to be wearing my Zanerobes as when he reached into the elastic waistband, pulled out my hard dick and proceeded to play with it.

When I fought my way into his jeans, I was blown away by the most beautiful dick that matched the beautiful everything else. As we gripped each other's boners, I asked if he'd like to head to my bedroom. He said that he would like that.

Upstairs, we stripped each other naked and hopped onto my bed. I pushed him backwards and gazed at him in wonder. I was amazed that this gorgeous ginger giant had chosen to head to bed with me. I counted my gay blessings.

We had a blast sucking each other's dicks, making out and feeling each other out in bed. Mike confessed that he would love to bottom for me but not that night. Not yet. I was happy to wait, no pressure.

With my dick in his mouth, I warned him that I was about to come, but he didn't back down. He took it greedily. As Mike rose up, he kissed me with the taste of my own come on his tongue and jerked himself to an orgasm on top of my torso. It was glorious to taste myself on his lips and watch him reach climax on top of me. Nice work, young man.

We lay naked side by side, cuddling and stroking each other's bodies, and talked about how neither of us were looking to date or have a boyfriend. Phew. He was too fresh out of a relationship to even think about dating and was happy to have a new fuck buddy. Perfect.

Back downstairs, we finished the rest of *Set Yourself on Fire* and agreed that we would buy tickets to see Stars celebrate the tenth(-ish) anniversary of the album at the Phoenix Concert Theatre (RIP) the following week, followed by a sleepover. It wouldn't be the first time either of us had seen the band, but to watch them play *Set Yourself on Fire* in its entirety with a new fuck buddy was too good an opportunity to pass up.

The week passed slowly and Mike and I were both pretty giddy at our dodgeball game. We agreed to keep whatever our new status was from our dodgeball buddies so they wouldn't tease us relentlessly. I wanted to shout to the world that I was having sex with this beauty, but I respected, and understood, the desire to be clandestine.

We'd planned a few drinks at my place before the Stars concert, and we attacked each other the minute Mike arrived—we were both primed and ready to go. Watching this beautiful giant straddle me and ride my dick was a shock of bright ginger light and warmth in the December dark and cold. It was glorious. I was glad to finally fuck Mike in advance of a shared concert experience the week before Christmas. Quite a nice gift from my new friend.

En route to the Phoenix (RIP), one of my least favourite venues in the city, we ate some pot brownies a friend had made to enhance our enjoyment of the show. As we entered the club, we both started zooming in the nicest way.

The place was overcrowded with more than a thousand fans, so we cozied up near the back of the room, stage right, where we could have a half-decent view of the stage and not be crushed by the masses. As I scanned the crowd, I realized this album must have really resonated with college kids when it came out; almost everyone in the audience was in their early to mid-thirties—a decade younger than me and a decade older than Mike. Watching the two lead singers, Amy and Torquil, re-create some of our favourite songs along with the rest of the band was a real treat. The drugs didn't hurt, either.

While the show lagged a bit by the end of the album run-through, I knew that we would soon be treated to a set of their best songs from other albums. The show really came to life at that point, and the energy in the room swelled. The band has a great catalogue of tunes, but sadly, Stars never reached the popular or critical heights of *Set Yourself on Fire* again.

Mike was the perfect concert date. He was there for the music, not to hang with his pals or chat, as so many other folks there were. We shuffled together, and as I bumped into him, he took my hand in his. I am here to tell you that holding hands at a rock concert with your cute date was as thrilling at forty-six as it was at any age. Maybe more so, because I knew how precious it was. When Mike positioned himself behind me, I leaned back into his massive body. I felt protected, safe and cared for—especially high on a pot brownie. He was like my own personal protection bubble.

When the house lights went up, we got the hell out of the venue as fast as we could. While everyone out front of the venue tried to figure out which Uber was theirs, we hopped into a waiting cab and sped westward back to my place, holding hands the

entire ride home. Sleep came easily to us both after some great
sex, a great show, a bit of dope and a few overpriced beers. Maybe
getting to know someone wasn't so bad after all?

THE HURTING

In the weeks that followed, Mike and I fell into a pretty regular
routine: we played dodgeball Thursdays and then had a sleepover
date at my place on the weekends. While playing dodgeball, I could
barely concentrate on the game, I couldn't keep my eyes off
Mike. I had always admired his skills and his body, but now that
we were fucking, I looked at him through a different set of eyes
as I watched him leap around and push his body to the limits. It
was beautiful. He was beautiful.

And boy, did we fuck. Mike was like a walking boner
when he got to my place, and I was only too happy to oblige
him. More often than not I was able to practise my new-found
topping skills, but every once in a while I satisfied my need to
get fucked too. Though Mike identified as a bottom, he was
twenty-two—you just had to look at his dick and it got hard.
I could lie him back, blow him for a bit and then climb on top
of him and ride to my heart's delight.

We made a pretty great match.

It was during these same weeks when I was seeing Mike
that I was told I was being downsized from my corporate gig
at Disney. There was a massive culling of 50 percent of the
Canadian office by the American overlords, and my name was
on the list. Ugh. Merry Christmas to you too, Walt.

I had spent most of the year in a protracted separation from
Everett that included a lengthy spell with lawyers after he served

me with papers. It was a nightmare—a very expensive night-mare. And just when everything got settled and I thought, "Phew, now I can just coast for a little while with no massive upsets," the goddesses had other plans.

I was terrified about what would come next. I had just assumed financial responsibility for my house, and employment opportunities for marketers were very youth-oriented. I was fucked, and not in a good way. Mike shocked me by how much he stepped up as a friend, more so than a lot of folks close to me. He constantly checked in with me, bought me dinner as he knew I was panicked about money, brought me wine and listened to my fears and concerns about money and employment. Mike really demonstrated a maturity way beyond his years, and I will be forever grateful for those nights when we fucked and then lay in bed as he comforted me. We played records, we played games, we laughed and we fucked.

What a prince.

It was on one of those nights that Mike asked me to play him one of my favourite albums from my teen years, something he was likely never to have heard before. Hmmm. This was the kind of challenge I lived for. Inspiration struck and I asked if he'd ever heard Tears for Fears' *The Hurting*. He hadn't. Perfect.

Within the first couple of seconds of the album's title track, I could tell Mike's interest was piqued. He was keen to listen to the record but also wanted me to tell him about the band and my experience with them as a fan. My favourite kind of invitation.

The Hurting came out in March 1983 and created a significant buzz in Canada. It made it to the Top 10 via play on alternative radio, meaning CFNY 102.1 in Toronto. In America it didn't find the same success, peaking at number 73 on the Billboard chart. With two handsome singers, the band was tailor-made for the video age. Roland Orzabal and Curt Smith—great songwriters, great singers, great hooks. British and cute. Slam dunk. I was obsessed.

The band always presented as a duo, but I later realized there were a few other consistent members, as well as one secret weapon: Chris Hughes. Chris played percussion and produced both *The Hurting* and its follow-up *Songs from the Big Chair* (1985). Before that, he was one of the two drummers in Adam and the Ants, and produced that band's two biggest records, released in 1980 and '81, before hooking up with Tears for Fears. This one man was responsible for some of my favourite beats and for producing four of my favourite records between 1980 and 1985. No small feat.

As we sat on the couch, I pointed to the wall behind us where I have a selection of ticket stubs from my favourite shows from the eighties framed. Among Adam Ant, Depeche Mode, the Clash, U2 and General Public, to name but a few, there are three Tears for Fears tickets from consecutive nights.

"Three nights in a row?" he asked me as he settled back on the couch and I nuzzled into him. "That's insane. Tell me about it." So I did.

My friend Lorna had camped outside Roy Thomson Hall (Massey Hall's sister venue) overnight for three nights to be the first person in line to buy tickets for the band's 1985 residency at Toronto's Massey Hall, and I was lucky enough to be her partner in crime. I only spent the final night in line with her, and we had an absolute blast. There were hundreds of fans, all similar in age, queued up around the block, and to kill time we would walk up and down the line and meet fellow fanatics and new friends to talk about our favourite band and other music we were listening to. A community of fans all banded together, most of us lying to our parents about where we were overnight and sharing our teen fandom and lives for a brief period. It would have been the perfect setting for a John

Hughes film. The sense of community was real. So much nicer than today's online Ticketmaster queue.

The tour was for the band's second album, *Songs from the Big Chair*. Between the time we bought the tickets and the date of their first show in Toronto on May 30, 1985, the album had exploded. Lorna and I were massive fans of *The Hurting* from the get-go, and now the world had finally caught up with our ardent fervour. Tears for Fears were one of the hottest bands on the planet that spring, and we were lucky to have front-row tickets to three nights of their residency.

We counted down the days to those shows as though we were awaiting the second coming of one of the goddesses. At the time, those upcoming concerts were the only thing that mattered to us.

I had just turned sixteen and remember wearing a new pants-and-jacket combo I had bought in Los Angeles. It was rather fashion-forward for a kid like me, who mostly wanted to blend into the shadows. I never wanted to be seen at school, but that night I guess I wanted to feel like a dandy. With my McDonald's shoelace bracelet and navy-blue plastic Ronald McDonald wristwatch, we headed out for night number one. I was 1980s perfection.

We got off the subway at Queen Street positively vibrating with excitement. As we turned onto Shuter Street, the neon glow of the decades-old Massey Hall sign came into view. The street was cluttered with fans, scalpers and unsavoury-looking dudes selling unauthorized T-shirts. It was a world so far from our neighbourhood fifteen subway stops away. I immediately fell in love with it.

Nope, we didn't need tickets, thanks, we had the best in the house.

The usher led us down the centre aisle and I felt like a rock star. As we got closer and closer to the stage, it felt as if every eye was on us as we took our two seats, and I felt like the luckiest sixteen-year-old boy in the world. We were only a few feet from the lip of the stage where our teen dreams would soon be standing. Thank you, Lorna Downie. Your efforts can never be properly repaid.

As the place started to fill up, our excitement grew. We watched for any hint of activity onstage, and with every roadie plugging in a cord, with every mic check, we almost leapt out of our seats. The mass murmur and mumble of expectation from the crowd that night became one of my favourite sounds—the anticipation of thousands of fans.

When the house lights went down, the place went berserk—teen spirit writ large. Lorna and I lost each other in the mad rush to the stage as everyone pushed to be as close to Curt and Roland as possible. It was completely disorienting, and as exhilarating as I found it, I was terrified too. I managed to find my way to the stage directly in front of Roland. The lip of the stage pressed against my chest as the crowd pushed and swelled behind me. I couldn't see below my chest and started to feel my feet lifting off the ground. The adrenalin was mainlining to my brain.

Other kids in the same position as me got pulled out of the crush by security, oftentimes at their own request, but I was not going anywhere. I'd waited months for this moment and I planted myself as best I could. Minute by minute, song by song, the terror dissipated and sheer joy and wonderment kicked in.

The band had only two full-length albums to draw from, so we got to hear almost every song from our two favourite albums. And as luck would have it, the band was using these shows at the historic, and quite frankly very photogenic, Massey Hall to document their 1985 world tour. They made recordings of several of the shows during their Toronto residency, which were used for the VHS release *Scenes from the Big Chair*. All of my 1985 glory is captured at dozens of moments throughout the show.

"No way!" Mike proclaimed. "You have video evidence of yourself at this show?"

I didn't have time to get out my VHS copy or find a player, so I pulled out my phone, which had a screenshot of a freshly sixteen-year-old me gazing at the stage in wonder. You can't help but laugh at the mix of terror, awe, lust and surprise. I would love to know how many other closeted queers were there that night, gazing up at the stage just like I was.

If only sixteen-year-old me could have seen the two men looking into the phone at him—one of them a future version of himself, living a life that was completely unimaginable to him at the time. A happy version of himself thirty years later. Still listening to the Tears for Fears records he so cherished, with a beautiful red-headed man, yet to be born, cuddled up on the couch with him.

By the time *The Hurting* was nearing its end, I was mostly asleep with my head on Mike's chest as he tapped out drumbeats on my back. It was heaven. I let myself drift away, safe in the knowledge I'd converted another fan to the sweet, sweet sounds of Tears for Fears. We travelled back to 1983 and 1985 with Tears for Fears and then crawled into bed near the end of 2015 happy men, all the better for sharing music, stories and sex. Life was good.

FAIRYTALE OF NEW YORK

Mike was busy with family obligations over the holidays, and while we were both enjoying our time together, neither of us wanted to be exclusive. We checked in regularly and were both clear that we were still not in the boyfriend market.

With Mike AWOL for the better part of a few weeks, I planned a good old-fashioned date on Boxing Day 2015 with a fellow named Adam. Adam was a thirty-three-year-old teacher on holiday from his job, and he was Jewish; his holiday season obligations weren't too extensive. We started a nice exchange on Scruff and discovered we were both pretty rabid music fans. Adam and I planned the kind of date where you meet a nice gentleman for the first time at a cocktail bar to see if you like each other. It was a cute idea and I was possibly caught up in the holiday spirit. Though not a fan of the Christmas season, a cocktail with a new friend on a snowy night felt like a charming idea.

When the twenty-sixth of December rolled around, the weather threatened to turn nasty. A winter weather warning had been issued. As darkness fell, so did the snow. We were in for a doozy. With the storm gaining momentum, Adam and I agreed to meet at Civil Liberties, which was close to both of us. They also mixed a damn fine cocktail and we both confessed to a fondness for bourbon-based treats.

Our first drink went down easily as we talked about our shared interest in music and vinyl. He had a small but growing collection of albums and impeccable taste in music, perfectly aligned with mine. When he asked what I had been listening to lately, the first thing I thought of was Destroyer's recently released album *Poison Season*, which I had just picked up. They were one of his favourite bands, naturally. Adam directed me to Destroyer's prior release *Kaputt* for further listening and suggested it was their best work. Best or not, he was right in pointing me towards it; it's a fantastic record and I had been a fool to overlook it upon its release a few years earlier.

We had two more drinks and discovered more shared interests: Bowie, dogs, making art, spending time in nature, running, beards, butts . . . the list went on and on. Our bar stools kept inching slightly closer and our bodies connected with increasing frequency.

The hour was getting late and another drink would have turned me from tipsy to drunk. We both agreed it was time to leave. Outside the bar, the streets of Toronto had transformed into a fairy tale. Gigantic flakes of snow were falling and the entire streetscape was coated in a layer of white snow and ice. Toronto can be disgusting when the snow turns to slush and melds with the dirt of the city, but at this moment it was a pristine white.

At this late hour the streets were barren save for a few taxis struggling their way through the snow along Bloor Street. I despise winter, but even I couldn't help but love the scene. I half expected a horse and sleigh to pull up to take us on a ride. With Dolly Parton driving it.

As much as I hate winter, Christmas music is worse. I think there is a special place in hell where only Christmas tunes are played. First track on that playlist: Paul McCartney's "Wonderful Christmastime." That's probably the only track on hell's playlist. There are a few exceptions, though, including the Pogues and Kirsty MacColl singing "Fairytale of New York"—despite the troublesome lyric "you scumbag, you maggot, you cheap lousy faggot" sung in the fifth verse. The falling snow and the festive season made me think of the song when Adam and I got out on the street, and I told him so as we stood in awe of Mother Nature.

The song was released in November 1987 as a single and appeared on the Pogues' album *If I Should Fall from Grace with God*, which was released the following year. The track was written by two members of the band, Jem Finer and Shane MacGowan—straight white guys, unsurprisingly. The inclusion of the homophobic slur *faggot* in the song wasn't that shocking in 1987. The use of *faggot* was sadly still commonplace in

day-to-day use and also seemingly okay in popular music of
the time; see also Dire Straits' liberal use of *faggot* in "Money
for Nothing" from 1985, which I have less forgiveness for.
Kirsty felt like a friend, but the old geezers in Dire Straits
came across more like the bullies in high school, sharing a joke
with their aging target audience and using that word to taunt
and shame me.

Despite the slur, I can't help but love the Pogues' song. It's
a dirty and downtrodden Christmas lullaby for those of us
who have mixed feelings about the holiday. Though I still
cringe every time I hear Kirsty MacColl sing *that line*, it's been
part of my holiday season in some way, shape or form every
year since its release. Maybe time has softened it, or maybe my
love for Kirsty overcomes the bigotry. It's also possible that I've
been called faggot so many times in my life that it just rolls off
my back now.

Adam and I turned to each other to say good night, and as
we lingered a little, I leaned in to kiss him. It was the right
move. We stood on the miraculously quiet corner of Bloor and
Ossington and French kissed like we had invented it—buff-
ered by our giant parkas, the snow falling all around us as our
lips continued to meet. It was our own little Fairy Tale of
Toronto. A quieter, calmer Toronto. I liked it. It felt like I was
experiencing the song in that moment and heard Kirsty's
remarkable and unmistakable voice sing the timeless, and
much less offensive, lyric "We kissed on a corner, then danced
through the night," in my head.

We didn't dance through the night, though. We pulled apart
and said goodbye. I ambled home with a grin on my face—a little
unsteady on my feet due to both the bourbon in my belly and the
snow on the ground. A new friend found on a cold winter's night
was sweet, but I would have loved to fuck Adam that night. There
is something about the typical traditions of the "holiday season"

that needs some subverting; gay fucking feels particularly joyful during that time of year. New ideas, new traditions.

Instead of my having any future with Adam, though, our fairy tale ended as soon as it began. After several unreturned texts, I got the message. I'd been ghosted, and this ghosting was going to hurt. Though I was learning to enjoy sexual connections with no strings attached, my emotions didn't have an off switch, or a Stop button. There were still a few guys who got under my skin. Adam was one of those men. I had discovered that hopping into bed immediately with someone from Grindr or Scruff was fun and frivolous, but I was also learning that "dating" or getting to know a person was when I was at my most vulnerable.

Fuck Christmas and its stupid music anyway. And fuck Adam too.

MIRROR MAN

The fairy tale with Adam wasn't my only new connection over the holidays. A few days before Christmas I met a very handsome gent named Jason for lunch after a few messages were exchanged on Scruff. He was in his early fifties and from his profile pictures looked as if he was built like a Mack truck.

He had arrived a couple of minutes before me at Fresh on Bloor Street, near Spadina Avenue, to grab a table during the busy lunchtime rush. His pics didn't lie—he was a hunk. As I started getting settled, I noticed we were wearing the same jacket from Mountain Equipment Co-op, the same Blundstones and the same Levi's. It was kind of like looking into a funhouse mirror, one that adds thirty pounds of muscle and changes your eyes from brown to blue. I didn't hate it.

During our "get to know you" conversation, I discovered that Jason also grew up in Toronto and that we had pretty similar backgrounds and experiences. Our social circles had some overlap, but Jason was six years older than me; we must have just missed out on being in the same place at the same time. But barely.

Lunch passed very quickly, and the more we talked, the better-looking he got. We soon found ourselves outside the restaurant in the pre-Christmas bustle. We hugged, kissed and both lingered a bit. I suggested a tea at my place, which he quickly accepted. We both knew what "tea" really meant.

Finally home, we eschewed the tea, got naked, and Jason gave me the best blow job I have ever received in my life. Hands-down. He had a gift. With his massive chest and arms, I felt that I'd found a true treasure.

We lay naked in bed after sex and got to know each other's stories more. Similar to me, Jason had pushed down his sexuality and came out late, well into his twenties. Those of us who hid in the closet until our late twenties really did a number on ourselves. The closet is a damaging place: it destroys one's self-esteem, makes you second-guess every move you make and every word you speak. The long tail of the closet's carnage can't be over-stated. Both Jason and I were still dealing with the collateral damage of living in there too long.

Like me, Jason was also raised in a very WASPy community, Toronto's tony Rosedale, and was still intricately tied to that privileged white world, working for a very exclusive social club that catered to rich straight folks. Jason knew he didn't fit into that world but was having a hard time finding queer connections and friends he felt a kinship with. His experience sounded all too familiar to me, just with more money. In a weird way, it was nice to share these common experiences; most of the guys I'd been spending time with came out in their early teens, with support systems at school and the encouragement of friends and family.

How great that the world has changed so much.

Jason never mentioned AIDS, but I couldn't help but draw parallels to my own experiences. I suspect that AIDS informed as many of his decisions about sex and sexuality as it did mine—leaving both of us scarred and terrified. I think that the combination of AIDS fear and denying a true self did the same kind of damage to Jason as it did to me, and he was still clearly struggling with it. He was envious of my experience on the dodgeball team and even more so that I was growing such a robust queer social circle. He was a sweet guy, but Jason still had a lot of work to do to find an authentic queer life, which he professed to want.

After he left, I immediately texted Carolyn: *I think I just fucked my future self.*

My middle name is Jason. No offence to the Jasons out there, but it's not my favourite name. All these commonalities and almost the same name? What kind of coincidence was this, exactly? It felt as though I had just experienced the X-rated middle-aged gay man's version of *A Christmas Carol*. As Carolyn and I texted back and forth, we riffed on what the ghosts were telling me.

The Ghost of Gay Christmas Past

After the best blow job I'd ever had, we both confessed we had broken hearts in our recent past. Jason's was from a guy several decades younger—a star university athlete, still hiding in the closet. It was a story eerily similar to me and Dave: he fell in too far, too deep and too fast and couldn't get out. When his version of Dave split, he was crushed. Do I want to be chasing that dragon when I'm Jason's age?

The Ghost of Gay Christmas Present

It felt as if we had lived parallel lives as younger men but were now on different paths, each hovering on either side of fifty. He was experiencing a ton of anxiety about spending time with his family for Christmas, whereas I was looking forward to a quiet week by myself in my own home, visiting with some of my chosen family (my parents and brother had left Toronto many years before). He hadn't done the work to start finding his own tribe yet, and was still struggling to fit a queer peg into a straight hole. Was I ready to be his guide when I still hadn't quite figured myself out yet?

The Ghost of Gay Christmas Future
Was Jason a window into my future self? Future Pete? A warning? In six years' time did I still want to be chasing guys in their twenties and thirties? For sex: yes. Falling for a closeted dude way younger than me? No. Still looking for validation from family and traditional role models while struggling to fit into a world I wasn't sure I wanted to be part of? No thanks.

We traded several texts over the holidays and they only served to highlight our differences. Jason's messages were riddled with the stress and anxiety of dealing with his family and staying at his parents' home. Mine described how happy I was to be on my own, having a Christmas by myself with chosen family. Though we started out in similar places, we were now truly worlds apart.

Despite my hesitations about Jason, we saw each other a few more times in the new year. I just couldn't resist his epic blow job skills. Sue me. But the differences between where we were at in our lives only got more pronounced each time we saw each other.

I looked at my friendship with Jason as a cautionary tale. The ghosts of past, present and future Pete were sent to tell me, "No, no, no—do not fall into that trap again, those same patterns." I had started the work to find my people and my path, and to finally accept who I was, not what someone else wanted me to be. I didn't have the energy to carry another person along with me on that journey. I didn't want to date an alternate version of future Pete. It was time to keep doing my own work. By myself.

ZIGGY STARDUST

Dodgeball Mike and I had been slowly drifting apart since the new year began. There were no hard feelings, we were both just carving out different paths forward and seeing other men. We still played dodgeball together every week and our relationship had seamlessly morphed from fuck buddies to good friends.

Time to find someone new to play with.

Martin was one of those guys I had met online but had almost written off. We had chatted intermittently for the better part of a year on Grindr and seemed to have a connection, but whenever we tried to make plans to meet, it always fell apart. It would definitely not be the first time an online conversation and stated mutual interest went nowhere.

On a cold Saturday morning in February, while I was reading in bed, Martin sent me a message on Grindr, and after a brief exchange he invited me to meet spontaneously for brunch. That sounded kind of quaint. He was already at a restaurant around the corner, so I quickly rinsed off in the shower and hopped on my bike to meet him.

I spotted Martin immediately upon entering and wow, he was a total babe. His profile pic was a little unclear, but I had a hunch he was very good-looking, and I was not disappointed. Fifty-four years old, he had slightly grey and thinning light hair, gorgeous blue eyes and an amazing body, not just for a fifty-four-year-old but for any age cohort.

Martin smiled from across the restaurant and rose to greet me. Not only a fox but a gentleman too. We shook hands, and as we sat down, it felt as if I was meeting an old friend. We were immediately comfortable, and it was clear we had a pretty strong connection too. It turned out Martin was a contractor who did his own design work and flipped houses in Toronto after renovating them. It was an incredibly time-consuming endeavour, and what little free time he had, he spent at a country house in Stratford (about two hours outside the city).

Brunch passed quickly, until Martin announced he had plans to go pick up his dog (a yellow Lab!) in his pickup truck (really?) and head to his place in Stratford for the rest of the weekend. A sexy fifty-four-year-old man with a house in Toronto, a getaway place outside the city and my favourite dog breed from my youth (RIP Chelsea)? Who was this dreamboat I had just discovered? He was the handyman dream.

Martin and I exchanged phone numbers and agreed that a second date would be planned quickly. An honest-to-goodness date. Nice.

We touched base later that day and agreed how nice it had been to connect. We quickly fell into a pattern of daily texts and check-ins to see how the other was doing. Martin's direct and regular communication style was very different from that of the other men I had met recently. I liked it.

Within a week of our first meeting, we planned a Friday night dinner date. Major real estate. With a bit of time to kill before my date with Martin, I started to go through my phone and delete old messages and photos from exes or hookups. Dick pic from Dave, deleted. Text from Magnus, deleted. Dozens and dozens of text messages to and from Dave, deleted. Delete delete delete. This was a better use of my time than flipping through

Scruff for an hour. Maybe I was ready for a new winter cuddle buddy? Maybe I was ready for something else?

I'm a punctual guy, but Martin was already at the restaurant when I arrived. He was dressed for a date—nothing over the top, but he was sporting a classic blue button-down shirt (that served to highlight those beautiful fucking eyes) tucked into a pair of nice-fitting jeans. I was actually on a date with a man . . . a grown-ass, respectable man. A curious turn of events.

He ordered a gin and tonic and we were off. I love anyone who is a fan of a gin and tonic in February. Throughout the meal, I could tell our attraction was increasing. We shared stories easily and shifted into each other's bodies, slowly but steadily. Knees connected under the table. His hand on my knee. Our hands brushed against each other on top of the table. All the while I gazed at those baby blues and he shyly smiled and returned my gaze . . . and held it. Two middle-aged men flirting is as cute and as awkward as watching two teenagers try to figure it out.

I invited Martin back to my place for a nightcap after a decent meal, a few G and Ts and some thoughtful conversation. He agreed a glass of port might be nice, so we bundled up for a chilly three-block walk to my house.

When he entered my front door, the first words out of his mouth were, "Do you know how easy it would be to turn your upstairs into a two-bedroom apartment?" This was music to my ears. Since being downsized at work, I was trying to figure out what to do with my house on my own, and some rental income from the second floor would allow me to keep it. Maybe I needed to date more tradesmen. Not trade. Tradesmen. Sometimes the right people come into your life for the right reasons.

I escorted Martin into the kitchen to crack open the port and he spied my record collection in the neighbouring room. I'd mentioned the collection and my passion for it, but no one truly understands until they see it with their own eyes. He stood in awe and remarked that the collection reminded him of a different time, a different place. Again, my album collection proved its worth. When my parents asked me as a teenager why I wasting my good money on buying albums, I'm sure that none of us ever imagined that the answer would be to get laid in thirty or forty years.

I poured the port and played it safe with an album choice. I dropped David Bowie's *The Rise and Fall of Ziggy Stardust and the Spiders from Mars* on the turntable. Bowie's death in early 2016 was still fresh, still painful, and I was still trying to process it by constantly playing the albums of his in my collection. How can you go wrong with Bowie? And if, somehow, playing Bowie makes something go wrong, I quite simply never need to see that person again for the rest of my life. Period. David Bowie is divine.

Martin and I started to make out pretty heavily on the couch and I thought, "Fantastic. It was worth douching for." We kissed. We listened. He remarked, "I'm not sure I've listened to this record in its entirety, it's fantastic." I ignored this blasphemy and kissed Martin harder. How is it possible a peer, one a couple of years older than me even, hadn't taken the Ziggy ride yet?

Side one ended and we pressed against each other to the final beat of the needle stuck in its final groove. The beat went on for a few minutes until he asked if it was the heartbeat of the album, a coda to side one. Cute. I was charmed by his naïveté, but no sir, it was the sound of side two crying to be heard.

We broke apart so that I could flip the album. Martin followed me to watch, and after I dropped the needle on "Lady Stardust," we stood face to face. Anticipation. I finally moved to unbutton that beautiful blue shirt to get a look at his chest. I was not disappointed by what I saw. He had massive pecs and biceps and his entire torso was sprinkled with salt-and-pepper chest hair. Swoon. I suddenly understood why all the twentyish-year-old boys I had been fucking liked my chest hair so much.

I swiftly pulled my shirt over my head and tossed it in a corner. Shirtless, we faced each other and slowly pulled together. Like Bowie, this too was divine. We kissed as our chests and torsos joined together, and my knees went weak at the sensation of our two bodies connecting. Lip to lip. Chest hair to chest hair. Hip to hip.

We slowly moved to the music. The record skipped as we stepped too heavily together, and he laughed at the reminder of that jarring sound. For him, it was the sound of grade eight dances, high school make-out sessions and college parties. For me, it was the soundtrack to my life.

We danced awkwardly for a few minutes, but Martin soon pulled back and announced he should go home and take care of his pup. It was an abrupt mood shift and I was taken completely off guard. I wanted nothing more than to continue groping him, to unbutton his belt and pants and have him fuck me, right there . . . or anywhere.

Most of my recent dates had ended with nudity and sex, and while I was hoping this date with Martin would end the same way, I could accept this alternate ending too. I knew that sex would come soon enough, and I didn't feel the need to try to persuade him otherwise. I wondered, is this what "dating" feels like in middle age? A good old-fashioned courtship? Was I actually embarking on something that was about more than just sex? And if so, was that a good thing?

I saw Martin to the door and sent him off into the cold night to go and tend to his dog. I poured myself a little more port and started up *The Rise and Fall of Ziggy Stardust and the Spiders from Mars* all over again. "Five Years" took me slowly to another place while I drifted away and dreamt.

Bowie's influence on popular music, on the wider culture and on me is almost impossible to overstate. He is a legend, a lodestar for all who came after him. *The Rise and Fall of Ziggy Stardust and the Spiders from Mars* is the crown jewel in an astonishing collection of twenty-six studio albums over the course of his music career. He's appeared in dozens of films, plays and television programs, including the iconically cheesy *Labyrinth* that I must have watched dozens of times in the late 1980s. That codpiece he wore as the Goblin King sparked my imagination in ways I wasn't ready for yet!

Neither Bowie's music nor his acting were his true gift to me, or to the queer community. Bowie claimed in a 1972 interview that he was gay. Whether he was or he wasn't, if he was bi or if he was straight, has been debated ever since, but it doesn't really matter. What mattered was how he presented to the world. Bowie played with gender in a way no one in the mainstream had ever done before. He wore dresses, he wore makeup with glitter and sparkle, he flirted with men and women, he invented characters and created fashion and visual masterpieces with dozens of collaborators that will never be equalled. When the touring exhibit of his life's work (up until that point), *David Bowie Is*, came to the Art Gallery of Ontario in 2013, I went three times and cried each visit, surrounded by Bowie's work. It was a massive archival exhibit of costumes, photos, lyrics, film posters, video installations and so much more. It was extensive and completely overwhelming.

I remember standing in awe in front of a video loop watching his star-making turn on BBC's *Top of the Pops*, hanging off gold lamé–clad guitarist Mick Ronson while singing "Starman" with fuck-me eyes—glaring at both Mick and the audience at home through the camera. The world would never be the same.

Bowie taught me to dream. He taught me to believe that otherness matters. And holy shit, did he write a staggering number of incredible songs.

The douching for my date had been in vain, but something told me I wouldn't have to wait too long for sex with Martin. Meanwhile, a date with Bowie was better than almost anything else the physical world had to offer.

WHERE WILL I BE

After our first two dates, I was anxious to see Martin again. Our regular texts continued, but we struggled to find a date we were both free. Recently unemployed, I had nothing but time on my hands, but Martin was a busy fella. After a few failed attempts, he finally asked, *Do you want to come to the house in Stratford with me this weekend?* There was actually nothing I wanted more. An overnight stay for date three was a bold move on his part. There was no escape hatch in this plan—for him or for me.

The two-hour drive passed quickly and our conversation was effortless. We both admitted to feeling very comfortable in each other's company and found words came easily. This was pretty unusual for me. There are many people in my life I can dive in and have long and deep conversations with, preferably over a bottle of wine or two, but for it to happen with a brand new acquaintance while driving was a very uncommon occurrence.

We were constantly connected the entire drive. Martin's hand found its place on my knee. When he had to pull away to change gears, afterwards he would take my hand to hold. I changed the radio station and my hand landed on his thigh. On and on it went as the kilometres passed by.

The house was adorable. There was a fireplace (amazing), a hot tub (as advertised) and, in the living room beside the fire-place, a turntable with an album collection (fuck, yes!). Now we were getting somewhere.

Martin took my bag upstairs and plopped it in his room with a sly grin that answered the question I had been asking myself all week: Would we or wouldn't we? It most certainly seemed we would.

After getting settled, he turned on the hot tub to warm it up and we agreed to enjoy an afternoon cocktail while we waited. The G and Ts went down fast and easy, and I jumped at his suggestion that we put on our swimsuits, grab a bottle of wine and hop into the now-warm tub. We changed rather chastely in separate rooms, which I found positively Victorian in its quaintness, if not a little curious. The tease would be drawn out a little bit longer.

Thankfully, Martin had a portable speaker and asked if I'd like to plug in my phone to play some music. He was open to anything as long as he didn't have to choose. Great . . . except, holy shit, what to play at this particular moment? I picked an old playlist with some xx, Blood Orange, St. Vincent and some of my other favourite artists at that time—a compilation that contained something for everyone. We hopped out onto the freezing-cold deck in our bathing suits and into the warmth of the tub as quickly as we could.

In almost no time we were snuggled in a corner of the tub overlooking a huge yard that sloped downward, steeply, to the neighbouring fence, which was almost out of sight. It felt as if we were at the edge of the world. With glasses of a delicious Cabernet in hand, the Wild Beasts' "Hooting & Howling" played softly behind us. I tried to reason with myself not to fall too hard for this man; the last thing I needed was a boyfriend or to have my heart crushed again. But holy shit, it was impossible not to swoon for this handsome devil in this very delightful moment.

Our chaste touches in the car now turned into some pretty serious groping. As more wine was consumed, our inhibitions were lowered. Martin leaned onto my chest and kissed me while St. Vincent sang "Cruel." We shifted positions and I pressed on top of him as Lou Reed asked us to "Walk on the Wild Side." Martin pressed his erection against mine as the xx serenaded us with "VCR."

We were grabbing, groping, kissing and grinding when I started to feel the need for release and asked, "Surely we don't have sex in the hot tub?" to which he laughed and admitted that "Yes, that's not ideal." Fair. We jumped out, left Kate Bush "Running Up That Hill" and raced upstairs, where we could finally see things through.

The sex was a little stiff. Okay, very stiff. With most of my recent lovers I had found a quick and easy groove, each partner discovering a rhythm and a pace that worked for the other person—wordlessly and effortlessly. With Martin it felt a little like a naked game of Twister, with me asking him to place his hand or dick somewhere on my body instead of a coloured circle. The confident and direct man I had come to know over the last few dates sort of fell apart when we finally got naked. It was almost as though he was intimidated by the sex, scared of it. Still, it felt great to finally be naked with Martin after a few weeks of anticipation. Maybe we were just getting the first-time jitters out of the way? It made me wonder if I had been that awkward during my first hookups with Antonio, Matthew and Ian twelve months ago, when I was still figuring out what sex meant to me.

While Martin lit a fire, I started to flip through his records. I wanted to get at them almost as badly as I wanted to get at the sex. It was a small collection of his old albums with some additional vinyl he'd inherited from members of his family. There were some oddities from an earlier generation than ours, but I found some gems from his college years: Echo and the Bunnymen, New Order, Simple Minds and others of their ilk, all directly in my wheelhouse.

As I continued to dig further, I felt as if I had found the holy grail—a 45 of the Normal's "Warm Leatherette." A masterpiece of early electronic music fused with punk, "Warm Leatherette" is about finding a sexual thrill in watching a car crash . . . counterculture material writ large. Grace Jones later covered it, but the original is dirtier and sexier than her version, and it sounded like nothing else blasting out of a club's speakers in 1978, when it was released. It is also the first single released on the incredibly influential Mute Records—later home to Depeche Mode, Yaz, Fad Gadget, Cabaret Voltaire and others. Its importance in the canon cannot be overstated.

I was impressed.

We played records in front of the fire as we shared stories of what some of the songs meant to us and the period of our lives they most strongly reflected. The shit I lived for. Our conversation turned to mixtapes, as these conversations so often do with people of a certain age group, and Martin claimed to be an aficionado of the art form. I had the art of creating a mixtape down to a science, a wild and unpredictable science, so I was a bit suspicious of his claim, but I could hardly say so as he gleefully ran down to the basement to retrieve a box from his past.

I poured more wine as he dumped a boxful of old cassettes across the Persian rug. We both raced down a memory lane of plastic and tape as we dug through the assortment. Martin was a rather clinical fellow, and many of the tapes were numbered from one to somewhere in the high thirties, and it was amongst this pile that I got a better sense of his taste . . . and I liked it. A ton of interesting alternative eighties bands that I loved, including the Jazz Butcher, the English Beat, Devo and Aztec Camera, as well as a vast selection of Australian artists from his time living overseas for the better part of the nineties. Listening for a later date.

The power of a mixtape is impossible to parlay to a younger generation. For those of us who were raised in the seventies and eighties, they were an incredibly important part of our lives. From the early days of waiting for a favourite song to be played on the radio so you could record it live to tape—the track was often soiled by a DJ intro or outro, but you didn't care, you just wanted to document a favourite song.

Tapes were communication tools—to court a potential romantic partner, to woo a friend you wanted to impress, to stay connected with friends from afar. There was a mixtape to be made for any purpose, and boy, did I make them. Ad nauseam. Each and every one took HOURS to craft. The effort cannot be overstated. There are no shortcuts—from the song selection that created a specific mood, to the mathematics or pure dumb luck

to ensure said songs would fit on a sixty- or ninety-minute tape
(and honestly, only the lazy and uninspired made sixty-minute
tapes). You would have to listen to each song in its entirety to
ensure a clean edit that didn't include a snippet of the prior
song or fade to the next . . . It was truly a labour of love. But
the best mixtapes had legs. You remembered them. Your friends
remembered them. And if anyone ever made you one, you sure
as fucking hell remembered getting it. There was no higher
honour than to receive a mixtape from someone.

While we littered the rug with albums and cassettes, I learned
that Martin had a fifty-fifth birthday in a week and that he was
planning to spend it in Mexico. Time was short, materials were
scarce, but I was determined I would make him a mixtape for his
birthday.

We finished the wine, tidied up and let the dog out for a pee
before the three us trudged upstairs, took off our clothes and
crawled into bed. A cuddle sandwich with a new lover on one
side and his pup on the other, I thought I'd died and gone to
heaven. Sleep did not come quickly as I buzzed on the feeling of
warmth and comfort on a cold winter's night. Maybe it was the
flush of a new crush, but I could get used to this.

Back at home the next day, I contacted a few close friends in
the hope of tracking down a tape deck. Mine had gone AWOL
somewhere during a move or cleanup—I guess I thought I would
never need it again. Big mistake. The ancient courtship rituals
don't die, they just lie dormant for a while.

Carolyn was the first to reply that hers was up for grabs, for
keeps. No surprise there. We had made each other dozens of
tapes when we first met in the late nineties. When I biked down
to her apartment to pick it up, she even had a Maxell ninety-
minute blank tape ready for me—the gold standard of all blank
tapes. It saved me a city-wide and internet-wide search. You can
always count on good friends.

Finding long-dead technology was the easy part. Now the real work began. Picking the songs. Setting the tone. What song says too much? What song sounds too flighty? The pressure was on. I was an artist staring at a blank canvas.

I started with the only sure bet, a song I'd introduced Martin to the prior weekend—Emmylou Harris's "Where Will I Be" from her outstanding 1995 album *Wrecking Ball*. She enlisted Daniel Lanois to produce it, her eighteenth record, and they created possibly the best work of her career. Emmylou collaborated with a crack team of musicians and songwriters including Neil Young, Lucinda Williams, Steve Earle, U2's Larry Mullen Jr. and a whole host of others. It is a spectacularly beautiful and atmospheric record, and "Where Will I Be," a song written by Mr. Lanois, kicks off the project in fine fashion. It's one of my favourite songs, and Martin instantly loved it.

Track one decided. In accordance with my usual modus operandi, there would be a healthy dose of Canadian artists and a strong selection of queer ones too. Ladies, gentlemen and non-binary folks, may I please present *Tape #55—Martin's Birthday Mix*:

Side 1

Emmylou Harris—"Where Will I Be"
David Bowie—"Starman"
Lou Reed—"Satellite of Love"
Wild Beasts—"Wanderlust"
Kate Bush—"Hounds of Love"
New Order—"Age of Consent"
Calvin Love—"Girl"
The xx—"VCR"
St. Vincent—"Cruel"
Blood Orange—"You're Not Good Enough"
Malcolm McLaren—"Madame Butterfly"

Side 2

Blue Peter—"Don't Walk Past"
Grimes—"California"
Hidden Cameras—"Carpe Jugular"
Austra—"Lose It"
Caribou—"Can't Do Without You"
Röyksopp and Robyn—"Do It Again"
Stars—"Hold On When You Get Love"
St. Vincent—"Surgeon"
Yaz—"Nobody's Diary"
Amy Winehouse—"Valerie"
Ohbijou—"Thunderlove"

I arranged a quick visit to "drop off a little something" on the day before Martin's birthday and to join him for a walk with the dog. When he opened the bag and found the tape, he was flabbergasted. Floored. He kept repeating, "This is so thoughtful," again and again in a bit of a daze. It was exactly the reaction I had hoped for. He wasn't just impressed, he was blown away. Only one who has gone to the effort of making a mixtape truly understands the process. As they say, it takes one to know one.

We shared a brief kiss and a promise of a weekend in Stratford to listen to *Tape 55* soon, and I left Martin to enjoy his birthday weekend down south. I walked home safe in the knowledge I had hit a home run.

IT DOESN'T MATTER TO HIM

It was March and spring was within sight with slightly longer days and warmer temperatures. The long freeze of winter was ending. I was excited about what was developing with Martin while also seeing a variety of other guys—some new recruits from Scruff and Grindr and a few ongoing affairs with men I had met over the prior few months. Martin and I hadn't talked about exclusivity of any kind, and seeing him on Grindr regularly suggested he was still playing around too.

The last thing on my mind was Dave. But, out of the blue, I got a text from Dave asking if we could connect because he "needed to talk." It had been almost a year since our fateful fuck in a generic hotel room, so I was pretty taken aback. Part of me wanted to tell him to go fuck himself, but the more I thought about it, there were a few things I wanted to say to him too. Like "go fuck yourself," but to his face.

The last time I had seen Dave was the previous October. I had a spare ticket to see John Grant at the Mod Club (now the Axis Club) on October 19, 2015, and I needed a date. Dave and I would still check in on each other once in a while and would bump into each other at parties or bars. I still felt that strange pull every time. Against my better judgment, I asked him if he wanted to join me. For better or worse, he said yes.

Dave came over for pizza and some drinks before the show and I was nervous, jittery, on edge. So I drank a lot and took a pot brownie, thinking it would settle my nerves. It did. But I was starting to get wasted. To combat the dope, I made another Manhattan—surely that would help. October 19, 2015, also marked a federal election in Canada. The votes were coming in and Stephen Harper was going to lose badly and the Liberal party under Justin Trudeau was headed for a landslide victory. The two of us left for the show safe in the knowledge that the country was under a Conservative government no more. Optimism (somewhat unfounded, in retrospect) was in the air.

John Grant was touring his new record *Grey Tickles, Black Pressure*. I was mad for his prior release *Pale Green Ghosts* but had not been quite as taken with the new one. Still, to see a queer artist in a venue that was only a few minutes from my house was a no-brainer.

A couple of songs into the show, I started feeling woozy. I don't know if it was due to the crowd, the noise or the dope, but I dropped like a stone in the middle of the floor. All I remember is Dave down beside me asking, "Pete, are you okay?" as a circle of concert-goers cleared around me. I got up, dusted myself off and insisted I was fine. More than anything, I was embarrassed. We moved to the back of the venue so I could have a little more space and a little more air.

The rest of the show went by with no further surprises, but I was distracted and felt out of sorts the entire time. I think that had more to do with my confused feelings about Dave than anything else. He had broken my heart, he had treated me like shit, and I knew I should have kept my distance, but I simply couldn't turn off my attraction for Dave. Add in the mix of pot brownie and booze and it all combined to make a pretty toxic stew.

Showing more care than I thought him capable of, Dave wanted to make sure I got home okay. I was feeling perfectly fine by that point but agreed to the escort. I invited him in, and much to my surprise we quickly ended up in a sexy situation on my couch. I did not see that coming. We were down to our underwear, our hard dicks pressing against each other, when Dave reared up and put a stop to the proceedings. In retrospect, I'm glad he made that choice. Having sex with him again would have been terribly confusing for my brain and my heart, but in that moment I was deflated. I loved the feeling of his cock in my hand again and was so ready to be fucked by him again. A hate fuck possibly, but still, I wanted it to happen. For some reason, I agreed to let him stay on my couch, and I went to bed confused, embarrassed and completely messed up.

The next morning I made enough coffee for the two of us and while we sipped it in my bed, we agreed the prior night was a bit of a mistake. Off he went. I figured that was the end of the Pete & Dave *90210* story.

But no, Dave wouldn't leave me, or the relationship, in the past. It was six months later when he texted me because he "needed to talk." I thought, "This should be interesting." It was time to get up, dust myself off again, and this time I needed to say goodbye.

We had agreed to meet at Northwood (RIP), a cute cocktail bar on Bloor Street, and we were both very awkward as we half-heartedly hugged. We settled into the window bar seat, and after two sips of beer I just got into it. I was prepared, I was direct, and I needed to say it all:

- You hurt me.
- You were not kind to me.
- You broke my heart.
- You acted selfishly and carelessly.

I went further and told him I wished he had been more honest with me. Had communicated with me. Had been fair. Dave knew that I was a neophyte in the world of casual sex and dating in the world of apps and cellphones; his rejection hurt all the more because of his disregard for my inexperience and my feelings.

Dave actually apologized. For the very first time, he took some blame for blowing up my life and admitted he acted poorly and selfishly. Dave elaborated that after our one night together in that anonymous hotel room he met someone else, fell in love and moved in with that person almost immediately. I silently said a little prayer to Yoko for that poor fucker.

I don't think I had ever been so forward and honest with anyone about a relationship in my life. Friend, lover or partner. It felt fantastic.

We ordered a second round of beer after airing all our shit and sipped them mostly in silence. I couldn't help but feel a bit of physical attraction. Dave was still incredibly good-looking. But for the first time, I wanted none of it. Thank heavens for objectivity.

When I got home, I turned on *Pale Green Ghosts* for old times' sake, mostly to cleanse myself of the memory of Dave and the John Grant concert, and to reclaim the artist and his music for myself. As John sang "It Doesn't Matter to Him," featuring the incomparable Sinéad O'Connor, I heard a truth I hadn't recognized before: John sang about trying desperately to win over a lover, being willing to do anything, to be anybody to win his favour, but ultimately realizing that the dream has died. John was never going to win the heart of his unnamed beloved.

Wasn't that the truth? I was never going to win Dave's heart again. I probably never had it in the first place. Most importantly, I had no interest in winning his heart again. Saying goodbye had never felt so good. While the rest of the record played out, I unfollowed Dave from all the social media accounts we shared, I deleted all the photos of him on my phone, and I finally hit Delete on the entirety of our text conversations.

There was no way I could avoid him in Queer Toronto forever, but I sure didn't need to see him online every day. He just didn't matter to me anymore.

I'M WAITING FOR THE MAN

After only a few dates, I had a pretty big crush on Martin. He was on my mind constantly. However, when my second long-term relationship with Everett ended, I had planned to enjoy my single status for a good long while; fuck a pile of men, go on dozens of dates and not let myself get entangled in any kind of relationship. I had been having the time of my life, and even though I was crushing hard on Martin, I wasn't ready to let go of my new-found freedom.

The day after Martin's birthday and the delivery of *Tape 55*, I started getting texts from Mexico. He was only going to be there for a brief vacation, but it seemed he was determined to keep our communication going strong. The twenty-something boys I was texting on the apps who lived down the block often couldn't reply to a text within a week, so to be getting communication from across the continent only served to warm my heart further.

We drove back to Stratford the week of Martin's return, as promised. Our drive mirrored the previous trip; holding hands or hands on thighs, we were in constant contact. The difference this time was that we had a cassette tape to play. Miraculously, his truck still had a tape deck! *Tape 55* entertained us as we cruised westward on Highway 401.

Once we arrived at the weekend house, I was feverish to jump him and enjoy our first proper fuck, but I could tell Martin was not quite ready for that. Instead, he buzzed around from room to room getting things ready for the weekend. Once the hot water was turned on, the heat turned up, and a few drapes were opened, we made a cocktail, sat by the fire and worked on a crossword puzzle together. Not exactly sexy, but pretty damn nice.

After a few hours of dozing by the fire, it was finally time for a soak in the hot tub. It was late afternoon and there wasn't much light left in the sky, so we grabbed some red wine, changed into our bathing suits and jumped in. This time, it was his turn to pick some music from his iPhone. The Wi-Fi didn't work well outside, so we were cockblocked from streaming, but it was sort of fun to be limited to the music on Martin's phone that hadn't been updated in several years. His face was locked in a grimace as he scanned and scanned his selections, with no obvious success. Finally, a grin lit up his face and he clicked his phone to start a track.

And what a track. "Sunday Morning" by the Velvet Underground started up, and my heart almost exploded. One of my favourite albums from one of my favourite artists. I told him so, and he nodded "me too." We both gazed off into the fading light and let the song wash over us.

I was taken off guard by the next tune. It was not "I'm Waiting for the Man," song two on their debut album *The Velvet Underground & Nico*. It was "White Light, White Heat" from their second record. I'm an album guy—I like listening to a piece of work as it was initially intended/created. Still, it was the Velvets. Who was I to complain?

My love affair with the band, and their first album, started back in the mid-eighties when I was in high school. I was at a party at my friend Sarah's house and my friends and I were all partaking in the usual antics of teenagers at a house party in the eighties—drinking booze, smoking dope and spinning records. A few of us were sitting on the front porch, the windows all open, music blasting, when my friend Joel went inside to change the record. He held up that iconic Andy Warhol–designed cover and announced from inside the house, "You guys have to hear this!" and he dropped the needle on side two, track one: "Heroin."

Jesus fucking CHRIST. What on earth was this? It was like nothing I had ever heard before and, quite frankly, like nothing I've heard since. The Velvet Underground was made up of Lou Reed (vocals, lead guitar), John Cale (viola, piano, bass), Sterling Morrison (rhythm guitar, bass) and Maureen Tucker (drums), and the band was managed by Andy Warhol. The group also served as the house band at Andy's famed

Factory. When it came time to record their first album together, Andy insisted they include the German model Nico on vocals for three tracks, resulting in the Rosetta stone of indie rock: 1967's *The Velvet Underground & Nico.* The top-selling records that year came from the Monkees, the Beatles and the Supremes; tunefulness ruled the airwaves, and the Velvets sounded as if they came from the basement of a dirty sex club. The Velvet Underground were not tuneful. A wild cacophony of experimental rock led by Reed's deadpan vocals and Cale's viola underscoring everything with a pulsing drone, they truly invented a sound uniquely their own. A sound as far from the mainstream as you could get. My kind of band. Thanks to Joel and that high school party, I have been in love with the Velvets and Lou Reed from that moment on. Joel was always cooler than the rest us. I'm forever indebted to him for that introduction.

Back in Stratford, Martin and I relaxed in the tub, cuddled in the warm water and listened as the playlist ran on. When the bottle of wine was almost finished and there was only a hint of light left in the sky, the playlist goddesses delivered us "Venus in Furs." An ode to kinky and dirty sex, it's classic Velvet Underground. The lyrics can still raise an eyebrow or two, but in 1967 it was like nothing else that had ever come before. Bondage. Leather. Blood. Whips. Yes, please.

The energy in the hot tub finally shifted and we started to kiss and paw at each other. Maybe it was thanks to the Velvets? Martin and I didn't have the same fever to fuck as I had with some of my younger lovers, but I was happy to be patient and wait for the right moment to arrive.

At the song's conclusion, we parted long enough for Martin to sigh deeply, look up at the sky and state, "This is such a nice moment," as he stroked my thigh under the water. I couldn't have agreed more. I was loving being in the company of this gorgeous man and listening to one of my favourite bands. It's nice to sit back and let someone else choose the music for a change.

Sadly, the "no sex in the hot tub" rule was still in effect, so we quickly towelled off, ran upstairs, kicked off the suits and got down to business. We were feverish in the tub, but something was lost on the trip upstairs. We fucked for the first time, and while I was thrilled to have Martin inside me finally, something still didn't feel right. It was a bit lifeless, a bit routine. He closed his eyes and banged away methodically and I felt a bit like a sex doll. I could have been anyone. It was connect-the-dots sex until I came . . . and as soon as I did, it was over.

Sex was important to me—at that point more so than ever before in my life—so I was pretty unsettled. I was starting to really invest in Martin emotionally, but I wasn't ready to give up great sex. Here was another man, close in age to me, still trying to make sense of sex and his queerness in middle age. The shadow of AIDS loomed large for those of us who survived and watched it with horror. I was finally recognizing that fear in myself and was trying to move past that collective trauma, but I had a hunch that Martin hadn't confronted those demons yet.

The rest of the weekend was delightful, and maybe with sex out of the way we both relaxed a bit. During the drive home we talked about future plans and introductions to each other's family and friends. It all felt very boyfriend-y, but were we boyfriends? Were we moving in that direction?

I couldn't quite get a read on Martin, and it flummoxed me. What was really going on here? Only time would tell.

SEXY MF

While riding high on my crush on Martin, I was still keeping an active life in the Scruff pool. I had learned from many of my new friends and sex partners that there was an unwritten set of rules around gay sex and dating, which didn't take me long to adopt. Sex does not equal dating. Sex does not mean any emotional entanglement. Sex does not equal love. And until a couple explicitly states they are dating or monogamous, it's open season to see other partners. The concept was still pretty new to me, but I was having way too much fun meeting new friends and having sex with new fuck buddies; I wasn't ready to truly settle down with anyone. You can't put all your eggs in one basket, as they say.

I had spotted Patrick online early in the new year and we spent several weeks messaging each other fairly regularly. When we connected online, he was keen and communicative, but would then disappear for a few weeks. It was incredibly frustrating; just when I thought I had him hooked and about to commit to a date, he'd be gone. And then he'd be back. It was a bit of a roller-coaster ride with Patrick.

During our online conversations I found out he was a law student, hence the regular absences. I also learned that he was new to Toronto, a recent transplant from the prairies. He had left his boyfriend back home, but they were going to try to make a long-distance relationship work.

"Good luck," I thought. I'm all for open relationships, but long-distance? Yikes.

Maybe I could continue to enjoy the comfort and connection with Martin and secure a cute, smart twenty-nine-year-old fuck buddy at the same time. Perfect.

He had a few extra days off from school over Easter and had headed back home to see his parents. It was during his trip that we moved from Scruff to texting each other's phones, a big move in the sex app world; it's a subtle distinction, but sharing a cell number is like an invitation into someone's private world.

With Patrick bored at his parents' house and me unemployed, we both had a lot of free time for texting. And text we did. We sent countless messages back and forth, slowly getting more bold in sending pictures to each other. Cute pictures of us doing fun things in the world with friends turned into pictures of us in our underwear and jockstraps and then, finally, with nothing on at all. What a treat those photos were. Over six feet tall, Patrick was long, lean and muscled from regular gym visits—he was a beautiful man.

It wasn't all sexy photos, though. When Patrick mentioned he loved queer stories from the turn of the last century, I pulled my well-worn paperback copy of *Maurice* off the shelf, snapped a pic and sent it in reply. *Like this?*

I think I heard his gasp through the phone. I may have impressed him with a picture of me in a jockstrap (I hope I did, anyway), but it was clear by his reaction that a shared love of *Maurice* was golden. We agreed the book was a pivotal "coming out" read and we also shared a fondness for the 1987 film based on the novel. There were not many films in 1987 tackling forbidden gay yearning helmed by Academy Award–nominated directors like James Ivory. There still aren't. *Maurice* made its mark on both of us, decades apart. You have to admire art like that.

Neither one of us looked particularly like actors James Wilby or Rupert Graves, but I imagined us as Maurice and Scudder, embarking on a life-changing clandestine romance, one where we both had lives outside our trysts (a.k.a. boyfriends) but could bang each other like animals every once in a while. Many a joke was made with Patrick about meeting at the boathouse, as well as sipping gin and tonics on the lawn after playing a rousing game of tennis. We both really leaned into creating this fantasy

text by text by text. We promised each other a joint viewing of
Maurice in the near future.

Once Patrick was home from out west, we continued to text,
but with far less frequency. I found it hard to get him to commit
to a date. School was busy again for Patrick and it was difficult
for him to find free time. We persevered, though, and finally
made a date towards the end of the month. The weekend after
Prince died, as it turned out.

Fuck. First Bowie, then Prince. What else did 2016 have in
store for us? Oh right, the nomination of the most disgraceful
president in the USA's checkered history . . . but that was still
months away. In April, we just had to mourn the loss of two
music legends, not the end of America.

Prince was one of the few geniuses of our time. Dead at fifty-
seven, he left behind a staggering body of work: thirty-nine
studio albums, and rumours of thousands of unheard songs
recorded and stored away in a vault in his home studio in Paisley
Park. No doubt his estate would be milking that treasure chest
for years to come.

As a teenager, I was an idiot. I didn't appreciate Prince. It seems
impossible to me now, but he was just too popular. I lumped him
into the same category as Madonna, Michael Jackson, Cyndi
Lauper and other hitmakers of the era—music made for the
masses. It was easy to do at the time, his music was everywhere,
listened to by everyone. Anything the jocks and popular kids
were listening to, I wanted to steer clear of. Sometimes it's easier
to define yourself by what you don't like rather than celebrate
what you love. My opinion was solidified when I bought the
Batman soundtrack in the fervour over Tim Burton's film in
1989. It's not Prince's best work.

The thing I most admired about him when I was younger was
that he wrote Sinéad O'Connor's smash hit "Nothing Compares
2 U," released in 1990. It's a killer song and holy shit, does she sing

the hell out of it. It's one of the great vocal performances ever put to record, and it took the world by storm.

As I got older, I realized the error of my ways, and without the baggage of high school I could listen to Prince more objectively. When I finally listened—really listened—to his music, I was astonished. How could I have heard "When Doves Cry," "Kiss," "1999" or "Little Red Corvette" and not recognized his genius? Like I said, I was an idiot.

I always recognized that Prince played a mean guitar, but I never realized that, like Stevie Wonder (also a genius), he released entire albums where he played every single instrument. Was I too young to appreciate how far he took genderfuck and played with the binary in a way no one in the mainstream had ever done before? Bowie teased genderfuck with makeup, hair, high-heeled boots and fashion, but Prince perfected it. Few humans look better in lingerie than Prince.

While he embraced and celebrated the femininity in himself, he also put women on a pedestal. During his creative and commercial peak he partnered with and promoted several women, sharing the burning white-hot spotlight that was shining on him. Wendy & Lisa were two women in his studio and touring band, the Revolution. Queer women. They were a prolific powerhouse themselves and both highly visible members of Prince's entourage. They contributed to the albums *Purple Rain* (1984), *Around the World in a Day* (1985) and *Parade* (1986) and toured with Prince to promote them. Wendy & Lisa even got a couple of co-writing credits on those records—a rarity on Prince albums.

Meanwhile, Prince partnered with Sheila E. to record and promote her first record. It's rumoured that he wrote every song on Sheila's debut album *The Glamorous Life* (1984), though she is credited as writing most of them. He even invited her to open for him on tour. There simply wasn't a better platform for any artist at the time. *The Glamorous Life* was a huge hit.

During this same period he also wrote smash hit songs for the Bangles, Sheena Easton, Chaka Khan, Patti LaBelle, Martika and others; he co-created duets with Kate Bush and Madonna on their records; and he even played the synthesizer part on Stevie Nicks's hit song "Stand Back." Prince was a very busy man in the 1980s.

So many of Prince's songs are about sex, but unlike most songs written by men, they're not all about conquering women, or male pleasure. Prince wasn't afraid to explore a woman's point of view in his songcraft, exposing himself as not just a lover but a thinker and a feeler. Prince went so far as to create an alter-ego named Camille, digitally altering his vocals to a higher pitch to sound like a woman. A few of those songs were released on Prince's *Sign o' the Times* record in 1987. I often wonder if Prince was living out his own fantasies around what it might be like to experience life and sex like a woman via Camille and in his songwriting for other artists, literally putting his words into the mouths of women collaborators. Taking his genderfuck to a whole different level. Only Prince knew for sure. I wonder, if his career were starting today, with our ongoing understanding of trans and non-binary experiences, would Prince try harder to explain exactly what he meant, what he felt? Maybe when Prince told us he was something that we would never understand, he really meant it.

Genius. There's just no other word.

At Patrick's suggestion, we planned to meet at Me & Mine (RIP) on College Street for our first proper date. Both of us confessed to being a bit nervous after the long lead-up to this date, but I was excited to connect. He beamed at me from across the room when I walked into the restaurant. Swoon. I'd seen enough photos to know Patrick was a babe, but wow, did he present well in person. He was gorgeous and his smile was out of this world.

Nerves fell away quickly and we both relaxed almost immediately. Everyone was talking about Prince, and so did we. To

Patrick he was a distant icon, sort of like how Stevie Wonder was to me. Still active and releasing records when I was a teenager, Stevie's best years were behind him. It took me a few decades to forgive him for "I Just Called to Say I Love You." (That shit is awful.) My memories of Prince were more personal than Patrick's, but still, we both recognized what a loss.

Prince didn't dominate the whole conversation, though. We talked about my album collection some more. Vintage porn. Theremins. A fondness for simpler times. Campy films. Favourite books. Wooden tennis rackets. It was a hell of a first date.

After a couple of drinks and some food, I asked Patrick if he wanted to come home and see my album collection. "I bet you say that to all the boys," he replied with a grin.

Back at my house, Patrick was a little closed physically. He kept his hands to himself and chose to sit in a chair opposite from me on the couch. So, I gave him some space. He flipped through the albums and asked me to put on Fleet Foxes' *Helplessness Blues*. Of course.

As the Foxes harmonized, Patrick scanned my collection and commented time and again on the quality of the curation. Music to my ears. He pulled out *1999* and *Purple Rain* for later consideration. I may have been an idiot in the eighties, but I've bought my share of Prince records since.

After I flipped Fleet Foxes to side two, Patrick finally moved over and joined me on the couch. He asked politely if he could kiss me. "Yes, please," I responded. From then on it was like a switch turned on. Patrick went from mild-mannered law student to aggressive and passionate lover. What a welcome turn of events. During our text conversations he had told me he liked being a top primarily and could get pretty aggressive if allowed. He was allowed. He took me to my bedroom and fucked me like an animal. It was amazing. Thankfully, our connection definitely included sex.

Lying beside me, sweating, still wet from sex, he announced that he should probably get going. It was after 2 a.m. at this point, but I was still a bit surprised. "School work tomorrow," he told me. I helped Patrick get his clothes together and gave him a farewell kiss, naked at the door. Sleep came quickly. I was sure I had just secured a hot and steady fuck buddy.

Wrong again.

Despite us both having had a great time, Patrick became impossible to pin down. We texted with some regularity for a while. We flirted and sent each other photos but barely met in the real world, despite my constant attempts. We met for beers and made out a bit once, played tennis once in the park, and bumped into each other on the street the odd time. We never fucked again, though.

Was I the first guy he slept with outside his relationship? I wondered. Maybe he liked me too much? That's what I told myself to help mend my bruised ego. Rereading all the messages to and fro, I wondered if he just liked the attention more than the connection. I was literate, gave him good recommendations in a new city and sent him photos of me in my underwear. Sometimes that's all a guy wants.

Months later, I got a notice from the Toronto Public Library that the hold I had placed on the *Maurice* DVD was finally available for pickup at my local branch. I chuckled to myself and picked it up the next day. I had long given up on Patrick, but couldn't resist texting him to ask if he wanted to come and watch the movie with me. In typical fashion he told me he did, he just wasn't sure when he'd have time. Sigh.

I watched it myself along with a few glasses of wine and lost myself in Forster's fictional world. Patrick's loss.

I never did get a chance to play Patrick those Prince records he pulled out. I'll share those with someone more worthy.

I CAN SEE CLEARLY NOW

My forty-seventh birthday, on April 5, 2016, was fast approaching and after the prior year's epic journey with Mintz I was thinking of a more low-key approach to celebrating the occasion. I could hardly ask my friends to provide a soundtrack for every birthday, could I?

Martin told me he wanted to help me celebrate, so I came up with a simple plan: a small dinner at my place with two old friends so that I could introduce them to the handsome lover I had gushed to them about. Work was busy for Martin, as always, but he told me he could shift a few things and was sure he could make it. Noncommittal, but I had faith in him.

As the day of the dinner party approached, we continued our daily texts. While he hadn't quite sorted out his schedule, Martin was still planning on coming. I have to say that my confidence in him was waning at this stage. When my two friends arrived for dinner, they could barely conceal their excitement.

"Is Martin coming?"

"I think so, but . . ." I still wasn't sure.

It wasn't until an hour after they arrived that I got the final text. It was full of apologies and excuses, but the bottom line was that he wasn't joining the party. I was crushed. What a dick.

I put on my best "happy face" and explained to my friends that we would just be a trio, while clearing away the fourth setting at the table. The three of us enjoyed a good meal, delicious wine and some great music. I went to bed sated, but sad. While I wasn't expecting *Mixtape 47*, I figured showing up to dinner wasn't too much to ask. Maybe there was something else going on with Martin?

Immediately after my birthday, the texts from Martin began to slow in frequency. His attention became far tougher to grab.

When dates were suggested, he refused to commit. Work was busy. Life was busy. Spring had sprung. When we did connect, sometimes we had sex, sometimes we didn't. On the occasions we did have sex, it never rose above the mundane. Don't get me wrong, I still loved sharing physical intimacy with such a handsome guy, but the sex just never really clicked.

With no job and too much time on my hands, I over-analyzed the situation. Was opening up to me too real for Martin? Was emotional intimacy as tricky for him as physical intimacy? Was meeting a couple of my friends too much of a commitment? Martin and I still enjoyed the odd date in Toronto, but the invitations to Stratford ceased to come.

I didn't see Martin for months, and I was pretty broken-hearted about it. We continued to check in on each other, and he helped me figure out an easy way to renovate my house so that I could rent out my second floor. I had reservations about giving up part of my home and moving my bedroom from the second floor to the dark basement, but Martin assured me I would love it. He had done the same thing years ago. The extra income would help me afford to pay my mortgage while I was looking for work. I'll be forever grateful for that.

Near the end of the summer, I got Martin to agree to a glass of wine after we hadn't seen each other in several weeks. I needed some closure and wanted to ask him what the hell had happened between us. With some wine in my belly I finally mustered up the courage to ask Martin directly what went down. It turned out that our brief romance upset his routine too much. He loved his life exactly as it was before he met me. Morning gym. Dog walk. Day at work. Client visits at night. Bed at nine. Repeat. Weekends were for chores and catching up on sleep.

I was speechless. Who couldn't carve out a little time for someone whom they clearly liked and had a connection with? Shutting down any kind of connection at fifty-five, that was sad.

I'd imagined making *Tape #56, #57* and many more, but I wasn't going to get that chance now. I was getting better at enjoying casual sex without emotional entanglements, but this level of intimacy? That was hard to shut off. I was hurt, and I couldn't help but ask myself, "What did I do to mess this up?"

But maybe I was the better for it. After only a few months with Martin, I thought my life as a single man was potentially over after sowing my oats for only a year. I wasn't sure I was ready for a relationship exactly, but this one felt like a special connection. Sadly, sex got in the way of intimacy . . . or intimacy got in the way of sex. Sex definitely got in the way of something.

After the experiences with my "future self" Jason, and now Martin, it was time to give up hanging out with men my own age. Too many scars, too much baggage. Bring on the young ones. Please, Dolly, Yoko and Grace, bring on the young ones. I needed to have some fun.

BROKEN ENGLISH

I was feeling pretty sorry for myself after Martin and I had our final conversation. More sorry for Martin, quite frankly—who eschewed real human connection and chemistry because of his "routine"? I just couldn't understand it.

What better salve for a wounded heart than sex with a young man? If there is one, I've yet to find it. I made a harmless "Woof" at Nat on Scruff as I scrolled through the profile pics of guys who were online. The "Woof" button is sort of a "Like" button to let a fellow Scruff user know you're interested in him, or that you think he's hot. Nat and I had chatted online a few times before, but he told me he was looking to spend more time with guys his own age—twenty-six. So I had written off our ever meeting, but it was the woof that changed the game. I was shocked to get a message in return: Nat had been stood up. Some foolish lad had led him on, got him all wound up and left him "All Revved Up with No Place to Go" (bless you, Meat Loaf). Perfect. Timing has never been my forte, but that day: right woof, right time.

Nat arrived at my place by bike within half an hour. He was tailor-made for me. Nat had beautiful brown eyes, short brown hair and an unkempt beard to match. Dressed in all black—T-shirt, shorts, socks and Vans—he was a sight for my horny eyes.

Small talk was brief as we both knew exactly what he had come for. After a few exploratory hands on knees and hands on shoulders, we were kissing and groping at each other under our clothes. I peeled off his shirt to discover tattooed across his well-defined chest: *Religion: Old Dogs.* One could not help but ask. He told me it was something he had seen on a Facebook profile in the early days of the site, and it resonated with him—not only because of the dig at religion (excellent) but also because it captured his affinity for dogs (most excellent) and for older men (most excellent of all). Maybe he had lied to me in our previous message exchange about dating men his own age, but did I care in that moment? A cute, bearded boy who knows how to kiss and likes older gents? I was all in.

Before long we were both topless and grinding against each other when Nat asked to go to my bedroom. It was not easy to untangle ourselves from each other, but we managed the feat and I led him by the hard-on down to my new bedroom in the basement. At the foot of my bed we peeled off our remaining clothes and stood facing each other completely naked. Nat had a killer body from regular gym visits and biking around town, and he looked beautiful with his erection pointing straight at me.

We hopped on the bed and pushed, pulled and teased each other's bodies in an adult wrestling match. I'm not sure who suggested it first, but we discovered we both enjoyed a bit of spit play. We spat into each other's open mouths. On each other's chests. On each other's cocks. It was obvious that it heightened the experience for both of us. Seeing a twenty-six-year-old grin as he licks your spit out of his own beard is something you may have to experience for yourself to understand how much of a turn-on it is, but to Nat and me, it was queer magic. Otherworldly.

As I lay back on the bed, Nat got on top of me. He straddled me and ground his ass against my dick, which was sandwiched between his butt cheeks. I grabbed his hard-on in my right hand and we moved in tandem, rocking back and forth, until he came. As I watched Nat convulsing and shuddering, he completely disappeared from his body; he was all sensation, giving in to desire, feeling and pleasure. Nat was beyond fear, beyond doubt, beyond thought and judgment, past shame. That was a place I wanted to get to.

Once he recovered his senses a bit, he continued to stroke my dick and I quickly jetted my come up his back and on his ass. With him still straddling me and both of us covered in sweat, spit and each other's come, we looked at each other, smiled and kissed a bit as we cooled down. There is nothing hotter than great fucking sex chemistry with a complete stranger.

Martin who?

We both partially dressed and climbed back upstairs for a "get to know you" beer. Nat was a New Jersey boy working on his PhD in behavioural sciences at U of T, and while he loved Toronto, he didn't have long-term plans to stay in the city. I also discovered he had a twin brother who was a professional musician in Brooklyn, and that his training and appreciation of music had rubbed off on Nat . . . He loved music and was more than a little intrigued by my record collection. A cute, bearded boy who knew how to kiss and shag, had both right and left brain firing on all cylinders, plus he liked older gents? Definitely all in. All of which made picking an album a tricky proposition. After a round of sweaty and dirty sex, however, it felt as though Marianne Faithfull was the right place to go.

Marianne's story is one of those stranger-than-fiction tales. Not only was her first single written by Mick Jagger, Keith Richards and Andrew Loog Oldham (the Rolling Stones' manager between 1963 and 1967), but she released her version before the Rolling Stones did their take on the song. "As Tears Go By" was released in 1964 and cracked the top ten in her native UK while she was still a teenager. The Stones' version followed the next year. From there, Marianne's career and life took untold twists and turns, including:

- A marriage and son with a major art dealer.
- A tumultuous romance with Mick Jagger that lasted for years.
- Becoming a fixture of London's sixties scene and a fashion icon of the time.
- Recording five full-length LPs in the sixties after her initial single.
- Overcoming an addiction to heroin.
- Co-writing "Sister Morphine" with Mick and Keith Richards (recorded separately by the Stones and by Marianne) about said heroin addiction.
- Performing in countless stage, TV and film roles starting in the late sixties.
- Being caught in a police raid wearing only a bearskin rug.
- Enduring a bout of homelessness for several years because of the addiction to heroin.
- Surviving a battle with anorexia.

And I would be remiss if I didn't mention a televised duet of "I Got You Babe" with David fucking Bowie while dressed as a nun! (Do yourself a favour and look that one up on YouTube.) There was even an urban legend about Marianne, a Mars bar and her vagina that, while reeking of total bullshit, somehow became "fact." I certainly believed it as a kid. The stories about Marianne are endless, and she's told many of them in the several autobiographies she's written.

Somehow, someway, at arguably her lowest point, she cobbled a team together to record and release her masterpiece, *Broken English*, in 1979. With Marianne having lost all credibility in the music industry due to her addiction issues, Island Records' Chris Blackwell took a big risk in underwriting the record. It proved to be a very astute decision: after fifteen years in the public eye for all the wrong reasons, Marianne finally found her voice.

And what a voice. It was completely ravaged by smoking and drugs. If she was an unremarkable pop singer in the sixties, she was a new woman in the seventies. Rough and raw, her vocals on this album are those of a woman who has lived, and lived HARD. Marianne's a survivor, no matter how many punches she had taken. It's no wonder the queer community gravitates to her. We've all got our demons.

The album kicked off with the title track, and within seconds I could tell that Nat was intrigued. The record is a curious blend of seventies rock and soon-to-be-eighties new wave sounds mashed together with that inimitable voice. The backing band comprised Barry Reynolds and Joe Mavety on guitars, Steve York on bass and Terry Stannard on drums, a lineup Marianne had formed for a tour several years before. Steve York's work in particular stands out on almost every track; his bass lines are incredible.

There were several other collaborators on the album, but bringing in Steve Winwood to play keyboards was truly inspired. Yup, that Steve Winwood. The guy who played with Eric Clapton in Traffic, was part of the Spencer Davis Group and had some really big cheesy hits in his later career ("Higher Love," anyone?) is the musician contributing keyboards across the album. I love his classic seventies-sounding electric piano/organ playing on the record, but it's his synthesizer playing that seems so ahead of its time.

The whole team was clearly taking in the late 1970s punk and early new wave music scenes and creating something completely unique. But, ultimately, the album is all about Marianne and that voice. When she repeatedly croaked out and asked the listener, or herself, what they are fighting for midway through the title track like a war cry, I could tell Nat was hooked. I've never figured out what the song itself is about exactly, but with Marianne's plea repeated again and again, I hear her asking all the big questions. What are we here for? What is worth fighting for? Who is it that's worth fighting for? Is it love? Art? Politics? Beauty? Why do we make the choices we do?

It's a great song and a great entry point to the record. The next three songs on side one are meditations on witches, addiction and guilt. Like Nat, it was tailor-made for me, and so many queers just like me. Side two starts with "The Ballad of Lucy Jordan." It's an oddity on the album, but arguably its best-known song. Used famously in the 1991 film *Thelma & Louise*, it became something of a touchstone for me. It's a little bit more poppy, as much as anything on this album can be poppy, and written by Shel Silverstein, a celebrated author and singer-songwriter. One of Silverstein's best-known works is the children's book *The Giving Tree*, which he wrote and illustrated, first published in 1964. A sweet parable about love and the joy of giving, it couldn't be further removed from Marianne's world if it tried.

In the chorus, Marianne describes a middle-aged woman who realizes she's never going to zip around Paris in a convertible with the wind blowing through her hair. It's a beautiful metaphor depicting a woman who is coming to terms with the fact that her life is not going to play out the way she hoped;

her dreams are dying. The image is great, but her phrasing of the lines is masterful; the hurt and the frustration are palpable. Though Brad, my first long-term boyfriend, had taken me to Paris before my thirty-seventh birthday, I realized one day hearing Marianne croak that line that I was never going to feel that sense of freedom and release with him. It was a pivotal moment in my assessment of that doomed relationship.

The next two songs are written by dudes too. "What's the Hurry" is a pretty cool rock 'n' roll jam, followed by a beautiful version of John Lennon's "Working Class Hero." Hearing a woman's voice take a turn on this chestnut is a nice twist, and she owns it. It may be blasphemous to suggest, but her version might be better than John's.

The final song is likely my favourite on the record. "Why D'Ya Do It" is a tour de force by a woman scorned, someone who has seen it all. Marianne is credited as co-writer with five other people, all men, but I sincerely hope it was her who came up with each and every one of the bons mots contained in the lyrics. The song is dirty, raw, and full of pain and hate. Give it a listen and look up the lyrics; a song that includes mentions of bitch, dick, cunt, fanny, pussy, cock, hash, snatch and more is not commonplace on an album aiming for (and missing) the mainstream. It was a brave choice by Marianne. Forty years before Cardi B's "WAP," Marianne showed the world how it was really done.

The song is crass, filthy, and I was absolutely astonished when I first heard it as a young teenager a few years after it was released. This is a woman who was not mincing words about being betrayed by her lover. Midway through the song, she sings about an act that Nat and I had unknowingly tried to re-create. Marianne asks why a lover spat on her snatch! As a teenager, my interpretation of the lyric was full of contempt: How could someone spit on their lover, on their sex organs no less? I was only too pleased to have this opinion rebuffed over time. As Nat and I lay together on the couch and let Marianne's glorious filth waft over us, we smiled knowingly when we heard the line detailing a bit of spit play. We each realized we'd found a new friend, and Nat a new favourite record.

Broken English peaked at only number eighty-two on the Billboard chart, but it found its way into the hearts of so many of us outsiders and fighters. I was only fourteen or fifteen when I first heard it and was starting to question my sexuality and where I was going to fit in the world. This woman's voice, this survivor's voice, resonated with me because I think she made it clear: "It's not going to be easy, kid."

The world may not have been ready for *Broken English* in 1979, but it has finally been recognized as the masterpiece it is by the folks who decide these things. The queers have known it all along.

Marianne definitely had some more ups and downs after the release of *Broken English*. She's released more than a dozen albums since, and collaborated with PJ Harvey, Nick Cave, Beck, Blur and many other incredible artists. Her two most recent music releases, 2014's *Give My Love to London* and 2018's *Negative Capability*, rank among her best work, and her reputation as a film actor continued to grow with appearances in feature films and on TV. One of her more memorable roles was God in the BBC comedy *Absolutely Fabulous*. If God has to sound and look like someone, my vote gets cast for Marianne. She was also one of the first celebrity cases of COVID reported in 2020 and nearly died from it. But she still hangs on.

When the album finished, Nat admitted he was floored. He was shocked to have never heard of Marianne Faithfull, let alone of this masterpiece. A new convert was born that day, and I was happy to be his tutor.

LIKE A PRAYER

I thought I was getting catfished by Douglas. Catfishing is pretty commonplace on the apps, I discovered—using a fake photo of a handsome man to bait a fellow user into a conversation. Douglas had one of those profile pics that made me a little suspicious. A couple of years younger than me, he had gorgeous salt-and-pepper hair, stunning blue eyes and a big, beaming grin. I had been burned the odd time by guys with clearly too much time on their hands, once going so far as to wait in front of a Starbucks only to discover that my Prince Charming had deleted his profile between setting up our date and the time of its arrival. Douglas seemed genuine, though, so I took a chance and set up a date for a drink.

The only time he was free that week was the day I was starting my new job. After months of employment worry and panic, I'd landed a pretty good gig as the director of marketing for an animation company owned by a massive Canadian media behemoth. What better way to end the first day of work than a drink date with a handsome stranger? And what a handsome stranger! When I walked up to the patio of the Rivoli, there Douglas was, no catfish, no bullshit. He was gorgeous.

And so began a series of cute dates.

Date 1. Over martinis on the Rivoli patio, we found out we both worked in media and had several shared contacts and friends. We each agreed we found the other very good-looking. At the end of the date he gave me a friendly kiss on the cheek and I watched his beautiful ass walk eastward along Queen Street.

Date 2. Douglas wanted to treat me to a dinner to celebrate my new job, so he took me to a Queen West classic: Peter Pan. Over wine he explained he wasn't sure what dating looked like for him, or should look like. It had been years since he'd had more than casual hookups and he wasn't sure what he was looking for exactly, but he liked me. Uh-oh. We parted with a half-hearted hug and chaste kiss.

Date 3. In a very sweet move, Douglas planned a picnic in Trinity Bellwoods Park. It was a gorgeous early summer evening with the late-day sun throwing long shadows over us and our blanket. We shared a bottle of wine, ate some delicious takeout and finally kissed on our little pocket of the jam-packed lawn. It was a beautiful moment, and he must have felt it too—he invited me back to his place nearby. Giddy-up.

Riding our bikes along Queen, I spotted Carolyn walking in the opposite direction and had to stop. I hadn't seen her for a few weeks so I wanted to say hi, but I also wanted to show off this gorgeous guy I was about to have sex with. In an instant, she knew exactly what was going on and sent us on our way with a clandestine wink for my eyes only.

When Douglas let me into his place, we didn't waste time getting naked. I'd wanted to see him without his clothes on since the second I laid eyes on him. The sex was fun and uninhibited— the perfect end to a picnic. While we lay on his bed, he picked my underwear up off the floor, covered his nose with the crotch and inhaled deeply. He admitted he loved the smell of another man's underwear, and who can blame him? We traded underwear that night. I slipped his black Calvin briefs on and left him with my Dri-FIT trunks.

I rode home in his summer sweat–soiled underwear through the quiet streets of Toronto.

Now, that was the kind of frisky fun I signed up for when I woofed Douglas. I still had no interest in anything resembling a proper boyfriend, but finding a new hot fuck buddy was definitely at the top of my to-do list. When I got home, I sent Carolyn a text: *I just rode home in that hot guy's underwear, the one you just met.* It was a boast neither one of us would have believed twenty years prior.

A week later, it was my turn to host for date four, and I was certain this was the night I was going to get to fuck Douglas. He was a bit standoffish upon arrival and I was a little puzzled by that. No pressure, I figured he'd warm up after some wine and dinner.

We chatted while we ate and drank wine, but there was a definite shift in vibe from our previous meeting. My physical advances weren't spurned, but they weren't exactly warmly received. Hmm.

As we settled on the couch, he asked if we could put on one of my Madonna records. Sure, why not?

Oh, Madonna. She, the revered queen of so many gay men my age, of any age really. I'm not entirely sold on Madonna and it makes me a bit of a traitor to my people. I have a lot of mixed feelings about her. The one-two punch of her eponymous debut album and her follow-up record *Like a Virgin* resulted in over 30 million records sold. An astonishing sales figure in any era and downright impossible anymore in the age of streaming. Madonna's first record came out only two years after MTV launched, and she knew how to take advantage of the fledgling music video medium—her clips were played incessantly. Ubiquitous on radio and TV, Madonna was everywhere you went.

I had a soft spot for Madonna when I was a sixteen- and seventeen-year-old. So did my good friend Anita. We pretended to like her ironically, though I suspect we both secretly loved her. We told each other that her work was trash and it was cheesy, and we weren't wrong. But it was good trash. The best kind of trash. And I love some good guilty-pleasure trash. Madonna was not in keeping with our usual tastes of that time. We were playing the Violent Femmes, R.E.M., Tears for Fears and all sorts of other alternative stuff of the time. Madonna was beneath us.

When *True Blue* came out, early in the summer of 1986, Anita went to buy the album on the release date and brought it over to my house. My parents were out of town and that always meant party time. We spent the entire day listening to the record—ironically, of course—and as the house filled with our friends later that night, we couldn't resist playing it some more. While my friends watched, I high-kicked my way across the living room à la "Lucky Star," drunk out of my mind, cigarette in one hand, beer in the other. I told myself it was just for fun. My friends laughed and that sound was contagious.

I couldn't admit that I actually liked Madonna, though. What would that make me? In retrospect, I'd love to take a survey of friends at those parties to see who thought young Pete just might be gay. Hands up, everyone!

Madonna has an amazing catalogue of songs that I think are outstanding examples of the quintessential pop song—great hooks, universal themes, catchy melodies. Really, some of the best pop songs out there. I actually don't think she gets enough credit in the songwriting department. In 2020 she celebrated her fiftieth number one song on the Billboard charts, more than anyone else in history. It's an astonishing statistic.

But do I think she's an amazing artist like she claims? No. Can she sing? Barely. Can she act? Nope. Can she dance? A little. Does she know how to stir up controversy and attract attention? Hell yes. It's her greatest weapon. Her instincts for self-promotion and her marketing savvy are unparalleled. I totally respect this about her—that is not a dig.

Douglas chose *Like a Prayer* from 1989 as the album he'd like to hear. I pulled the record out and we both sniffed the faint scent of patchouli; the first pressing of the record came out with a scented inner sleeve. I'm not sure if that was to indicate Madonna had become a hippy—she did have long brown curls all of a sudden—or just a cute marketing ploy, but I was sold. I loved it. I still love it. It's nice to think of a time when record labels had that kind of money to spend. I put the record on the turntable and thought, "This should be fun, maybe it'll loosen him up."

How wrong I was.

The first two tracks are killer pop songs—"Like a Prayer" and "Express Yourself"—and we bopped along and enjoyed the great songwriting and production. They are two of Madonna's best tracks. During track three, "Love Song," her ill-fated collaboration with Prince, Douglas started crying. Madonna clearly meant a great deal to him, and hearing *Like a Prayer* on vinyl for the first time in decades was striking a chord. He talked about travelling downtown on the GO train from the Toronto suburbs to see Madonna's Blond Ambition tour in 1990 at the SkyDome and having his own private coming-out party. Emotional territory for anyone.

I never saw that tour, or any Madonna concert until my thirties. I did, however, see the documentary film she made during the Blond Ambition shows. *Truth or Dare* came out in theatres in 1991 following the end of the concert tour. I was twenty-two and my good friend Lorna and I went to the movie as fans. Somewhere along the way I was able to admit I liked Madonna, but I still wasn't able to admit I was gay. Twenty-two and still in the closet. Sigh. Similar to my friend Anita, I think Lorna and I had a tacit understanding that I was gay. Thank the goddesses for both of them, they helped me get through my teen years with some hope for the future.

Madonna was at the zenith of her popularity when the documentary was released. Following up *Like a Prayer* with the singles "Justify My Love" and "Vogue," she was white-hot and everything she did made the news. Madonna got a lot of attention for fellating a bottle of water in the film, but for me, watching two of her backup dancers make out during an onscreen game of truth or dare was revolutionary. Two gay men kissing onscreen at the multiplex was totally unprecedented at the time. Gay men on any screen was unprecedented, period.

Yes, she stole "Vogue" from the trans and queer Black and Latino communities.

Yes, she stole most of her "reinvention" tricks from Bowie and Grace Jones.

Yes, she stood on the shoulders of so many artists before her without acknowledging them.

But she helped countless gay men get a glimpse of what it could be to be queer. Watching Madonna, when she was the biggest pop star on the planet, not just accept those two men kissing onscreen but celebrate them and their desire was game-changing. That was major. For me and for millions of other closeted homos like me. And for that, I love her.

She never quite reached the heights of *Like a Prayer* and *Truth or Dare* again. *Ray of Light*, from 1998, may be her creative peak, but she would never have an album as popular as *Like a Prayer* again. Maybe Madonna should have spent less time fruitlessly trying to win an Oscar and pumped out a few more good records instead. There are more duds after *Like a Prayer* than there are winners. It would be so great if Madonna could do something truly revolutionary again. To hear her do an acoustic record or something stripped down and really address what it's like to be Madonna, or a woman aging in the public eye, would be so fascinating. There could be real meat there. Sexy. Strong. Original. But instead, we get *Madame X*. Sigh. If anyone can name one good song on *Madame X*, they might be as delusional as Queen Madge herself.

Listen, Madonna can do whatever the fuck she wants, and I am here to support her. But we've seen her play the sex kitten, or dominatrix, thousands of times. One of the things that was most interesting about her at the peak of her career was her constant drive for reinvention, to be seen in different ways, in different roles. A real reinvention in her sixties would be a game changer. Sadly, Madonna's grasp on reality seems more and more tenuous with every passing year, and my hope for anything interesting from her faded long ago. I'll still cough up the cash to see her in concert, though!

With Douglas, I listened to *Like a Prayer* from front to back, maybe for the first time in my life. Definitely the last time for me—there are a lot of lame tracks on the damn thing. The longer the album played, the more withdrawn Douglas became, and I could tell something had shifted between us. As he sat on the couch, hugging a pillow for comfort, I knew I didn't stand a chance against Madonna. I would not be fucking anyone that night.

We traded a couple of texts after date four, but there was no date five. Maybe opening up to another gay man over Madonna was too much for him? Or maybe Douglas was another guy still struggling to make sense of growing up in the eighties and nineties and carrying around AIDS baggage? Whatever the reason, Douglas and I were done. It was time for me to find somebody fun, somebody young . . . someone ready for a meaningless fuck. I wonder what Madonna would do?

BIG TIME SENSUALITY

Before I took Dustin to see Adam Ant in concert, we both attended a killer James Blake show at Massey Hall on October 8, 2016. Dustin and I didn't meet that night, but it was during an online Scruff conversation after the show where we both raved about James's performance that he finally agreed to our epic first date. In between that first date at Lipstick & Dynamite (RIP) and that monumental Adam Ant show, Dustin and I had been having a blast with each other.

We were both often busy with work and school, so finding time to connect wasn't always easy. However, each of us made time at least once a week for a ritual that became a spectacular routine, a hallmark of the Pete & Dustin friendship. Dustin would arrive at my place, one of us would fuck the other, we'd partially dress, then we'd sit at the kitchen island in our underwear and eat takeout Portuguese chicken, sip wine and listen to music. I'd get the chicken, Dustin would buy the wine, and we'd each bring our desire for the other.

During one of our post-sex snuggles on a dark winter Wednesday night, Dustin asked me if I had ever seen Björk perform live. She was one of his favourite artists of all time and seeing her perform was one of the biggest items on his bucket list. The goddesses have been good to me and I told him that I had been blessed on more than one occasion to be in an audience when Björk had performed. I picked Dustin's briefs off the floor, took a sniff, tossed them to him and said, "Let's go listen to her."

We started with his favourite album, 1995's *Post*.

Before I told him about seeing Björk live, I needed to tell him about the time I didn't see her live. The minute I heard the Sugarcubes' first single, "Birthday," in 1988, I fell in love with Björk and her band. It was instantaneous. I needed to hear more, and I bought their first LP, *Life's Too Good* (1988) and followed the band through their second and final albums, *Here Today, Tomorrow Next Week!* (1989) and *Stick Around for Joy* (1992). The second record was a bit lacklustre, but I was a big fan of the other two.

After living with a friend for a few years, I moved back to my parents' house in early 1992. I was about to turn twenty-three, was still in the closet and was back living in my folks' basement. Ugh. Life wasn't great at that time. Back in the old neighbourhood, I had the opportunity to connect with some old friends, and on one of those nights I went to see a local band at a shitty bar on Queen Street East with my Madonna dancing pal Anita. At the gig, she introduced me to her friend John and I could tell two things right away: 1. he was gay; 2. he took a shine to me.

We chatted, and the longer we did, the more nervous I got. Could anyone tell he was gay? Or that I was? Did Anita know? I kept drinking.

At the end of the night, John asked for my number. Yikes. Emboldened by the booze, I scribbled my number down on a piece of a cigarette pack (don't judge—it was the early nineties, everyone smoked) and gave it to him, explaining I was temporarily at my parents'. At least, I hoped it was temporary.

Several days later, the phone rang. It was John. We had talked about the Sugarcubes the night we met and he had a spare ticket to see their upcoming show at the legendary Masonic Temple (now Concert Hall)—a beautiful concert hall on Yonge Street that many bands played early in their careers—including Led Zeppelin and the Who! Did I want to join him?

Holy shit.

I wanted to go so badly. For so many reasons. The band (amazing). The guy (cute). The venue (small and special). Björk, mostly Björk; she was always too big for the band. They were touring their latest album, *Stick Around for Joy*, which would prove to be their final one as a group.

But I said no. I wasn't ready for any of it. I completely chickened out. I was still in the closet. I didn't want to admit to my friends that I was gay and, most of all, I was terrified of other guys, of sex and of getting AIDS. It was all irrational, but it was real to me. Imagine seeing Björk performing in such an intimate and historic venue, playing the best of the Sugarcubes' three records? That's the stuff that dreams are made of.

There are a lot of bands I wish I had seen before it was too late. But this one was in my grasp. It's one of my greatest concert regrets. I might have finally gotten laid too; I had barely kissed a boy by twenty-three, let alone had sex with one.

The idea of seeing the Sugarcubes was almost too much for Dustin. He hadn't even been born yet. He was also surprised that I was in the closet at the same age he was as he sat on my couch. Times have changed, my young friend.

After *Post*, it was time for me to pick my favourite Björk record: 1997's *Homogenic* all the way. For me, this is when everything came together for the creation of one consistent artistic statement. The fusing of classical strings with electronic beats and that incomparable voice was breathtaking when it came out in 1997, and it still is today. It is a musical high-water mark for one of the true originals. A genius.

My redemption finally came when Björk announced a show on Toronto Island for September 3, 2003. Her most recent album at the time was 2001's *Vespertine*, which made me hesitate on buying tickets. It's an album that takes time to open itself up and greet you, and I hadn't put in the work yet. It's a pretty quiet record, short on any bangers, and I was further worried the concert would be a bit of a bore. I wasn't sure I wanted to lay out on a blanket and be lulled with gentle Björk lullabies.

Thank the goddesses I went for it. It was a rager. One of the best and most exciting concerts I have ever seen in my life. Bar none. There were shooting flames at the sides of the stage. There were fireworks blasting above her and the Toronto harbour. Björk had a massive band with her that included an eight-piece string section. The show was epic, and I don't think anyone in attendance was truly prepared for it. I sure wasn't.

Björk's voice was the real revelation, though. She seemed so tiny, so waifish to me that I figured her voice was equally small. A studio instrument. An amazing studio instrument, but still, I expected the live experience to be wanting. How wrong I was. Björk is one of the belters of our time. She has a HUGE voice.

Vespertine figured in the playlist, but she punched those tracks up to match the occasion. I think she played more tracks from *Homogenic* than anything else, and in fact the concert felt more like a career retrospective than a tour to promote any one album.

For years afterwards, that epic Björk concert was like Toronto's version of Woodstock. Everyone wished they had gone, everyone claimed they had, but for those of us who made the trip, it was breathtaking. Shockingly, the show didn't even sell out.

Dustin could only dream. I would have loved nothing more than to take him back in a time machine and have him take the place of Brad, my date that long-ago night. Dustin would have enjoyed it so much more.

The next chance I had to see Björk was after her *Biophilia* album, on July 16, 2013, at Toronto's Echo Beach, named after the indelible Martha and the Muffins hit song, on the waterfront. Let's be honest, *Biophilia* is not Björk's easiest record. From my island experience, though, I had learned you just go to see Björk live if you have the chance.

There were a couple of musicians onstage, but it was her ten- (or so, I kept losing count)-person Icelandic choir who stole the spotlight. They were a force to be reckoned with, and it was the first time in my life I realized how powerful a choir can sound. It was as though a wild, magical coven from another planet had descended on Toronto for the night. It was otherworldly.

Lesson for all: when you can, just go see Björk.

I think poor Dustin was ready to cry at this point, he was so envious. I am sure that Dustin's time will come with Björk. I just hope I'm there with him. But snuggling up to him on the couch while listening to *Homogenic* was a pretty great placeholder until that time comes.

DREAMS

January 1, 2017, I woke up ready to take on the world and get laid. Dustin was on holiday in Mexico with his family, and while we didn't talk about it explicitly, we both knew we were meeting other guys; seeing each other pop up on Scruff regularly was a pretty strong clue.

Every year, Carolyn hosted a massive party on December 30 known as Fake New Year's or FNY. It was a doozy; her place was always jam-packed with queers and queer adjacents getting their party on like nobody's business. It was my favourite party of the year, and I always commited to the whole experience, no matter how late it went. As a result, I was always more exhausted and hungover on December 31 than on any other day of the year—and I loved it. On New Year's Eve I would make a nice dinner for one, have a few glasses of wine and go to bed at about nine thirty while the world was gearing up to "have the best night EVER," or at least hoping to. The best part of the whole experience was that I woke up the first day of the new year feeling like a champ! It was a fantastic way to start the new year.

After a run and a shower I was hoping to meet a new friend in the new year, so I opened up Grindr. I was surprised to hear back from a very cute twenty-five-year-old blond fellow I had messaged. William was one of those cute instagays with 2,500+ followers—scruffy blond beard and a killer smile. He was beautiful, and way out of my league. Or so I thought.

He was crashing at a friend's place for a few days and couldn't invite me over there, so it was agreed he would come to my house. William arrived about half an hour later and was ready to get down to business. He started kissing me the instant I opened the door and continued to do so as he took off his coat, kicked off his shoes and entered my house with his face attached to mine.

Stripped down to our underwear, William took my hand, led me to the kitchen island and turned me around so that my stomach was pressed against the counter. He pulled my underwear off, got down on his knees and spread my legs. He spit and dove in—licking, kissing, nibbling at me as I pressed my ass backwards against his face. It was divine. I turned around, dropped to my knees and, with my back pressed against the island, took his dick in my mouth and leaned back as he face-fucked me for a few minutes. William was turning out to be a very fun trick.

He lifted me up by the chin and pushed me back towards the kitchen counter. With a wee boost I found myself perched in a corner of the counter, legs up, with the ninety-degree angle of the counter pointing directly at my butt. He bent down and went to town on my asshole again. My head continued to bump back into the overhead counter, and I could not have cared less. This was fucking amazing.

From the kitchen counter, I led him downstairs to my bedroom and was shocked when he asked if he could fuck me. It was unusual for younger guys like William to want to top me, and in that moment only my desire outweighed my surprise. On my back, with my legs spread, he pressed his dick against my asshole and, in a surprise move, took the big toe of my right foot into his mouth and sucked on it. We both laughed at the shock value, but I liked it.

To exert a bit of power from my delicate position, I mashed my foot against his face again and forced him to take my toes back in his mouth. I was surprised by my own actions, but William obliged. It gave me a feeling of power and control as he was about to force his sizable dick inside me.

At this point I was basically begging to get fucked, but William was not done with the teasing yet. He gave my ass a few good spanks and then tentatively slapped my balls a few times to make sure I was okay with that. With my consent he really gave my balls a good fucking with—both spanking and squeezing them to a point where I almost couldn't take it anymore. I didn't ask him to stop. He squeezed a giant drop of precome out of my dick and licked it, creating a long trail from my dick to his mouth as he rose above me. Queer magic.

William sheathed his hard dick and finally slammed it into me. I was more than ready for it after the epic rimming and teasing he had been giving me. With his dick inside me, he asked if he could spit on me. I told him to go for it, and as he slowly started to pump inside me, he spit first in my mouth then, judging by my enthusiastic reaction, onto my chest and my face while he fucked me. He pulled me over to the side of the bed, positioned me face-down and pounded me doggy-style. We were both feverish, and before long William pulled out and we both spewed come everywhere.

I was covered in sweat and spit and come. I felt filthy and sexy and amazing. And it was barely noon.

Happy New Year.

We had barely said two words to each other during the entire hookup, and as we both lay back and caught our breath, we started to chat. We soon discovered we sort of liked each other. After a quick shower together, he agreed to an afternoon beer to celebrate the new year. William eyed my record collection with awe. He told me that he loved the idea of a curated collection, a tangible, touchable thing. I think so many people of his generation feel the same way, having grown up in a digital age. I did the math. He was born in 1992 and would have been seven years old when Napster launched, changing the consumption of music forever. Shawn Fanning's little experiment Napster, which gave folks the ability to share music files online for free, killed the music industry as we then knew it. Sadly, it killed a lot of artists' income streams too. Forever altered. Just . . . gone.

I pulled two tall cans of beer out of the fridge as he perused the collection. William's first request? *Rumours*. He told me it was a family classic and that he and his parents listened to it all the time. Sadly, I ran the math on that too, and it checked out that his parents would have been first-time Fleetwood Mac fans, like me.

Fleetwood Mac's *Rumours* is one of my all-time favourite albums, hands-down. It's unlikely I have heard a single record more in my life than *Rumours*. It is positively astonishing that I have not sickened of it. The record was released February 4, 1977, just two months shy of my eighth birthday. Though I was only eight, it was impossible to escape the cultural tidal wave of *Rumours*. It was everywhere: radio stations, basement rec rooms, dances and, perhaps most importantly for me, my older brother's album collection. When he left home for college in '83 or '84, that baby became mine, and it has never left my possession since.

That kind of ubiquity is exceedingly rare, air the likes of which only artists like Michael Jackson breathe. It also doesn't happen anymore. The splintering of radio and Spotify demos and the sheer firehose of content that gets blasted at us every single day has sadly made the collective attention span very, very short. *Rumours* sold a gazillion copies (over 40 million and counting) and was the number one album for an astonishing thirty-one weeks! Non-consecutive weeks, mind you, but still, 60 percent of an entire calendar year. Beyoncé, Adele and Drake can only dream of that kind of run.

William knew all the songs but had never really paid attention to them. I figured everyone on the planet knew the twisted alchemy that brought us *Rumours*, but I guess there is always a new generation who need the knowledge passed on. *Rumours* is the eleventh album released by Fleetwood Mac but only the second to feature California golden couple Stevie Nicks and Lindsey Buckingham. The membership of the band had been in constant flux since its inception in the mid-sixties, but something magical happened when Stevie and Lindsey joined Mick Fleetwood (drums), Christine McVie (keyboards and vocals) and her husband John McVie (bass) in early 1975 as the band looked to explore a new sound.

Within six months of beginning to work together, this new quintet recorded their first album as a band and released it a few months later, in July 1975. It was an instant smash and completely revitalized the band. It introduced Fleetwood Mac to an entirely new audience and also introduced the world at large to Fleetwood Mac's biggest star, Stevie Nicks, via the hit song "Rhiannon."

The toil of touring and promoting their breakout album left a long trail of devastation. Stevie and Lindsey broke up. Christine and John ended their marriage. Mick left his wife Jenny and was soon to embark on a sexual and romantic relationship with Stevie. Drugs and drink were being consumed aplenty among the quintet, and the press spotlight was shining intensely on this upstart new band, touring their tenth album. There was a lot of pressure on this new and improved version of Fleetwood Mac.

It was during this insanity that they all agreed to head into a studio in a remote town in California to record a new album together. With emotional wounds raw and still bleeding, drug and drink addictions mounting, and interpersonal relationships at an all-time low, they somehow created a masterpiece, writing songs eviscerating each other, telling their side of the story and celebrating new loves, all the while playing and singing on those exact songs that were directed at each other.

Bonkers. Yet, as a team, they created one of the greatest pop musical masterpieces of all time. Thankfully, I have the famous 1977 *Rolling Stone* magazine cover of the band, shot by Annie Leibovitz, all in bed together in various stages of undress, framed and up on my wall. It proved an invaluable aid in opening up young William's mind to the magic and madness of *Rumours*.

All interpretations and opinions are entirely my own.

Side 1

TRACK 1: "Second Hand News"

You see, it's Lindsey (I pointed to Lindsey) singing to Stevie (point) about feeling tossed aside by her. Listen to her harmonize on the lyrics basically calling her a soulless cunt. Beautiful.

TRACK 2: "Dreams"

Stevie's reply to Lindsey; every story has two sides. When the song fades out with Stevie's last line, it almost sounds like a curse: You go have your fun, Lindsey, but you are going to pay, big time. Mick's drumbeat lurking down below as Stevie is singing about the heartbeat driving her mad . . . If they're not fucking yet, you can tell they're damn close. They are in sympatico.

TRACK 3: "Never Going Back Again"

Ostensibly about not going home again, one can read this one pretty clearly: Lindsey ain't never going back to Stevie. No way. Nohow.

TRACK 4: "Don't Stop"

Christine wisely let Lindsey sing the first couple of verses of this one, and it's kind of a nice break thematically after the Stevie vs. Lindsey pissing match. A song of hope, about looking forwards and not backwards at our mistakes, but honestly, let's just get back to the Stevie vs. Lindsey war of words.

TRACK 5: "Go Your Own Way"

That's more like it. This is one of the most gut-wrenching songs in the rock 'n' roll canon. Sadly, it is so overplayed, almost no one pays attention to the lyrical content. After several decades I am still 100 percent on Stevie's side in the couple's breakup; by all accounts Lindsey is an insufferable asshole, but wow, he really makes a strong case here when he basically begs Stevie to accept his love. The whole band is blasting on this song, and they collectively take flight into a new world by the end. The drumming is astounding, the bass holding everything together, and the combined vocals of Stevie, Lindsey and Christine create a harmonic magic unlike any other in rock music.

TRACK 6: "Songbird"
Skip. I know people love this song, but mother Yoko, please put us out of our misery. Maybe Christine is saying goodbye to John, maybe she's in love again, who cares. It's a bummer and a buzz-kill. Next.

Side 2

TRACK 1: "The Chain"
It's anyone's guess why this insane group of people are still making an album together. It's a chain? It's a pact? Maybe they're all blood siblings? Doesn't matter. The lyrics are secondary to an epic jam that positively explodes at the end of the song.

TRACK 2: "You Make Loving Fun"
Rumoured to be about Christine's new paramour at the time, it's the best of her contributions to the album, in my opinion. It's a pretty sexy jam with some cool organ/electric piano work by her, and there are some early glimpses of the approaching 1980s in the spacey production of her and Stevie's vocals during the chorus. There's enough room on this one to let the band rock a bit too. Christine gets a pass from me on this one. It's a C+, though, not a B.

TRACK 3: "I Don't Wanna Know"
While Stevie's least interesting contribution to this album, it's still a fun, bouncy blues jam. It does hint at some of the drama of her relationship with Lindsey, but I suspect it's the excellent bass line and generally upbeat sound that helped push this one onto the album when she had a far, far superior contribution to make. More on that later.

TRACK 4: "Oh Daddy"
Dear goddesses above, make it stop. This song is fucking terrible. Full stop. Awful. Christine's last contribution to *Rumours*, the only reason this monster made it onto the album was to give each of the songwriters an equal voice on the final album. There can be no other reason. This track is garbage.

TRACK 5: "Gold Dust Woman"
I actually have no idea what this song is about. None. It's rumoured to address Stevie's cocaine addiction (I mean, the silver spoon line is kind of telling), but it truly doesn't fucking matter. This song is insane. The vocal is from another, deeper place than anything Stevie has ever put to tape, the drumming is harrowing, and all the instrumentation just builds and builds to this scary, awesome and dark place. The coyote-like howls near the end can scare the shit out of me if the circumstances are right (a.k.a. if I'm high). It's a band taking a groove and an idea deep, deep, deeper than many songs dare to go. What a way to close an album. The end. Or is it?

"Silver Springs" – The song that never was. Written by Stevie, this tune was relegated to the B-side of "Go Your Own Way" due to the time constraints of a single vinyl album. There just wasn't room for it on *Rumours*. I had to pull out my 45 copy to play the track for William. The song is a masterpiece of heartbreak. In direct opposition to Lindsey's claim in "Go Your Own Way," Stevie suggests that it was Lindsey who would not accept her love, not the other way around. The song is an interesting counterpoint, and the pain and suffering you can hear in Stevie's vocal is extraordinary. She's positively living this experience in the studio, singing it to her ex, who is likely staring at her from the sound booth. "Silver Springs" is a magnificent track and would have transformed *Rumours* into something even more special than it already is. That we have to live with "Songbird" and "Oh Daddy" for the sake of appearances, or Christine's ego, is one of the most egregious crimes in rock 'n' roll history.

My effusiveness for *Rumours* bordered on embarrassing, but William loved hearing it.

It's amazing to me how many songs and albums lose their potency after you hear them many times. Do yourself a favour and try to listen to Aretha's "Respect," Sinéad's "Nothing Compares 2 U" or Marvin's "I Heard It Through the Grapevine" as though you are hearing them for the very first time, and play them loud. Masterpieces all, dulled by repeated playing or reproduction through shitty sound systems or poor radio signals and by their use as background music for TV commercials. They, like many of the songs on *Rumours*, deserve so much more.

As I shared all these stories, William eagerly asked questions and listened to the songs. He'd heard the album hundreds of times but never actually listened to it. It wasn't the last record we shared that day, nor did we stop at one tall can. I learned about William's upbringing in Boston, his current life in Calgary and his desire to relocate back to Toronto. I told him about my life and I let him know I was kind of dating Dustin, or maybe dating Dustin, or hoping I was dating Dustin, at least.

It was a spectacular way to start a new year. We traded numbers and continued to text throughout the rest of the day and evening as he prepared to head back west the following day. Before he left for the airport, his last text to me was: *Dustin's a lucky guy*.

HOW SOON IS NOW?

In Toronto, the tough months of February and March send us all indoors to hide. It's cold, it's dark, and it's tough to get excited about much of anything. Thankfully, Dustin and I were still happy to have each other as a distraction during the most depressing months of the year. During the first weeks of our Scruff courtship, he sent me a photo of himself in the cutest green 2(X)IST briefs that fuelled my dreams for months, in the best possible way. They still do. We had planned our first sleepover and I made a special request that he wear them for our Saturday night date.

He arrived a little bit late. I was learning to expect Dustin to be a little late, but he was always worth the wait. We were still in the early days of a new sexual relationship and couldn't keep our hands off each other. I love that kind of excitement. I loved that he still felt it too. I peeled down his too-tight jeans and, sure enough, as promised, there were those hot green briefs.

As much as I loved looking at him in them, I could not wait to get them off him. Once I got Dustin naked, he crawled on top of my bed and turned to smile at me with an impish twinkle in his eye. Most of the time when I fucked him it was missionary-style. I really liked looking down at his amazing body and connecting with him eye to eye as I entered him. That night, however, Dustin had other plans. He positioned himself on his hands and knees, asshole facing me, and told me to fuck him, and fuck him good.

Yes sir.

I sure didn't mind that view either. His ass was one of the seven wonders of the world as far as I was concerned. He was clearly happy to have me fucking him from behind, and I loved having an unobstructed path to his ass. We both learned a good lesson that night: Ask for what you want. Everyone wins.

Once we'd cleaned ourselves up and made it back to the couch, I poured Dustin some wine. It was time to pick an album, and I was stumped. Dustin was a tough customer, and I really wanted to nail the selection, especially after nailing him with such ardour. Panic. Panic. Panic. Oh right . . . "Panic." The Smiths.

I reached for an old favourite, *The Queen Is Dead*. As I pulled the record out of the sleeve, Dustin laughed a bit and admitted he'd never quite cracked the code on the Smiths. I was aghast. Based on everything I had learned about his musical tastes, the band seemed entirely up his alley. He recognized the disconnect and acknowledged that, by all accounts, he should be a fan. But he wasn't. He understood the musicality, he got the wry humour of Morrissey and the killer Johnny Marr riffs. He couldn't deny their importance in the indie rock canon and to queer culture, but it just didn't click for him.

Huh?

I think that unless you were there for the initial ride, the Smiths are a tough sell. Morrissey has become such an insufferable asshole, spouting all sorts of inflammatory nonsense to anyone who will listen, it's impossible to separate the art from the artist. His ego was always stadium-sized, but his opining has led to accusations of racism and right-wing sympathy from a variety of sources. And while he released some great material as a solo artist, his work has been reaping diminishing artistic returns as the years go by. I'm not sure he actually believes half of what he spouts. Rather, I think he's acting out a character named Morrissey, and trying to spark conversation and grab attention. I also think the relative anonymity that musicians and celebrities had back in the eighties served the Smiths well. When I see footage now of Morrissey from that period, he kind of reads as a twat back then too.

I stood up to pull the record off the turntable, but Dustin told me not to. He wanted to hear it, give it another chance, and hear about why I thought the band mattered.

The Smiths arrived in my life at a rather fortuitous time. Like so many closeted kids, I was a confused and depressed teenager when I first heard the band. When I hear some of the Smiths' tracks now, they remain a comfort to my still-healing teen heart. They only released four proper albums in a white-hot spurt of activity from 1982 to 1987, when the band dissolved. These same years coincided with my teenage years from thirteen to eighteen. I was primed to mope.

The band's first album, *The Smiths*, was released in 1984, during my grade nine year. I was the classic ninety-eight-pound weakling when I first heard that record. When I look back at pictures from that era, I can't believe how tiny I was. In hindsight, it was cruel to send a kid like that to high school. Like sending an unprepared soldier off to his certain death. Bullying existed for me in grade school, and I was no stranger to being called a faggot. That insult was tossed around in the grade school yard liberally to all. But in high school, it was really directed at me. Squarely at me. It hurt because it was true. Kids insulted me. Boys pushed me around. Taunted me. I just wanted to hide from it all.

When I heard *The Smiths*, it was like hearing from a friend I didn't know I needed. A miserable, lost and confused friend from across the ocean. My people. That first record was also the band's most overtly queer one, and quite honestly, the songs all sailed completely over my head. Hearing the record now, it's hard to believe I didn't pick up on some of the lyrics, but I suspect subconsciously I was taking it all in. I'm sure I wasn't the only one. "Hand in Glove" and "This Charming Man," in particular, contain overt homoerotic imagery and references to male connection. I just didn't want to hear it in 1984.

What connected for me was the melancholy and the voice—the singing, the wailing and the moaning of young Morrissey. It didn't hurt that I found him to be pretty damned hot. Morrissey felt of the "other." Queer, though I didn't have that word yet. He was never out, but he and the band always positioned themselves as outsiders, beyond the mainstream. In the UK they were massively popular, but on this side of the Atlantic they were truly for the outcasts. I responded to that. Back in the mid-eighties, you could have all the Cyndi Lauper and Madonna you wanted, I would take Morrissey and company.

The band followed up that first record with *Meat Is Murder* in 1985, which featured the iconic "How Soon Is Now?" Has there ever been a more obvious queer anthem? Morrissey sings about going out to a club in hopes of meeting a stranger who might love him, but he moves through the space unable to find connection and finally goes home by himself, depressed and expressing a desire to die. I wouldn't know the experience of going into a gay bar for many years to come, but my first forays into gay space left me feeling much the same way. Alone. Alienated. Again, the lyrics sailed over my head.

Only sixteen months after that release came the band's magnum opus, *The Queen Is Dead*, in 1986. I'm positive there was no other album that got played more during my eighteenth year.

Finally, their fourth and last album, *Strangeways, Here We Come*, followed in 1987, after the band had officially split up. It was an album I didn't really warm to until much later in life. Like many fans, I felt betrayed that they had broken up . . . How dare they? It felt as though my parents had divorced, but worse.

At parties my friends would spin "Panic," "This Charming Man," "Bigmouth Strikes Again," and we'd dance and laugh and talk about the band. The girls wondered if Morrissey was gay and I quietly and very attentively listened to their debate. And we'd drink. A lot.

Mostly, though, I listened to the Smiths by myself. Alone. Depressed. Those same years coincided with me finally figuring out that I was gay, and I really didn't want to be. Not one bit. Back then, I stayed in bed for days, skipping school and sleeping, blissful sleep, escaping the world and the torment at school. There was many a day when I would get up just in time to be presentable for my parents when they got home from work. I would pull my bed across the room next to the turntable so I could listen and flip the albums without having to get up out of my nest. I was committed to my misery. Morrissey was my constant companion.

It got so bad that, in grade twelve, I received a report indicating I had been away eighty-one days in one scholastic year. The biggest surprise was that I still managed to get two credits out of the eight courses I started with. I stumbled along in school, and in five and a half years I managed to cobble together enough credits to get a grade twelve diploma. Not a stellar accomplishment, nor one I am proud of, but I am also not ashamed of it. I was a struggling kid who fell through the cracks and no one seemed to care all that much.

I surprised myself by being so vulnerable with Dustin and sharing all of this with him while listening to *The Queen Is Dead*. I was on the verge of tears a couple of times recounting my history with the Smiths, and I was a little worried I'd freaked him out. He held my hand and told me he loved that I could be so open with him. My emotional availability was something he really liked about me.

What a sweetheart.

I didn't change his mind about the Smiths that night, but I did give him a better understanding of why they mattered so deeply to me. I know I am not the only queer person who grew up at that time who feels this way.

Funnily enough, listening to the band and sharing these stories with Dustin may have altered *my* opinion, not his. My love for the Smiths still exists, but with each passing year it gets harder and harder to listen to their music objectively. Morrissey just keeps digging himself a deeper and deeper hole with his asinine and inflammatory comments about politics and immigration and his trashing of other artists, to name a few hot buttons. Maybe I just didn't want to be that sad sixteen-year-old anymore? Life was way too good for that shit.

After *The Queen Is Dead*, Dustin and I were done with the Smiths. It was on to more joyful things. I spun a set of twelve-inch singles from that same era that was way more fun. Out came old records by the Cure, Yaz, Simple Minds, Eurythmics and many more great bands of my youth. My teenage years weren't all doom and gloom; there were some bright moments.

We danced in our underwear. We drank too much wine. We ate. We stayed up too late. We made out ferociously. We smoked some pot. All to a soundtrack of records I had bought thirty years before, never dreaming that a future like the one I was living was remotely possible. Talk about sweet dreams.

Dustin had to be at his part-time job the next morning so we both got up earlier than we would have liked. He showered and I sent him off with some coffee and toast in his belly. He left me the green underwear. What a charming man.

YOU WILL BE LOVED AGAIN

Every time Dustin agreed to another date, I let out a small sigh. Phew. I hadn't spooked this magical boy yet.

Life was good with Dustin. Our fuck, chicken, wine and record dates were the highlight of every week and I loved getting his daily texts. Most days those texts included photos: Dustin fresh out of the shower; Dustin picking out his underwear for the day; Dustin looking cute at the library. I was a very lucky man.

One night we bucked routine and had a proper date. We went to Reposado on Ossington for a couple of drinks. The winter was dragging on and we thought some tequila might remind us of the long-absent sun?

Dustin looked devastatingly handsome when he walked into the bar. He was wearing a fitted cowl-neck sweater that showed off his chest and arm muscles, and jeans that hugged that amazing ass and sweet bulge up front.

To our surprise, Reposado also had live music that night. A cute little guitar, drum and bass trio was soundtracking our night with some smooth grooves. Part jazz, part rockabilly, they were the perfect accompaniment. We gazed across the table and held hands as though it was our first date again. Damn. After two delicious tequila cocktails Dustin asked for the bill and pulled out his credit card. He wanted to treat me. What a sweetheart. I loved that he didn't expect me to pick up the bill. Dustin was not looking for a sugar daddy, and I was comforted by that.

Drinks weren't the only thing he treated me to that night. My good fortune took a turn for the better, and when we got home, Dustin fucked me with a vigour and determination he had never displayed before. More often than not he liked to bottom for me, and I was more than happy to practise my topping skills on him. He was gorgeous—I'd be mad to be upset about that arrangement. This shift was welcome, though. Getting fucked by a hot twenty-three-year-old is one of life's greatest joys, I've discovered.

Post sex, we retrieved our underwear and headed upstairs from my new basement bedroom to enjoy some wine and smoke the heel of a joint he'd brought along.

"Play me something chill so we can snuggle and listen."

Have sweeter words ever been spoken?

I was browsing around the *O* section of my record collection, wondering about maybe introducing him to another Yoko Ono album, but no, that was hardly chill. My eye wandered a few album spines to the left, passing O'Connor, Ohbijou . . . O'Hara!

"Do you know Mary Margaret O'Hara?" I asked him.

"Mary Margaret who?"

Bingo. Game on.

Dustin had welcomed my introduction of Yoko via *Take Me to the Land of Hell*, but Mary Margaret's first and only real record, *Miss America*, is not always an easy sell for some folks. I warned him that a lot of people found the record a challenging work, but he was up for it. I knew my instincts were right almost immediately. Dustin's body relaxed into the couch and he said quietly, "Oooh, this is nice," as he invited me to lie down beside him.

Miss America was released in 1988 after a tortured birth. It took several years and a few different producers to wrestle the record out of Mary Margaret. I like to think that she stuck to her guns and didn't allow anyone to tell her what this album would sound like; it would sound exactly the way she wanted it to. And it sounds like nothing else on earth.

Mary Margaret is a member of the storied Toronto O'Hara family. Actress and SCTV legend Catherine is the most celebrated, but I think Mary Margaret is the more talented sister. Don't get me wrong—I think Catherine is a total genius, full stop, but Mary Margaret is from another plane. More ephemeral being than human, Mary Margaret floats around and drops in wherever and whenever she sees fit. Totally unpredictable. But when she lands, wow.

When the album was released in 1988, it was not a hit. After I bought it, I remember a friend asking me why I would want to listen to that squawking and screaming. We are no longer friends. Mary Margaret's delivery is never predictable, but she does not squawk. She does not scream. She bends and swoops and soars through a song. She puts you off kilter immediately and you never see what's coming next. She's like a cabaret singer from a future that hasn't even been imagined yet. Maybe for when Berlin relocates to the moon.

I'm sure O'Hara's record label had no idea what to do with the album. It's genre-less. It was not going to get played on any radio station. It was just never going to happen, not in 1988 and certainly not today, after the enormous media conglomerates have bought up all the radio stations and homogenized their playlists. While the masses mostly ignored it, Mary Margaret found her way into many an artist heart. Into many a queer heart. Her emotional bareness resonated with those of us who cared to listen. For those of us who were struggling and bleeding emotionally, we heard a kindred spirit.

Her songs have been covered by Perfume Genius, Cowboy Junkies, and This Mortal Coil amongst others, and her fans are many in the music community. One of the smartest things Morrissey ever did was get Mary Margaret to contribute, in her inimitable way, to his track "November Spawned a Monster." It's one of his best solo tracks, in no small part due to Mary Margaret's vocal contributions. Toronto's own Hidden Cameras somehow got her more recently to contribute some vocals to a few songs on their *Age* album, released in 2013. They even got her to perform at a gig during Toronto's Luminato Festival the following summer. I'd never seen Mary Margaret live—very few have. She rarely performs, she never toured *Miss America*, and there was no way I was going to miss this chance to see her onstage. The perfect combo: one of Toronto's best-known queer bands with one of Toronto's least-known geniuses.

The minute she opened her mouth, I started bawling. She wasn't even singing words or lyrics, more a mumbled kind of scatting that is uniquely her own. It's indescribable. Emotional and artistic truth standing onstage and doing her thing. Transcendent. It made me love her even more.

Mary Margaret never released a proper follow-up to *Miss America*, sadly. One album and she peaced out. She's done some acting work, some soundtrack work, and recorded a few things here and there over the years, but *Miss America* was the only proper album we ever got from her. I can't help but wonder what else she might have created, given the time and resources. How many more beautiful songs and records. Let's not get greedy, though. She left us with one masterpiece, and most artists are lucky to manage that with decades of work under their belt.

Dustin was ready to hear it all. Instantly, he understood Mary Margaret's genius. He was one of the blessed few. As we let the effects of the wine and the joint wash over us, he curled up into me, put his head on my chest, and we lay there listening. Mary Margaret set the perfect mood.

When I got up to flip the record over to side two, he proclaimed, "I have to get this album." Hearing that was more exciting to me than the tequila cocktails and the sweet fuck put together.

Side two passed much as side one had. Wordlessly. We shifted our bodies, nuzzled into each other, shared the odd kiss here and there, but mostly we listened. I was in heaven.

With the album stuck in its final groove after "You Will Be Loved Again," it was pretty late. "Let's get to bed," he announced, and I was more than happy to oblige. He snuggled into bed beside me and was soon breathing in blissful sleep.

I was exhausted, but sleep eluded me. I kept thinking about Dustin, about Mary Margaret, about all the choices that had led me to this place. What a beautiful life I had created for myself. I'd ignored joy for much of my life, but Mary Margaret's gorgeous work reminded me that joy was the aim, and I was finally paying attention to that message. Was I actually falling for this twenty-three-year-old beauty?

REAL LOVE BABY

I have spent a lot of time passing on my love of music and musical artists to men, but it hasn't always been a one-way street. I have been introduced to a lot of great music in return.

Dustin had exemplary taste in music, and he brought many great new bands and artists into my life: Sylvan Esso, Japanese Breakfast, Yaeji and so many more. The list is endless; he and I trading music and bands was a hallmark of our relationship and our most regular topic of conversation. Several times a week we would text each other: *Have you heard . . .* We would share links to videos, songs, articles. I cherished each one. I hope he felt the same.

He also made me re-evaluate a few artists I had never quite connected with, Pixies and the Breeders in particular. They were his two favourite bands, and while I bought the Breeders' *Last Splash* album on its initial release, I really zoned in on the most well-known songs, "Cannonball" and "Divine Hammer." Dustin made me realize they had so much more to give than I realized. He introduced me to their first album, *Pod*, which is arguably better than *Last Splash*, and he took me to see them play live at the Phoenix (RIP). They were a killer live band. As for the Pixies, they were just one of those bands I never connected with until he made me pay attention. When a twenty-three-year-old insists you sit down, both of you dressed in your underwear, and listen to a record, you do as you're told. I was glad for the opportunity to re-evaluate and reassess.

I was also forced to take another good look at Father John Misty. When he released his second album, *I Love You, Honeybear*, in February 2015, it seemed everyone was mad for it. I gave it a spin or two online, but it didn't really grab me. That's often how it is when I interact with a band or artist on a streaming service: I play the album, I pay half-hearted attention, and then I forget about it, even if I like it. Owning a physical copy of a piece of music is a different experience. If you don't play it, it stares at you, taunts you until you do. Some of my favourite albums of all time took me ages to really appreciate. The digital experience is designed for short-term engagement, a brief flirtation, and then on to the next bit of content. This doesn't serve the artist or the listener, only the streaming platforms.

Dustin loved FJM, though, so I was determined to find a way into the music. He and his ex were crazy for the *I Love You, Honeybear* album, and I was bound and determined to make Father John *our* guy, not theirs. When it was announced that a third album was on its way and Father John was coming to Toronto to play a pair of dates at Toronto's Royal Alexandra Theatre, I was determined to get tickets and take my young lover.

Tickets secured, life resumed and we had months to wait until our date with Josh Tillman, a.k.a. Father John Misty. When the big night of the concert finally arrived on May 5, 2017, I was invited to Dustin's place for a couple of drinks. He made a mean cocktail and I was ready for it. I was ready to get laid too, but when I arrived, his roommate was there. Buzzkill. Dustin mixed us a couple of delicious Manhattans that helped soothe my disappointment.

In an effort to impress Dustin leading up to the show, I bought the vinyl version of FJM's *Pure Comedy* on its release date and was rewarded with a bonus 45 of "Real Love Baby" for my efforts. It was Dustin's favourite FJM song and it quickly became mine too—more so than the album, to be honest. The album is a bit of a bummer, which I'm never opposed to, but, for me, the record really drags. It's a little too long, and the thirteen-minute-plus "Leaving LA" smack dab in the middle of the record is like a cold stop. Kate Bush can get away with songs a quarter of an hour long, but sorry Josh, you're no Kate Bush. Still, I had heard FJM was great in concert, and I was delighted to be taking the beautiful Dustin as my date.

The Royal Alexandra was an odd spot for a rock show. Traditionally used for touring Broadway hits, the century-old theatre has a grandeur missing from a lot of concert venues in Toronto. We felt like a couple of fancy boys out on a nice date. We arrived at the venue with only a couple of minutes to spare, and when the show started with the first song on the new album, "Pure Comedy," I was captivated. In keeping with the special venue, FJM really turned it on. He beefed up his band to include fifteen musicians, with backup singers and an eight-piece string section. Wow. That was completely unexpected.

Josh was a real showman. Funny, charming, and damn, could he sing. When he dropped to his knees, swung his mic around or used the mic stand as a dance partner and prop, both Dustin and I swooned. I think even the straight boys in the audience swooned. Father John Misty was sexy as fuck. He sold the shit out of his new record that night. I love it when an artist takes their recorded music to a whole new level in a live performance setting. I was hooked. A Father John convert.

The concert was a really special performance, but I could tell Dustin was not entirely with me. He didn't feel cold exactly, but a little distant. Something was up. I invited him back to my place at the end of the show, but he declined. He told me he was feeling a little tired and needed a good night's sleep. No one appreciates a good sleep more than me, but I felt unsettled after he went home alone, without me.

We saw each other a few times over the next couple of weeks, usually at my place for the traditional chicken and albums in our underwear. We biked to see Sigur Rós at Echo Beach together for another evening of surprisingly awesome live music. I'd always assumed they would be kind of a bore in concert, but boy, was I proven wrong on that one too. I guess, like Björk, you can never count out the Icelanders for turning out a good show.

That funny feeling about Dustin never left, though.

A few days after the Sigur Rós show, I was sitting in the middle of a long work presentation when I got the text I was hoping wouldn't come but half expected. Dustin sent a long missive that boiled down to "let's be friends." He blamed himself, but it didn't help. My heart was broken. It was the end of an era for me and Dustin. I had loved being with him. I had loved fucking him. I think I may have loved him, period.

I played out the history of our relationship over and over in my head. I wished we'd had more time together. I wished we'd met after he had finished school. I wished our schedules hadn't conflicted so often. I wished I'd been more open about my own feelings for Dustin, but because of our age difference I discounted them, or didn't trust them. I definitely didn't trust that Dustin could possibly feel the same way about me. I swore I wouldn't make the same mistake again; if I had strong feelings for one of the men I was having sex with or dating, I would let him know exactly how I felt.

We promised to remain friends and still share music, go to shows together and stay in each other's lives. Staying friends with exes had never been my strong suit, but I really hoped it would work this time.

Father John wasn't Dustin's greatest gift to me by a long shot. Neither were the Pixies or the Breeders. Dustin gave me the belief that I could actually love someone half my age. The attention and affections he showered on me gave my self-confidence and self-image a boost I never saw coming. I'd had a ton of fun with a handful of younger men, but this was different. Not an infatuation. Not a tawdry thrill or quick ego boost. Love.

It may not have been reciprocated in the way I had wanted or hoped, but Dustin truly taught me that age didn't matter in relationships, or friendships. That's a gift I can't easily repay. But I'm hoping that the Adam and the Ants, Kate Bush, Grace Jones, Yoko Ono and Mary Margaret O'Hara albums that found their

way into Dustin's collection will help. We both discovered a few
beautiful things during our time together.

I sold my copy of *Pure Comedy* eventually, but I definitely
hung on to the "Real Love Baby" single. It is forever dedicated to
sweet Dustin.

SIDE TWO

GIVE ME BACK MY MAN

After our amazing *Rumours*-fuelled hookup on New Year's Day, William flew back to Calgary, but we had stayed in touch via text. I was a little disappointed he lived so far away, since we had such a great connection, but was happy to keep the torch alive in the event we were ever in the same city again.

Not long after Dustin sent me the text that put me in the friend zone, I got a very different kind of text from William. He was excited to tell me he had just got a job in Toronto. He'd be relocating a few weeks after Pride in June.

Well, well, what an interesting development. William fucked me when Dustin and I were starting our little romance, and now he would be here at its demise. The goddesses were definitely opening up a window for me. My heart was still a little wounded from Dustin and a new hot fuck buddy was exactly what I needed—great sex, few attachments and a pile of fun.

William was very keen to reconnect, and within his first week back in town we had a date. I was heartened to know I wasn't the only one who'd enjoyed our New Year's Day hookup and was pleased that William was making such an effort. He was one of those surprise encounters that had gotten under my skin—casual sex leading to feelings again.

Over wine on the back patio of the Walton (RIP) on College Street, we relived our long-ago date with *Rumours*, and he confessed it was one of the nicest hookups he'd ever had. He also admitted that Fleetwood Mac wasn't really his musical wheelhouse. He liked shitty music (my words, not his). Really shitty music. Celine Dion was his favourite singer (oh dear) and all his leanings were towards shitty pop sensations. Some old, some new, all terrible. Maybe I could work with this? It seemed like trying to fit a square dildo in a round hole, but the effort would be worth it. William was awfully cute.

While we debated a third drink, he asked if he could come back to my place for a nightcap instead. Forward. I liked that.

After a few months of sexting, we burst through the door and were almost instantly naked. It was my turn to fuck him, I was told, and I did. I fucked William every which way—on his back, on his side, with his face down on the bed . . . It was clear that he really, really liked getting fucked.

Before I'd even caught my breath, William told me he wanted to go upstairs to listen to some records. My collection had made a huge impression on him and he was keen to engage with it again. I was charmed by his enthusiasm, and with a playful slap on his butt, away we went.

What to play? How could I find some middle ground here? Something that would satisfy his pop leanings but also had some guts. I pulled out my well-worn copy of the B-52s' self-titled debut to see how that would work. Before I could even get it out of its sleeve, he excitedly told me that his family frequently listened to "Rock Lobster" and "Love Shack" together. Uh-oh. That's the worst kind of B-52s fandom in my estimation. The band has a wealth of great songs beyond their two biggest hits, and I can barely stand to hear either of those tracks anymore.

It was time to start William's education.

He watched with laser focus as I dropped the needle on side one. He told me that he had never put the needle on a record

before! I could hardly believe it, but when I did the math, someone born in the 1990s would never have had cause to.

"Do you want to try it?" I asked. His eyes lit up and I took
the needle off the record.

The process is second nature to me, so I forget that there is a
whole generation who have no idea how a turntable works.
William was so nervous, his hand was trembling. I held his shaking hand to steady it and explained that you just have to place
the needle gently on the outside edge of the record. It landed a
bit clumsily, but with a single skip the needle found its groove.

His first time. I was honoured.

I remember hearing the B-52s over the radio during the spring
of 1980 with the most unlikely hit song in pop music history. It
has been so overplayed that the shock and thrill of it are mostly
forgotten, but "Rock Lobster" is a crazy mess of surf guitar, the
wild cacophony of punk and a trio of vocalists spouting out
stream-of-consciousness lyrics like it was the most important
message in the world. Maybe it was.

The B-52s' eponymously titled first album had been released
the summer prior, in 1979. It was like a beam from outer space at
the time. After hearing the band on the radio, I trekked to
Eaton's department store at Shoppers World, a nearby strip mall,
to buy a copy.

While not openly queer for most of their career, the band still
screamed "otherness" to everyone who heard or saw them. It's
almost universal to gay folks of my age and era that the B-52s were
a touchstone to help them understand queerness and know they
weren't the only weirdos out there, that "different" could also
equal "fun." The Bs were a family of outcasts and misfits, and it
seemed as though anyone could join their party. John Lennon
famously said he loved the band's first record and recognized
Yoko's influence on it. It's rumoured that hearing "Rock Lobster"

was partly the inspiration for John to get back in the studio and make *Double Fantasy* with Yoko. Now that's high praise.

A quintet of friends, including a brother/sister duo, from Athens, Georgia, the band briefly took the world by storm. Kate Pierson (vocals, keyboards), Fred Schneider (vocals), Keith Strickland (drums, guitar), Cindy Wilson (vocals, percussion) and Ricky Wilson (guitar) were a team that sounded like nothing else the world had heard before. Four out of five were queer (Cindy was the sole exception), and while it may have been obvious in the early years, it was never discussed. Hidden, as so many of us were in the eighties.

Dressed in outrageous outfits and wigs cobbled together from thrift store visits, they were campy, they were silly, and they were fun—but they also released two of the most influential post-punk albums (and two of my favourites) of the era. In amongst the credits in the liner notes for drums, keyboard bass, guitar et al. on that first record, I found mentions of smoke alarm, toy piano and walkie-talkie. My people.

I spent countless nights of my youth dancing to the band's first several albums. Dancing with my straight crush Jim at three in the morning. Dancing with my friend Lorna after trips to the Goodwill, where we shopped for vintage clothes inspired by the Bs' mad outfits. Dancing on my own in my bedroom and dreaming of a fantasy technicolour future. The B-52s were a constant reminder that the oddballs can sometimes win, that to celebrate your "otherness" just might be rewarded. They were the antithesis to my obsession with the Smiths. When I was down, I listened to Morrissey and Marr, and when I felt good, it was almost always the B-52s. A burst of instant joy.

I didn't get to see the band live until 1989. At that point it felt as though almost everyone had given up on the B-52s. When the band lost Ricky Wilson to AIDS in 1985, they lost a lot of steam. A blow for any group, let alone one that included his sister. The band had trouble promoting their last album featuring Ricky in the wake of that tragedy. With no tour and limited airplay, 1986's *Bouncing Off the Satellites* was the least successful record of the band's career to date, and appeared to mark the end of the Bs. They seemingly disappeared.

During that downtime, the band must have been quietly grieving, plotting and, most importantly, healing. It took them four years, but in the summer of 1989, now a quartet, they released *Cosmic Thing* to almost zero fanfare. The world didn't much seem to care about a new B-52s record. To promote the album, the band started a club tour that didn't even bring them to downtown Toronto; I had to trek out to a shitty club in Mississauga, a suburb about an hour outside the city, to realize my lifelong dream of seeing them live. My fear was that if I didn't get to that show, I'd never have the chance to see the B-52s again.

Little did anyone know that the band had just released what was going to be the biggest album of their career and arguably the biggest album of 1990. I would see them two or three times in the year that followed as the world finally seemed to come around to my way of thinking (in large part due to the release of "Love Shack" as a single). They were the most fun party band around.

William and I drank wine and bopped on the couch through the entire debut record, and he asked for more. Their follow-up, 1980's *Wild Planet*, is just as good as the first, and he couldn't believe how fun the songs were and how contemporary they still sounded forty years later. He was not wrong.

William left me that night a little drunk from wine and a little intoxicated by his enthusiasm for my record collection and for the B-52s. Maybe there was hope for him after all.

He texted me on his way home: *I have a crush on you.*

Gulp. Was I ready for that? After Dustin, I was most certainly not ready for that, but . . . William was awfully cute.

CONSTANT CRAVING

How do you even begin to unpack an artist like k.d. lang? The idea of an out, butch lesbian, vegetarian, cowpoke singer having one of the most popular records of any year is a pretty unusual idea, but in the early 1990s it was downright preposterous.

1992's *Ingénue* was k.d.'s fifth album after a series of releases that kept creeping up on the mainstream, most notably her 1987 duet with Roy Orbison of his timeless hit "Crying." I am positive, though, that no one would have predicted the breakout stardom that befell her during the promotion and tour of *Ingénue* or the cultural impact this queer Canadian weirdo would have on the world. I don't fall into the camp of those who think *Ingénue* is one of the all-time great records—it's not even her best, listen to 2008's *Watershed* for that—but I have to give k.d. respect as one of the all-time great singers who has walked the face of the earth.

After I had introduced Nat to Marianne Faithfull's *Broken English* the night we met and had raunchy sex, we continued to get together a couple of times a month. Our sex dates were always spectacular, and we started to go see a lot of live music and share records too. Nat and I had a great thing going.

In bed one morning after Nat had slept over, I casually mentioned a TV interview I'd recently seen of k.d. during the promotion of *Ingénue*. In response I got, "Who?" Sure, Nat was an infant when the record was released, and he was further impaired by being an American, but still, how had he not heard of an artist so relevant and important to the queer community? I immediately pulled out my computer and found the interview in question; there was k.d. lang on *The Arsenio Hall Show*. She shocked the world by performing "Miss Chatelaine" in full femme drag—prom dress, makeup and beehive included.

Following the song, she sat down for an interview where the conversation turned into a dialogue about queerness, gender fluidity and k.d.'s place as a representative of all that. A black man and a butch lesbian talking about gender fluidity on a nationally broadcast talk show in 1992? Surprising today, revolutionary in 1992. Nat was floored.

I then pulled up the 1993 *Vanity Fair* cover with Cindy Crawford lathering up k.d. while dressed in a suit and spats, mocking a facial shave. It was hot. It was groundbreaking. It was like nothing I had ever seen before. I liked it. A lot.

Out came my CD of said album, and I told Nat, "There is no doubt you have heard this song," and I cued up "Constant Craving" on the CD player on my bedside table. He recognized the tune almost instantly, as it had become a staple of adult-contemporary radio—it was almost impossible to avoid. American or Canadian, queer or straight, "Constant Craving" is part of the musical vernacular. Nat was thrilled to discover this queer history, hiding in plain sight.

Back in 1992, I was still hiding in the closet, so I didn't spend much time with *Ingénue*. I was afraid that being a fan of the record would mark me as gay. Funnily, I had an album or two of k.d.'s weirdo cowpunk stuff in my vinyl collection from when she was still in the closet, just like me. Maybe our shared secret made me feel safe to be a fan in k.d.'s early days, but I was into different stuff in 1992. Different artists, different tunes. However, for a wide swath of queers, including my friend Matthew (he with the tusk), *Ingénue* was everything. It was an album that accompanied many queer awakenings. Just not mine.

Matthew and I had sort of lost touch after our days with *Tusk* and *Graceland*, but one day out of the blue I got a message from him asking me to be his guest at k.d.'s twenty-fifth anniversary tour of *Ingénue* when it hit Toronto. We had talked a lot about how important the album was to him, so I was honoured to accept his invitation. I had seen k.d. on her tour to support the release of her 1997 record *Drag*, and it was during that show that I realized the immensity of her gift. Her voice is a thing of wonder. I wanted another taste.

In a nod to our first date, Matthew and I met for a few Manhattans before the show and walked into the theatre a little buzzed on rye and a whole lot of excitement to see k.d. We filed in with the countless queer men and women—and, to be fair, a good turnout of hets—to see the show. Most attendees were in their forties and fifties, but it was good to also see a younger generation of queer folks out to support a queer cultural icon.

k.d. started the show with the first song on the album, "Save Me," and the crowd was rapturous. She sang every song from *Ingénue* in order . . . which to me only served to highlight the record's weaknesses. There is too little variation on tempo and style for my liking; it sort of becomes a test of will by the end ("Tears of Love's Recall," I'm looking at you). But still, it was k.d., she sang the hell out of it all. And by the time "Constant Craving" kicked in, the final song on the recorded album, the crowd was at her feet. As was I.

She finished her set with a variety of other well-known tunes from her catalogue, including Leonard Cohen's masterful "Hallelujah." For Canadians this song has become a kind of anthem and has taken on a life of its own. I had seen it performed on television and on YouTube and have listened to k.d.'s recorded version countless times, but I was wholly unprepared for it live. It was jaw-dropping. Every ounce of her body was invested and the sound coming out of her was entirely beyond description. I sobbed. Not cried—sobbed. And the audience sobbed with me. It was the kind of moment when an artist completely captures an audience of thousands and you all go on an incredible journey together. Magic. Queer magic. I expect that no one outside Canada has even heard her version of this song.

As we were leaving the venue with eyes, ears and hearts full, Matthew ducked off to go take a last-minute pee and I continued onwards to wait for him out front. Leaning against my bike, I saw him heading towards me with a massive grin on his face. I could tell he had news.

"I just got cruised in the toilet of a k.d. lang concert."

It seems that a cute older fella wagged his dick at Matthew at the urinal as they stood side by side with concertgoers swirling around. A couple of quick tugs and a smile was as far as they got, but it put my friend in a naughty mood.

As we walked through downtown Toronto on a warm late-summer night, me pushing my bicycle along, we strode right past his streetcar stop in search of a secluded spot for a queer nightcap. Matthew wanted to act on his sexy new mood and I was more than game. We walked for ages. Block after block of fruitless searching. Every park, nook or cranny was too bright, or gated, blocked from wandering queers. You don't realize how well-lit our city is until you want to have your dick sucked by an old friend in the great outdoors.

You would think we would have given up, but horny queers are nothing if not a determined sort! Finally, a beacon called— the shining light of Hooker Harvey's. Harvey's is a Canadian fast food restaurant and their location at Jarvis and Gerrard in downtown Toronto has long been rumoured to be a meeting spot for sex workers and their clients. Harvey's—they not only make a hamburger a beautiful thing, they have the distinct honour of housing a sex-for-sale hotspot in downtown Toronto.

Side note: I am 100 percent pro sex work and pro sex worker. I think they deserve the same rights and protections as any citizen, and abhor the degenerate terms often used to describe them, like *hooker*. However, Hooker Harvey's is bigger than my distaste for sex work shaming. It's practically a landmark for the Toronto tourist guidebooks.

A few feet beyond the restaurant is a residential alleyway where we found a bit of a cubbyhole—more accurately, a gate to someone's home where I propped my bike against a phone pole. While slightly hidden, it would have been pretty easy to spot us if anyone took a half-decent look—all part of the excitement. Soon, Matthew had my pants undone and squatted down to take my dick in his mouth. He worked quickly, as the thought of getting busted was on both our minds. He sucked, I moaned. He was always gifted at this particular act. I came in Matthew's mouth pretty quickly and my body shook as he swallowed the entire load. I zipped up and then bent down to return the favour. I stroked and sucked his dick for a short while, but he confessed he was unable to come while standing up—an affliction that had never crossed my mind but one I found rather intriguing. A challenge for another day.

We grabbed my bike and shared a goodbye kiss at the curb, the orange glow of the Harvey's logo lighting our flushed faces. We agreed that k.d. would be proud to know that two queer boys celebrated the experience of her live performance with an act of queer sex in a famed alley—a public display of "We're here, we're queer . . . and we fuck."

I hopped on my bike with the bright neon in my rear-view and marvelled at how wonderful it was to be a queer man hitting his prime in 2017. I felt sorry for those heterosexuals who sang along to "Constant Craving" at the show and reminisced about their prime twenty-five years prior, dreaming of their life before kids and mortgages.

When I got home, I discovered a text from Matthew: *I'm riding the streetcar and I can still taste your come on my beard.* Queer craving has always been and will always be.

HUG OF THUNDER

The summer of 2017 flew by too fast. Nat and I were spending a lot of time together over the summer and I had been lucky enough to meet a variety of new boys who helped my heart heal after Dustin, but no one seriously captured my attention. There was always room for more.

The first few days of a new month can be a little like Christmas morning on the hookup apps. New boys move into your neighbourhood on the first of the month and checking into your geographical area on Grindr and Scruff can yield delightful surprises. The key is to act fast and stake your claim—make the connections quickly, before the fellows find another shiny new toy.

So it was in September 2017 when Preston moved across town and into the Annex, a west-end Toronto neighbourhood abutting mine. We chatted online quite politely considering the medium, and wooed each other with a shared love of music. When he inquired about my album collection, he was sold. A date was set within days of our connecting for a respectable glass of wine at my place. I was moving fast. Staking claim.

The day before the date, I got a message from him: *We could just fuck first.* It was an abrupt change of tone from our prior conversations. When a twenty-three-year-old who has just graduated from dance school at Ryerson suggests we "fuck first," who am I to say no? I guess I wasn't the only one moving fast. Staking claim.

Upon his arrival, I was blown away. The photos I had seen did not do young Preston any justice. A towering six foot three with a long, lean body and a gorgeous face that reminded me of an old-school movie star—he could have doubled as a model, not just a dancer. There was almost no small talk. We were going to "fuck first," as promised. Immediately we were connected at the mouth, our hips, our chests. Grabbing. Groping. Pawing.

In contrast to most conversations on these apps, we had not pre-prescribed our sex act. Neither of us asked the other, "Are you a top or a bottom?" or the dreaded "What are you into?" Instead, we tacitly agreed that we found each other hot and would let the moment play out as the moment needed to. I cannot stress how much I liked this about him.

We stripped each other feverishly and were quickly naked on my bed. The discovery of a new body is always such a thrill, but Preston's was a true wonderland. We kissed. We stroked. We sucked each other's dicks, and before long it was agreed that he would fuck me. This was a most welcome surprise. Often guys so much younger than me wanted me to be the top, to be the aggressor. Preston flipped this script on its head, and I liked it.

Our fuck was next-level. He was an excellent and attentive partner, and I credit his history as a dancer for that. The man knew how to use his body.

Post sex, we lay naked on the bed and finally made some small talk and started to get to know each other. With sex out of the way, we both relaxed and shared stories and histories. While we chatted, we were in constant physical contact, and I continued to marvel at Preston's body. It was exquisite. His leg muscles, his ass, abs, chest and arms—a decade of dance training had shaped a thing of beauty, the kind of body seen in classical sculpture.

I was silently amazed lying next to this young man. At Preston's age I had one toe barely poking out of the closet and was an awkward and confused kid; I still had a lot of growing up to do. I had very little confidence, and when I see pictures of me at that time, I can barely recognize myself. It is no wonder that I had struggled to find a date, let alone a fuck; it didn't help that I looked thirteen years old until my mid-thirties. I am told that I have grown into my looks, that I am one of those men who get better-looking as they age. I don't really believe it. When I look in the mirror, I still see that confused and awkward kid;

the damage those bullies did in school has had a long and lasting impact. I still think I'm too short, that I should have bigger muscles, and now, with age, I think my hair is too grey and thin (instead of curly and untamed as it was in my younger years). Which made it all the more surprising to find myself lying naked with Preston, a man twenty-five years my junior.

"How about that glass of wine?" I finally asked.

We spent the next several hours on my couch in our underwear drinking wine, with me curating a playlist of albums both old and new. Preston was an eager student, and during our conversation I discovered he was also a musician! He played piano and guitar and spoke intelligently about chord progressions, time signatures and drum patterns—with much more expertise than I was able to summon up. I swooned. Hard.

The album we bonded most strongly over was the new Broken Social Scene record that was released earlier that summer, *Hug of Thunder*. Preston had heard of the band to some degree but never really connected with them. It made sense—the band formed in 1999, when he was a toddler, and their peak popularity would have been when he was in grade school.

The band is a collective numbering up to nineteen members depending on the day. They seem a uniquely Canadian phenomenon: a band formed by Kevin Drew and Brendan Canning that contains members of other bands arguably more popular than itself, including Metric (sometimes), Stars (most times) and, in the case of Leslie Feist (sometimes), one of indie music's biggest stars from the 2000s. With the number of egos involved, it seems a miracle that the band could manage one album, let alone maintain a touring schedule and record five albums over the course of sixteen years. Canadians, we play nicely together. Usually.

The band's fans are all the richer for it. With so many players and so many singers, their material hits you like a wall of sound.

BSS sometimes come across like a messy cacophony, but when you really dig in and pay attention, the individual contributions are incredible in the mix. There are beautiful melodies, exquisite instrumental passages, gorgeous vocal harmonies—often all layered overtop of one another to create a wild and gleeful noise.

I saw BSS in concert back in 2006 in a festival setting on Toronto Island with Feist, Bloc Party and a few other forgotten bands who played earlier in the day. I was so excited to see such a great lineup of bands with Carolyn and a close group of friends taking in some sun, some beers and a day of fun and music. My boyfriend at the time, Brad, felt rather differently. He professed to want to join in the fun, but en route to the show we had an epic fight where it became painfully apparent that he really had no interest at all in attending. I encouraged him to go home, but he proceeded to pout and temper-tantrum all day.

There is nothing worse than standing beside someone who doesn't want to be at a live show—arms crossed, mouth permanently in a scowl, radiating negative energy all fucking day. The event was spoiled. BSS put on a wild show with dozens of musicians onstage creating a magnificent and original noise. So many wonderful and surprising parts. But the only thing that stood out for me was the cranky boyfriend overshadowing the joyful sounds. A show and a day ruined.

Twelve years later, Preston and I sat on my couch and listened to four sides of vinyl and committed to Broken Social Scene for the entirety of *Hug of Thunder*. He was an instant fan. We tapped out rhythmic patterns on each other's bare legs. We stopped talking at times and drifted away through several songs. He gasped and commented again and again on how wonderful the entire project was. I sat gleefully watching an album transform this young man's face and body as he listened. He didn't dance on the couch exactly, but I watched the way his body responded with subtle movements to certain rhythms and his

face light up in response to sections of songs. I remember thinking back on that ill-fated BSS show in 2006 and deciding I
wanted a lover who could take the time to appreciate music in
the same way I did, but had resigned myself to never finding
him. Who knew that he would come in such a package?

After two bottles of wine, it was time to send Preston home.
Our intention to fuck was accomplished easily, but I think we
were both surprised to find the connection we had. He collected
his clothes and we traded numbers, agreeing to a repeat date very
soon. We kissed at my door and I sent him off into the night for
his walk home with BSS queued up on his phone. What a beautiful man. What a beautiful connection. What a beautiful
record. The holy trifecta.

CRACK-UP

After William and I reconnected over the B-52s, we started
seeing each other fairly regularly. Once or twice a week we would
get together for fuck dates, but our friendship extended outside
the bedroom for regular dates too. Sometimes I'd fuck William
on my living room floor. Sometimes we'd go to a book launch.
Sometimes he'd rim me on the kitchen island. Sometimes we'd
have a nice dinner on College Street.

We were having a nice summer fling, but we both continued
to see other guys. We were very honest about our exploits and I
loved his openness about sex. It was revelatory to me, in fact. My
former long-term partners couldn't be honest about their attraction to other men or talk about desire for others, even in a fantasy realm. Most of the guys I'd been fucking recently, single
and attached men, seemed to be working on a far more level

playing field. Being honest about attraction and sexual desire was a good thing, in my opinion.

Every time we connected, William repeatedly told me how much he liked spending time with me, how I calmed him. I had nothing to compare it with, but I found it a curious comment. What was he like when he wasn't with me? I remember being in my twenties and I was a total chameleon, code-switching by altering my language and personality to fit in wherever I went. Maybe that was William too?

Stuck between living spaces, William was in a jam for somewhere to stay at the same time I was going on vacation for a short break from city living. I told him to give me a portion of the cash he would have spent on an Airbnb and to stay at my place. It seemed like the perfect arrangement. When I arrived back home, William had left me a pair of his come-soaked Calvin briefs under my pillow as thanks. We had once joked about how nice it would be to come home to such a gift, and I loved that he went through with it.

We were having a good time together, but the initial excitement we shared on New Year's Day was waning. I think we both felt it. Our dates were beginning to be spaced further apart, and when we did see each other, we weren't as feverish to get naked.

With a Fleet Foxes show on the horizon, I waffled over inviting him. His music tastes and mine did not exactly align, but this concert was a pretty safe bet. When Fleet Foxes released their first full-length album in 2008, the buzz was instant. It's a gorgeous record from front to back, and I was charmed by it. I loved the folkiness. I loved the harmonies. Some of the lyrics are a bit twee, but still, it was a beautiful record. It was the perfect Sunday morning record. The perfect driving record. The perfect chill record. To me, the band felt like a New Millennium version of Crosby, Stills, Nash & Young.

Helplessness Blues followed in 2011 and was equally good, if not better. More gorgeous tunes, more gorgeous melodies. No "sophomore slump" for the Foxes. A band with the world at their feet, they finished touring the album and then seemed to fall off the face of the earth. That second album appeared to be the last we would hear from Fleet Foxes. Fans of the band were able to find solace in their drummer's reinvention as Father John Misty, but still, I was sad to see what I thought was the demise of Fleet Foxes.

When a new album, *Crack-Up*, and a supporting tour was announced almost six years after *Helplessness Blues*, no one was more surprised than me. I was not going to miss the opportunity to see the band perform live.

Dustin and I had planned to go together, but he changed his mind. I was still struggling with how to navigate a friendship with Dustin, so maybe that was for the best. I wondered if I should ask Carolyn; she was always a trustworthy concert date. Then I thought that maybe I should give William a chance. Despite my efforts at turning William on to some decent music, it was a struggle. I hadn't played Fleet Foxes for William but hoped that, in a live setting, he might be charmed by them, as I had been a few years earlier. Oftentimes people just need exposure to good art to enjoy it. I crossed my fingers and rolled the dice. William was free to go and was thrilled to be asked. Maybe I had underestimated him.

Even without the live music, we got the night off to a great start. We met at my place late in the afternoon so we could fuck, snack and have a drink before our dinner date. I adore a young man who is keen to fuck in the afternoon. There is nothing better than an afternoon delight.

I'm usually pretty lucky with obtaining concert tickets, but these ones weren't the best—up on the second balcony, looking down upon the band sideways. But Massey Hall is such an intimate and well-designed space, there really isn't a bad seat in the house. As a bonus, the acoustics are incredible, world renowned, so it truly doesn't matter where you sit.

Thankfully, the band sounded as good as I had hoped they would. Their gorgeous songs and harmonies filled every corner of the historic Massey Hall. Even a pop music–leaning fan like William was impressed . . . and not a choreographed dance routine in sight. Fleet Foxes were spectacular and held the sold-out audience in the palm of their hands. The crowd ate it up.

Outside on Shuter Street after the show, William asked if I wanted to go to Woody's for a nightcap and to see what was happening. Maybe he needed some Mariah, Celine and some drag queens to balance out the acoustic magic of Fleet Foxes? Or maybe he just wanted us to cruise some cute guys together? Not a chance, I was beat. I went home to bed and William went off on an adventure of his own.

I didn't see much of William after our Fleet Foxes date. Summer was slowly turning to fall and we had to take a break in our sexual activity. William had acquired a contagious STI, so he was on a sex blackout. He was on PrEP, and while PrEP provides almost foolproof protection against acquiring HIV, it doesn't protect the user from anything else. On many occasions William had invited me to fuck him without a condom, as had a few other young men who used PrEP, but I was absolutely not ready for that. In my mind, condomless sex was still out of the question, not something I was ready to consider no matter the protections in place. I was still suffering from decades-old fear and stigma of HIV. I wasn't ready to listen to science and logic just yet.

The first STI was not the last one to put a pause on our sexual activity. Things were falling apart, the cracks were starting to show. Without sex, the lack of depth in our connection was becoming more apparent, and both of us knew it. Maybe I should have heeded the omens from the records he bought me.

STRIKE 1—A Celine Dion French-language release, *Les plus grands succès de Céline Dion. En français ou non*, it still sounded like overproduced garbage to me.

STRIKE 2—Haim, *Something to Tell You*. "They sound just like Fleetwood Mac," he proclaimed. They decidedly do not.

STRIKE 3—Janet Jackson, *Rhythm Nation 1814*. I guess he forgot the night I played my copy of the album for him. A second copy of a classic is never a bad thing, I guess. But still.

The gestures were sweet, but three strikes and William was out. We were headed for a crack-up. We started playing squash together, which reinvigorated our friendship a bit, and we were able to find some common ground again. After a game one afternoon he asked me to come and have a coffee with him. There was something about how he asked that felt important.

He wanted to clear the air and officially call us friends. William admitted that he had liked me more than he ever let on to me and that he had hoped we might develop into a more concrete partnership, that we could even have become boyfriends. We were in that weird grey zone: we were never boyfriends, but we were more than fuck buddies. Knowing he was continuing to fuck other guys regularly gave me permission to not address what we were, but damn, I should have addressed it. At this point I still wasn't ready for a boyfriend, or a relationship of any kind. I should have vocalized my feelings and told him so directly. We both should have been more open and honest. I promised myself after Dustin that I would be transparent if I felt strongly about dating someone. I guess I needed to do the opposite too. I wasn't fair to William, and in that moment I knew it.

Our hope was to remain on good terms, as we had several friends in common. Tennis and squash could be our common ground. Being friends with your ex-lovers was still a new concept for me, but I was getting better at it.

He could have Gaga. I'd keep Fleet Foxes.

If anyone needs a few albums, I've got a couple to spare.

PLEASURE

In the wake of my crack-up with William, the calendar flipped from summer to fall. The leaves were inevitably starting to change colours, but I was still hanging on to summer, I wasn't ready to let go.

I had feared that my first hookup with Preston was going to be my last, despite our strong connection. I could barely believe my luck in bedding him once, and I was certain he would be very popular on the hookup apps. Our connection was intense, but I truly thought he was out of my league.

When I asked for a second date the week after our "fuck first" evening, I was shocked when he immediately said yes. Upon his arrival at my place, we got to sex right away again. I didn't get a "fuck first" message but was more than willing when he walked in the door full of intent, fuck energy written all over his face.

I wanted to be hospitable, so I opened a can of beer for Preston as he playfully slapped my butt while we alternately kissed, sipped our beers and sucked each other's dicks in my kitchen, only a few feet from the door. Preston pushed me towards the stairs leading down to my bedroom and fucked me almost the second we hit the sheets. Like a master. With his dick inside me, I barely needed to touch myself and I came all over my stomach and sheets.

He smiled and shared that he loved to watch me orgasm while he was still hard inside me. It had only been twice, so I hoped that was a promise of things to come, but we weren't finished yet. Preston slowly pulled out of me and with a few quick strokes it was his turn to finish—he spurted all over the place, his come joining mine on my torso and bedding. I was in thrall to watching this beautiful man jerk and moan and spasm. It was gorgeous.

Once our heartbeats returned to normal, we headed upstairs to finish the beer we'd left behind and to listen to some music. He was keen to have some more of my music "tutoring"—his word, not mine. I was in the mood for some Stevie Nicks so pulled out her 1981 album *Bella Donna*, her first solo record made while on hiatus from Fleetwood Mac. Admittedly, it's a bit cheesy, but it contains some of her best solo work and I've been a fan since it was first released.

Preston was into the late seventies grooves and bopped along to the beats; even though this record was released in 1981, it reeks of late seventies rock 'n' roll. When "Edge of Seventeen" started, Preston's eyes almost exploded. He'd never made the connection between Stevie Nicks and Destiny's Child's massive song "Bootylicious," which samples the guitar riff from "Edge of Seventeen." Preston was a little embarrassed by his oversight. Stevie deservedly got co-writing credit on that song for the sample that was used, and the royalties likely kept her in shawls and boots for a couple of years.

We were both vibing on the sounds of the seventies, so out came Bowie's 1976 release *Station to Station*. As the title track played, Preston could not believe his ears. He admitted he really only knew Bowie from the hits that got played on the radio and had never heard this record, or the incredible ten-minute-long title track. It seemed I had my work cut out for me.

It was getting late, but I wanted to play Preston one more album. I had been listening to Feist's new record *Pleasure* all summer long and had tickets to see her the following week. It would also be a nice continuation of our love for Broken Social Scene from our first "date."

"I love Feist!" he exclaimed. He reminisced about hearing "Inside and Out" when his dad used to play it when Preston was a kid. He was probably the same age when Feist scored a hit in 2004 from the song as I was when I was listening to the Bee Gees' original version on the radio in 1979.

Gulp.

Preston had mentioned his dad during our first date and it's clear his father had an influence on Preston's music tastes. In a good way. I learned that his dad was fifty-five and his stepmom was thirty-two. Wow, I was fifteen years older than Preston's stepmom and only a few years younger than his dad. You can't help but laugh, so we did. He took the news in stride and we joked what a great double date we'd all make, representing the age spectrum in our twenties, thirties, forties and fifties. What a crazy life.

I still hadn't found someone to come to the Feist concert, so I asked if he could join me. He agreed, and we had our next meeting planned. Our first proper date?

September 24 came quickly and we agreed to have dinner at the Hair of the Dog, a pub in the gay village, before the show. Immediately it was clear that our chemistry definitely extended outside the bedroom, and I felt more and more connected to young Preston as the minutes passed by.

Over dinner, I discovered that Preston didn't know any Bowie full-length albums and, maybe even more troubling to me, that he'd never heard of Divine or John Waters!?!? My word, Preston needed a queer intervention. In the shape of one forty-eight-year-old me.

He insisted on paying when the bill arrived. I had bought the concert tickets and he wanted to contribute to the night too.

I liked that he didn't assume I would be treating him to dinner and drinks. As much as I enjoy younger men, I had no interest in being anyone's sugar daddy. I let Preston pay.

I confessed that I was worried about inviting him to the show for fear of giving him the wrong impression. He replied sarcastically, "You're not my boyfriend? We're not in love?" and laughed. I chalked one up for Preston. I was immensely relieved.

As we walked down Church Street en route to Massey Hall, I shared some of the pot brownie I brought along. We cozied up to each other and walked arm in arm for a bit. We were both kind of giddy and were very much looking forward to the show.

Feist is a national treasure. While her last couple of albums haven't been as popular as her earlier work, they are so much more interesting to me. Her later work explores some tough emotional territory like heartbreak and death, focusing on subtle and quiet grooves without much concern for a "hit." A true artist, she has really stuck to her guns and released what she wants to, when she wants to.

Pleasure was only Feist's fifth full-length album in almost twenty years. She bided her time and released music when she was ready. It was always worth the wait. The show was breathtaking. As advertised, she played the entire *Pleasure* album from front to back. I adored her confidence in the work and that she trusted the audience to stick with her for the performance of a new record that many might not have been familiar with yet, some of whom were only there to hear Feist's more popular songs. But stick with her we did.

She followed up the run-through of *Pleasure* with a set of some of her best-known work. Sadly for Preston and me, "Inside and Out" was not included. Still, Feist was having a blast onstage and she sold it all full stop. Even "1234" sounded great—arguably the most overplayed song in music history. At least in Canada.

True to my instincts, Preston proved the perfect companion. He was 100 percent attentive and focused. I loved watching his enjoyment of the show. He showed it in his body as he turned and twisted in his seat while he listened and watched a performer at the top of her game. Unlike most folks his age, or any age, Preston let his phone stay in his pocket for the entire show. He was there to experience it, not document it. We held hands, we rubbed each other's legs, and we alternated tapping out beats and rhythms on each other's bodies. He had great rhythm in addition to all his other impressive qualities.

After the show, Preston walked me back to my bike and we parted ways after a quick hug and kiss. I rode home alone with Feist humming a tune in my head and Preston carving a spot in my heart. I rode away that night surprised by two things: 1. What a fucking great guitar player Feist is. People don't talk about that. Likely because she's a woman, but news flash: women play guitar just as well as men do. 2. I really fucking liked Preston.

SEXUALITY

The first single from Billy Bragg's 1991 album *Don't Try This at Home* was titled "Sexuality" and contained a message of support to the gay community, and a nod to safe sex. Both were a rarity in 1991.

It was a message I was desperate to hear. I was only twenty-one when the album came out and still in the closet, but well aware at that point where my sexual desires lay. To hear a pop song from a straight artist I had liked for many years condone gay sexuality was literally and figuratively music to my ears. Billy was never exactly a pop star, though. More a protest singer, he has a lefty streak a mile wide, and his songwriting leans towards commentary on politics, the state of England and social justice issues. He is kind of a modern-day Bob Dylan or Woody Guthrie, without the commercial success or mainstream adulation. Billy flirted with the mainstream now and again but has always stood on the sidelines, resolutely an outsider, and with "Sexuality" he cemented his status as a queer ally.

"Sexuality" was featured on his sixth full-length record and was co-written by Billy with Smiths guitarist Johnny Marr. Johnny played on the record, and the incomparable Kirsty MacColl contributed vocals—as well as some killer tambourine, if the video is to be believed.

Billy, Johnny, Kirsty. A trio of Pete favourites.

I remember hearing somewhere that Bragg wrote "Sexuality" as a challenge to "write a hit," and while it didn't quite storm the charts, it was his best-performing single in North America, climbing to number two on the Billboard Alternative Songs chart on October 12, 1991. Kirsty also had the biggest hit of her career with a Billy Bragg composition, "A New England," which she released in December 1984. The song first appeared a year prior on Billy's debut record *Life's a Riot with Spy Vs Spy*, but it's been Kirsty's song ever since she recorded it. It's an amazing cover, and it was likely her version of the song that was my first introduction to Billy's work.

There's more history to this trio too. Both Johnny and Kirsty are credited on Bragg's brilliantly titled 1986 album *Talking With The Taxman About Poetry*, and Johnny co-wrote two songs and played on Kirsty's 1989 album *Kite*. Three old friends and collaborators getting together in the studio to share a special moment and create a lasting song.

When Toronto's storied Horseshoe Tavern announced a series of seventieth-anniversary shows in the fall of 2017, I was shocked to see that Billy was doing a three-night residency. He had played the venue several times in his early years and developed a personal relationship with the owner. Though he could have filled a venue five or ten times the size, it seems Billy was doing the residency for the love of the venue, to mark his own history with it. It made me love him all the more.

I knew exactly who I wanted to go with. Soon after Ian instructed me to wear a Speedo so he could peel it off me and fuck me, we scheduled a late winter afternoon date at my place with a plan to enjoy some beers and music along with some sex. With the daylight waning on a rainy March afternoon, he gleefully pulled *Talking With The Taxman About Poetry* out of my collection, remarking, "I can't believe you have this!" Why he couldn't believe it I don't know; he was learning my music tastes by that point, and Billy fit within them perfectly.

Despite his love of Barbra, it was hardly surprising to discover he was a Billy fan. Two politically motivated and left-leaning activists who also happened to be poets, Ian and Billy were cut from the same cloth. Ian and I were each pleased to find a fellow Billy Bragg fan that day.

My sexual relationship with Ian lasted the better part of a year, but by 2017 we were simply friends. Our connection was deeper than the sexual chemistry we shared, so we had stayed in touch and allowed our friendship to grow, without sex involved. We shared book recommendations, did crosswords together, and I got to know his friends and partner. When I texted him to see if he wanted to join me to see Billy play live, the response was instant: *Absolutely*.

For Billy's run of shows at the Horseshoe, he was focusing on different albums for each evening, and I was waffling over which performance to attend. Ian and I agreed that *Workers Playtime* was our favourite of all his records, so it was decided we would attend the final show on Thursday, September 28, 2017, where he would be primarily performing songs from that album and the follow-up record, *Don't Try This at Home*.

Workers Playtime was released in September 1988 and remains my favourite album of his, my love for "Sexuality" notwithstanding. Ever the provocateur, Billy included the following text on the cover under the album title:

Capitalism is killing music

No fucking kidding, Billy. In 1988 we were at the beginning of an era when the music industry was trying to jam overpriced CDs down consumers' throats, convincing many of us to rebuy albums we already owned with a pitch of "more convenient," "better sound" . . . all at only $19.99 a pop. What a crock of shit. A greedy industry was trying to milk every penny out of its consumer base. I'm sad to admit that my first copy of *Workers Playtime* was a CD copy. I was an early adopter of this CD nonsense and regrettably migrated from vinyl quite early. Several years and thousands of dollars later, I finally reverted to vinyl, but I bought a shit ton of CDs in the 1990s. I desperately wish I had a magic wand to transform my CD collection into LPs. Is it any wonder the world said a collective "fuck you" to the music industry when Napster launched a little over a decade later?

I wonder what Billy would include on the album cover were it released today, in the era of downloading and streaming services.

Capitalism won.
Greed ruined the music industry, not Napster.
Artists are fucked.
Please, please, please buy a concert ticket or some of my merch
   so I can eat.
Streaming is nice for you all, but artists don't make any money.

There isn't a lot of room for artists like Billy in the world today, and we are all worse off because of it.

Workers Playtime was the record where I discovered that Billy was a bit of a romantic . . . and was not immune to a broken heart! The album leans far more heavily on songs about relationships and love, both new and failed, than any of his other work. I'm not sure about the personal history of what was going on with his life when the record was made, but it seems as though it was an emotionally fertile time for the young man.

Maybe I was a bit of a romantic too? Ian and I were friends now. Not fuck buddies. Not romantic. Not boyfriends. No chance. Never was a chance. But still, I kind of lamented the "possibility of Ian." He was never within my reach because of his long-term partner, but he was exactly the kind of guy I wished were in reach. His boyfriend was a lucky man.

After a few friendly beers at my place, we hopped on our bikes and headed over to the Horseshoe on a warm late-September night. The place was packed and buzzing when we arrived. If I'm not the oldest person at most gigs I go to now, I am certainly in the top 10th percentile. Not at a Billy Bragg show. I had never seen so many grey-haired, paunchy-bellied men in their fifties and sixties at a gig in all my life! I felt positively fresh-faced and youthful. Ian must have felt like a babe in the woods.

Billy came out to thunderous applause, the crowd primed and ready to go. He didn't have a band, nor did he need one. He's one of those musicians who can transfix a crowd with only a guitar and his voice. He started the evening with "Accident Waiting to Happen" from *Don't Try This at Home* but jumped into songs from *Workers Playtime* soon after with "Little Time Bomb" and "The Price I Pay." Ian and I shifted around in search of the best view of the stage and found ourselves arm in arm for a bit, but finally, since he's taller, Ian positioned me directly in front of him. We stood with my back pressed to his chest and I was comforted by this closeness to my friend. Sometimes we swayed, sometimes we stood apart, but it felt good to be so close to Ian again. Even clothed.

We were both surprised to confess to each other how hot we found Mr. Bragg. He was never a sex symbol, but boy, had he turned into a hot silver fox.

Billy dropped "Sexuality" mid-set and I couldn't help but cry a bit. So much had changed in the decades since the song's release, for both Billy and me. In 1991 it was a message of hope. In the fall of 2017 it was a nostalgic reminder of my time in the closet, of my work to break out of it and finally find not just comfort with my sexuality but real thankfulness for it. I had the presence of mind to look outside myself in that moment—standing beside my tall, blue-eyed ex–fuck buddy who was fifteen years younger than me—and it was a pretty great look. Better late than never.

After two hours of Billy standing at the lip of the stage with his acoustic guitar, he came out for a final encore. He blazed through a killer version of "A New England" and did a pretty good job of reclaiming the song for himself.

When the lights came on to signal the end of the show, all the grey hairs and Ian filtered out onto a Queen Street I barely recognized anymore: capitalism didn't just kill music, it killed a once vibrant and thriving arts scene on Queen Street West in Toronto. Music stores, live music venues, cafés and independent shops that I remembered from my teens and twenties had been replaced by US chain stores with gigantic neon signs. This was not progress.

Still buzzing from "A New England," I asked Ian if he had ever heard the Kirsty MacColl version of the song.

"Who? I've never heard that song before."

I filled in the details as we unlocked our bikes, looking forward to introducing Ian to Kirsty's version. He couldn't wait for me to play it for him.

Ian and I had started our relationship with a quick and anonymous Grindr encounter. After a lengthy relationship as fuck buddies, we found ourselves standing arm in arm a few years later as friends. We were great lovers, but maybe we could be even better friends. We could be whatever we wanted to be.

50 WORDS FOR SNOW

In the first chorus of the song "Snowflake," the first track on Kate Bush's *50 Words for Snow* album, she claims that the world is simply too loud. Kate's right: the world is loud. Too loud. All of it. Too loud. Too much. And it's so damned hard to remove ourselves from it.

When *50 Words for Snow* was released in 2011, it was only Kate's second album of new material in almost twenty years. The entirety of the album is the distinct sound of a fifty-three-year-old woman who just does not give a fuck, not about making hit records, not about finding radio play, not even about album sales really. I think she made this record to follow her own muse and to create a lasting piece of art. A quiet, reflective masterpiece that demands attention and reflection, it is not an album to be taken lightly.

It was the perfect accompaniment for a January date with Preston. Like *50 Words for Snow*, he too was a masterpiece, a thing of beauty. As was our connection. Both of us were juggling end-of-year commitments, so we saw very little of each other in December despite several attempts. Quietly, 2017 had shifted to 2018, so to celebrate the new year we carved out some time and planned a Sunday afternoon date.

Preston arrived around 3 p.m. on a cold and dark day, as they all are in January in Toronto. To toast our reunion we decided on Aperol spritzes, a splash of summer, to help combat our winter blues. As we caught up on holiday activities and life events, we started to touch and gravitate closer and closer to each other. In very short order we were making out like horny teens on the couch and ignoring our cocktails. At his suggestion we went to my bedroom. Goodbye winter blues.

Preston undressed quickly and then revelled in taking off my clothing, one piece at a time. As he always does when we are naked, Preston remarked on how spectacular my body was! Mine!?!? The twenty-three-year-old, six-foot-three dancer complimenting the forty-eight-year-old middle-aged man on his body. That felt nice. So, so nice.

Sex with him was always remarkable and that day was certainly no exception. While he continued to top me, to fuck me, Preston identified himself as a frustrated bottom. I was thankful to have him play a more dominant role when we fucked, though; he delighted in exploring and pleasuring my body. But we both dreamt of a day when we would switch positions.

We took our time exploring each other's body naked on my bed. Him on top of me with my legs splayed. Me on top of him pushing between his long legs. Then me on top of him, straddling his hips, putting pressure backwards onto his dick. He flipped me over, spread my legs and pulled my ass into the air. With my face down in the pillow, he started to lick my ass, tentatively at first, but then with increasing intensity. He took a breath. He spit. He dove in for more. He stroked my cock and played with my balls the entire time he ate me out. Unsated, he flipped me on my back and continued his work while making direct eye contact with me. There is something so sexy and so transgressive about staring your lover in the eyes as he eats your ass.

Preston began to tease my asshole with his cock, and we both moaned in delight. As he pressed against me more forcefully, I pushed backwards until we were both almost feverish. When he asked, "Do you want me to fuck you?" we both knew that asking the question was a simple courtesy. Preston stared at me as he slowly pushed his cock into me and almost instantly we were working in perfect rhythm. We were both pressing together. Faster. Slower. We kissed. We smiled. We smirked. We revelled in our shared connection. We did not break apart. It was a long and glorious fuck. I could not hold back a second longer, and he watched me from atop as I yelled and orgasmed all over my stomach and chest. He just kept saying, "Wow, wow, wow," from above me. Wow.

Preston pulled his dick out of me slowly and the withdrawal made my post-come body shiver. He began to jerk himself off while I squeezed his balls and fingered his asshole. He was moaning and twisting on top of me and in a minute or two his come joined mine on my chest. We both smiled again. And laughed. And sighed. Sex that good is hard work.

Preston was very tender afterwards and spearheaded the cleanup. After tossing the used condom in the trash bin, he went to wet a warm towel and brought it back to the bed to clean up my body. He gently wiped and caressed me as he removed the ample evidence of our fuck. Spent, we lay in bed together and talked, cuddled and kissed.

But Kate . . . what of Kate Bush?

We made it back upstairs in the dying light of the day and I prepared him a simple dinner of roast chicken, the aroma of cooking poultry and vegetables filling the room while we played several records and drank a few glasses of wine. Each of us had worked up a hunger that needed to be sated.

By the time we had finished our meal and the washing-up, it was getting late. I knew I should encourage Preston to go home, but we were enjoying each other's company so thoroughly, I wasn't ready to end our date yet. *50 Words for Snow* came to mind and I asked if he'd like to smoke a bit of dope and sip a Scotch while I played him a record. He was game.

50 Words was a gamble. Preston had proven himself to be a very eager student for almost every record I had played him, including some Kate Bush songs from her commercial peak. But

50 Words is different; it takes some patience to reveal itself. But he was an artist, I was confident he could handle it.

After we blazed, I got up and dropped the needle on side one. I was nervous. We sat entwined on the couch with our tumblers of Scotch and waited for it to begin. The album starts with a ten-minute song, "Snowflake," a duet between Kate and her prepubescent son. Preston was a piano player and was immediately drawn to Kate's playing. But as the song slowly, almost imperceptibly built, I could see he was falling for "Snowflake." Hard. His eyes opened, practically bulging, and he looked at me with his mouth agape. There were no words this time, but it was obvious . . . Wow. Wow. Wow. After only a few minutes in, I could tell he was absolutely smitten.

At the conclusion of song one, we finally spoke. Briefly. "This is one of the most incredible pieces of music I have ever heard," he told me as he put his Scotch down and got up to retrieve his notebook. He was so overwhelmed, he was visibly flustered. He needed his notebook to start writing down some of his thoughts and feelings about the work to calm himself as it played.

Song two, "Lake Tahoe," trumps song one by exceeding eleven minutes. It's about a ghost woman searching for her lost dog on a frozen lake. Song three, the entire second side of the record, goes one step further with a running time of over thirteen and a half minutes, and describes a love affair with a snowman come to life. And so it goes. So it goes. NOT for the faint of heart.

The songs are ostensibly about snow and winter, but I hear so much more in them—in each simple lyric a world unto itself. The playing is masterful. Kate's piano is restrained but exquisite, filled with meaning. Her backing band are total pros too, a combination of musicians on guitar, bass, drums and backing vocals; they are with her every step of the way. The mood is cold, but it draws you close, almost looking to the listener for heat, for warmth to survive.

Feelings of loss, memories of love and thoughts of love lost are all inescapable—but only if you pay attention. And listen. Really listen. And we did. For just over sixty-five minutes, we sat in wonder and let four sides of a quiet but complex work wash over us while we cuddled, held hands and very slowly, very quietly sipped our Scotch.

At the record's conclusion I think we were more spent than after the long and glorious fuck. We submitted. We felt it. We connected. We allowed Kate to take us on a journey outside our day-to-day lives, and we revelled in her company. In a world full of noise and distraction, to sit in a candlelit room with a twenty-three-year-old man and drift away to Kate's world was an extraordinary luxury. That night was magic. Artist and listeners conjoined in a long and glorious aural fuck.

I'm not sure where Preston fell from, but I'm sure glad I caught him.

LET'S GO TO BED

The planets had aligned to give me the best of both worlds on my forty-ninth birthday; I was going to have my cake and eat it too. I planned two separate celebrations—a date with a beautiful young lover and a party with Mintz.

The first evening was a date with Preston on my actual birthday, April 5. Everyone deserves an afternoon cocktail on their birthday, so it was arranged he would come to my place at four thirty for an Aperol spritz. Right on schedule, the beautiful man arrived, and much to my surprise, he brought gifts. Great gifts. A beautiful bottle of wine that he thought I would enjoy and, best of all, a new album. A new record for my collection was a gamble, and he knew it. Many have tried, most have failed.

I pulled it out of the bag to discover *Brasil '65*—a compilation album of samba and Brazilian sounds that was similar to what he and his dad had been listening to over the weekend (his dad again!!!). He'd long been a fan of Brazilian rhythms and wanted to add some to my collection. Preston went on to tell me that he wanted to give me a piece of himself, something that we could share and enjoy together. He elaborated that he detested the "have to give" kind of gifts that are not well thought out or are given out of obligation. My heart swelled for young Preston. I hate gifts with an agenda or any sense of obligation too.

The album hit the turntable and the wine was put away for later.

Brasil '65 was certainly a far stronger effort than any of the albums William had foisted upon me. As we sipped our spritzes to the South American beats, we started kissing on the couch with a wild fervour. Maybe it was the samba, but in no time we were both down to our underwear, with insistent hard-ons straining against the fabric. It was time for another long and glorious fuck. How great to enjoy my forty-ninth birthday on my hands and knees being serviced by a twenty-three-year-old beauty.

As we lay naked, covered in semen, I confided to Preston how delighted I was that he was still in my life. It had been seven months since our "fuck first" date and at this point I was amazed that we were still spending time together. Still connected. We were definitely more than fuck buddies, but we weren't boyfriends, and we both liked it that way. We simply agreed that we really liked each other and wanted to continue to do what we were doing. Sex. Music. Art. That felt good. Great, actually. I didn't want to make the same mistake with Preston as I had with William, or Dustin for that matter. With Preston, I would be honest about whatever I was feeling. Talk about having your cake and eating it too.

After we cleaned ourselves up, it was time to get dressed and go to dinner. The night was just beginning. My gift to Preston was dinner at one of my favourite restaurants on Ossington Street, Union. He had never been to the restaurant before and it became clear that he hadn't done a ton of fine dining, and he basked in the experience. The tastes and flavours, the odours coming from the kitchen, the incredible service and attention from the staff. It was a sensory delight! All through cocktails and dinner we smiled and talked about art and held hands at the table, in constant physical contact.

It was only a few weeks before this birthday date that I had been invited to join a small writing group with my friends Jen and Hil, both professional writers and storytellers, to begin exploring my nascent writing. I wanted to tell Preston about my new-found creative energy and outlet. He was eager to hear all about it and asked what I had been working on.

"Well . . . the current piece I've been writing is about . . . you." Yikes.

The excitement on his face was obvious. He was thrilled to be the subject of my writing practice, and when I told him it was about the recent night I had introduced him to Kate Bush's *50 Words for Snow*, he gasped. That night with Kate was as memorable for him as it was for me.

The Art Gallery of Ontario (AGO) was our next stop, and on the cab ride over I read him the first couple of paragraphs of the piece about him. I was shaking with nerves, but he held my hand and told me he loved it, he was honoured to be remembered this way. I promised I would read him the whole thing during one of our next dates.

For several years the AGO had hosted a night called First Thursday, on the first Thursday of any given month. It usually involved programming from different disciplines, with live music often serving as the anchor. It brought out a ton of queers and other cool folks from around the city, and it was great to experience the gallery at night while enjoying a few drinks. I had attended many of these evenings and been blown away by the music programming. Tanya Tagaq. The Rheostatics. My dodgeball friend Casey Mecija when she released her first solo record. The acoustics kind of blow in the main hall, but still, it was such a beautiful space to take in a show.

The program that night I attended with Preston was admittedly not great. The headliner in particular was rather lacklustre. The most exciting thing she had to offer was "Twitter shoes." That's right, platform shoes with a built-in LED screen that posted live Twitter messages from the audience while she played. She did not hold our attention for long. Instead, we roamed the galleries side by side and looked at art and talked about it in such a different way than I was used to. We really appreciated some of the work but gave ourselves permission to dismiss some of it too. This was a huge change of thinking for me. When Brad and I were together, he had very strict rules about how art was to be experienced. If I didn't read every didactic, gaze at every piece the right amount of time, I was doing it wrong. This was a refreshing change. This was how it should be.

My favourite part of the unplanned programming was watching Preston move. It was almost as if the pieces in the gallery brought the art in him to life. He did not walk through the space—he danced, he floated. Rarely in an obvious way, but he was in constant, beautiful motion. I wished I was wearing a T-shirt emblazoned with *This Guy Fucked Me Earlier Tonight*. I wanted everyone to know.

Preston's enthusiasm for the art and for the experiences of that evening was infectious, and he got me moving with him too—two queer men from different generations gliding through the gallery on a date. We held hands. We kissed. We snuggled in front of Emily Carr. It was insanely romantic and beyond what I had ever imagined for my forty-ninth birthday, for my life. I was swooning hard. And he was too, I think. We ogled some of the other cute boys who were also at the gallery and talked about the idea of having a threesome one day. Please, Yoko, Dolly and Grace, hear my prayer!

Neither of us was willing to say goodbye when the event was wrapping up, so we walked to a favourite bar of his on College Street, where Preston bought us a nightcap. We sat snuggled in a booth sipping our delicious old-fashioneds together while we recapped our evening and talked more about art, music and writing. Ever the gentleman, Preston hailed me a cab, gave me a fantastic kiss at its door, and, with a final pat on the ass . . . I was off.

He may not have been my boyfriend, but Preston was definitely something special. I had enjoyed one of the best birthdays of my life, and I still had a party to look forward to. Bring on the witch energy.

SPANISH TRAIN

I had a few days to recover from my birthday date with Preston before the main event—another living room gig with Mintz. It had taken us a few years to pull everyone back together again, but here it was: Audience of One II.

I always hope that my birthday in April marks the beginning of spring and warm, sunny days, but Mother Nature had a different idea that year. More winter weather. Thankfully, neither Mintz nor my friends were going to let a little late-winter storm ruin the night. Mintz arrived one by one, and each of them came armed with a surprise. As if honouring me with their gift of music, improvisation and art in my own home weren't enough, they all brought me a thoughtful and personal item to honour the occasion.

Celina arrived with a beautiful bottle of single malt Scotch. We both love a good Scotch.

Carolyn had in tow a witchy crystal that she saw and intuited was for me. A taliswitch to protect and guide me.

Christina brought me a spectacular bottle of red wine. Wine had fuelled many of our conversations about life and art, and she has exquisite taste.

Sarena arrived last with a copy of her band Rough Spells' first full-length release on vinyl, *Modern Kicks for the Solitary Witch*. Not just any copy, but one personalized for me by Sarena, bedazzled with a sparkling *P* for Pete on the cover.

The gift of my friends' music, nothing better. Good Goddesses. I was the luckiest little homo in town.

Many of the men I had dated or spent time with in the past few years were fascinated by my lesbian circle and a few had begged to be part of a Mintz happening. Sadly, Dustin and Preston couldn't make it that night, but Nat and William could. While hosting an ex–fuck buddy and a current fuck buddy at the party might have provided a bit of awkwardness, this was the new Pete, and I wanted to embrace the messy and the uncomfortable.

Once everyone I expected had arrived, we made our way to the living room, one by one. Mintz had been slowly warming up, greasing the chain. There would be no formal announcement, Mintz told us, we would just know the show had started when the show started. When it did start, it was the usual intangible magic. We went on an improvised musical journey and were all stunned at how Mintz could take a riff or a run and turn it into a song before our very eyes and ears.

During a break in the music, Sarena and Carolyn talked about a song they'd been trying to remember recently: Chris de

Burgh's "Spanish Train." I was a bit alarmed. I had never heard of the song, but just the mention of Chris de Burgh sent shivers down my spine. His biggest hit, "Lady in Red," is one of my biggest triggers—it is quite possibly the most cloying and saccharine song of all time. I've hated it every time I heard it—at every school dance, every wedding, in every elevator. The idea of an extended jam inspired by Mr. de Burgh did not thrill my heart.

But I trusted Mintz. I always trust Mintz. What followed owed virtually nothing to the source material, I suspect. The band used the title alone as a jumping-off point, and we were treated to a twenty-three-minute improvisation of pure genius. The music shifted and weaved as the jam chugged along, all following Carolyn's incredible improvised lyrics. During a mid-"song" bridge she treated us to an extended rant between the devil and the lord that was transcendent. It was an amazing thing to witness. We all chanted. We all sang. We were all part of an epic journey, courtesy of our four friends. As the train wound down, everybody needed a break to refresh and refuel for the second set.

Once my glass was refilled with red wine, I picked up Celina's kalimba. I had never seen one before, let alone heard one, but I was immediately drawn to it. The kalimba is a weird hybrid of percussion and "plucked instrument" and sounds a little like a xylophone, to me anyway. Throughout the night I had watched Celina play it and I had to pick it up and try. I experimented hitting the tines. Pluck. Ping. Pluck. It felt natural in my hands and I loved the sound. Before long my tentative plucking found a groove and I was playing something that resembled a rhythm, a pattern.

Celina jumped up and instructed me not to stop, so I didn't. I kept playing the pattern in a loop as she grabbed her berimbau and started to find her place alongside my little run of notes. The berimbau is a gorgeous and very primitive-looking instrument.

It looks like a backwards bow and arrow attached to a gourd that the player places on their belly. With the metal string of the "bow" facing outward, the player uses a stick and a stone on the string, while using the seal of the gourd on their belly to modulate the output. It sounds a bit like a primitive sitar. Find a friend who can play one: they are very fucking cool.

Almost instantly we had a hot groove going. I could hardly believe it was happening, and I was loath to stop. Lana poked her head into the living room and exclaimed, "How is it that Petey knows how to play that mystery instrument like a virtuoso?" I truly had no idea, but I felt the music and it sounded amazing. With Celina joining in, we drew our friends back into the room one by one. Our joyful jam helped transition into the next song: "Reluctant Joiner." Me.

My involvement with Mintz had always been as an observer and now, for once, here I was at the centre of a jam. The instigator. The reluctant joiner. I was always the guy too scared to join in. Afraid to raise my voice. Reluctant or not, it was my time to finally join the party, to abandon the fear of what people thought of me, to quell the anxiety I had in sharing who I really was, and to forget the worry that people would think my voice was bad or, worse, that what I had to say had no value.

At last, the reluctant joiner was coming to the table. It had taken me almost five decades, but I was finally getting to a place where I wasn't afraid of making an artistic contribution, nor of looking foolish trying. I needed four women to hold my hand and guide me along, but I was finding my place, finding my voice.

I wasn't the only one rocked by Mintz, we were all awestruck by their energy and their gifts that night. The Mintz magic touched us all. We were anointed.

The remainder of the evening was filled with our usual antics. Wine. Records. Joints. Laughter. Dancing. The joy from our living room concert lifted us all up.

Before I knew it, Nat and I were the last ones standing. I think my friends thought they were leaving me to a night of sex and passion, but Nat and I cuddled and napped on the couch instead. We were done. Sex with Nat could await another day. Lying with him in my arms, we drifted off to dreams of magic witches dancing in our heads.

Audience of One II was a smash. Amazing things were coming at forty-nine. I could feel it.

STORMY WEATHER

Just after my forty-ninth birthday celebrations, I received the most unwelcome news. Preston was leaving Toronto. He had landed a great summer theatre gig in Ontario cottage country and would be leaving town soon to start rehearsals. It was a great move for him, a logical next step in his career, but damn, I was going to miss him. The news of his departure hit me like a punch to the gut, but we decided not to dwell on it. We had one last concert to go to together, a favourite of Preston's, Baths.

When Baths' third album, *Romaplasm*, came out in 2017, it attracted a fair bit of attention in the music press. It was widely noted that Baths, a.k.a. Will Wiesenfeld, was gay and I am always ready to leap to support fellow queers making art and trying to survive in the music business. It was the album cover that sealed the deal, though, when I saw it on the record store shelf. The way Will was holding the hand of another man against his face, his expression unreadable as the light hit his eyes, was such an invitation. What was happening? Are they in love? Are they breaking up? Are they about to fuck? It was a gorgeous cover, and I had no problem dropping twenty-odd bucks to see if I could find any answers to the questions that the photograph raised for me. I didn't love the record immediately, but it slowly warmed its way into my heart. The opportunity to see it performed live with Preston was more than enough reason to go. On lucky Friday the thirteenth no less.

Preston was busy with packing and seeing a few close friends before he left town, so our plan was to meet at the show. It wasn't exactly how I would have planned our final night together, but I totally understood. The show felt like a bonus date, and a few more hours with Preston was gold. I would take what I could get. I arrived at the Horseshoe Tavern before the posted set time and was surprised to discover that Baths had already started.

Winter was still not done in our corner of the world and there was a wicked ice storm brewing. Baths needed to get the show done and get the fuck out of town. Montreal beckoned the following evening. I found Preston midway into the crowd, leaning against a support beam. From behind he looked perfect, outlined by the lights flashing up on the stage. That ass. Those legs. His stature. My date. Wow. I walked up behind him and gently placed my hand on the small of his back to announce my arrival. He turned, smiled and leaned down to kiss me in greeting. Wow.

We were there for the music and it was far too loud to engage in any conversation regardless. We held hands, drank a beer or two, kissed and snuggled into each other, happy to be in our own little world. A queer artist performing for two queer fans nestled up against each other. I'd like to think Will would have been delighted if he could have seen us. At one point in the show, my hand landed on what I thought was the post we had been leaning on, but no, it was Preston's fucking leg. His thigh muscles when engaged were rock-fucking-solid. I laughed at my own confusion and was amazed anew at the physical condition of my young date.

It was a fun show, but the finality of my time with Preston was catching up to me, so I wasn't entirely in the moment. I'm not sure Baths was either. His set was cut short and his crew started ripping down the stage set-up before he could even get off the stage. The storm was coming.

The freezing rain was just getting started as we stood outside the Horseshoe on Queen. Preston and I did the awkward shuffle in the rain, neither really wanting to say goodbye but not sure exactly what to say to each other. We exchanged goodbyes and promised to stay in touch over the summer. I was excited for him, but I was pretty sad. Preston was clearly a bit sad too. I gave him a final bear hug, a hearty kiss on the lips, a squeeze of that beautiful ass, and jumped into a cab home before my emotions got the better of me.

Would this be the deep freeze for Pete & Preston? I couldn't help but wonder if we were ever going to see each other again. Preston was embarking on a summer of creativity, new experiences, new romances, new sexual partnerships. With younger and far sexier guys than me, I was sure of it. Something about that night felt very final. The end of something beautiful. If this was our finale, though, we had a pretty great run.

TAKE THIS JOB AND SHOVE IT

The catchphrase "Just say no" was former first lady Nancy Reagan's sad attempt at getting teens to stay away from drugs in the 1980s. Nice try, Nance. As her intended target market, my circle of friends at that time and I thought it was the funniest thing we'd ever heard. Sure, bitch. It was almost as funny as her husband's sad attempt at running the nation south of us. We were all certain he would go down as the most vile and disgusting president the United States would ever see. How quaint that idea sounds now. Reagan is still a vile monster, but no one could have predicted the tornado of shit that would hit America in 2016. I've ignored Nancy's advice over drug use all my adult life, but at forty-nine years old I was about to "just say no" to something else entirely.

Having mostly flunked out of high school, I had worked full-time since I was nineteen, almost always in strict, conservative, corporate environments. One national bank. One mutual fund company. Two Hollywood film studios. A few minor blips in the not-for-profit world and Canadian film distribution worlds, but for the most part only gigantic multinational profit machines. By the spring of 2018 I was working at one of the few remaining Canadian media companies as the director of marketing for an animation studio. It was a pretty enviable career to most.

At every single job I'd ever had, I always felt I'd compromised myself. I decided what to share about myself and my life and, more importantly, what to hide. I always tried to assimilate as best I could. A master chameleon. Code-switching, blending in wherever we go, is something we queers learn from a very early age, and I grew up to be an expert in it. So many of us do. I spent so much time trying to fit in, to be someone else, I completely lost track of myself.

I have been very lucky that most of the corporate jobs I've had were decent to me financially. But they stole my heart and creative spirit for years. The "performance" of going to work, of hiding my true self and acting out a role I assumed people wanted to see every day, took so much energy, I barely had room for anything else.

I just couldn't do it anymore. I no longer wanted to trade happiness for money. I needed to stop "acting" and start living my life fully. My corporate malaise was further abetted by the fact that the company I was working for was in absolute tatters, leveraging public funding to churn out some truly terrible content and making some astonishingly bad business decisions. All the while they continued to ignore the reality that streaming services were taking over content delivery from good old-fashioned television. So, in addition to being sucked dry emotionally, I felt morally and ethically compromised too. It was time to "just say no" to corporate Canada.

After weeks and months of labouring over a decision about my future and saving a little nest egg, I finally found the guts to put my hand up and ask to be set free. The company paid me to leave. Bless their twisted corporate minds. I had only worked there two years, but at my asking, they agreed to package me out! I got what I asked for, proving that sometimes voicing your desires outside the bedroom can pay dividends too.

My plan was to spend the summer of 2018 up north at a cottage community where I'd spent many summers of my life. The goal was to escape the city and reset—go swimming every day, play tennis most days, and try to spend some time writing, drawing and dreaming about what my future life could look like. Maybe I would finally find a creative voice? Maybe I could finally figure out what I wanted to do next? Maybe I could take my nascent writing efforts and create something new? I had no idea what was going to come next. That terrified and excited me in equal measure.

While life by a lake was all fun, games and relaxation, there would be almost no opportunities for sex or queer connections. The small cluster of cottages was quite remote and never saw a lot of queer people visit. As if fate saw my months of limited sexual opportunity lying ahead, she dealt me an STI I'd never even heard of—*molluscum contagiosum*. Look it up. I know I'm not the only one who hadn't heard of it. Kids often get it in gyms or schools, and it typically manifests on their feet and hands. Mine most definitely did not manifest on my feet and hands. The clustering of spots was most conclusive: it was an STI. Thankfully, it's a pretty benign condition, but it is incredibly persistent, so my sex life was put on hold. *Que sera.* After the luck I had enjoyed over the prior few years, I could hardly complain about a little pause.

I hadn't felt so free since I'd said no to both of my long-term monogamous relationships. I had a clean slate. By saying no, I was finally embracing yes. Leaving a job never felt so good. Free at last. Thank goddess almighty, free at last.

Before a summer in the woods, though, it was time for Pride! My timing in just saying no was pretty damned perfect.

RISE UP

As soon as tickets for the annual Queer Songbook Orchestra (QSO) Pride show at Buddies in Bad Times Theatre (the largest and longest-running queer theatre in the world) went on sale, I bought a pair. Their Pride show the year prior had been one of the best in recent memory, so there was no way I was missing out on this event. Thinking I would have no trouble finding a date for such a special night, I was surprised it actually took me a few tries. Around that time I had been on a few dates with men closer to my own age who were kind of interesting, so I started off with two of them.

TEXT 1: *Anthony, hope all is well. I have a spare ticket to the Queer Songbook show at Buddies Sunday, can you come?*

He could not. Something about his sister. His loss.

TEXT 2: *Lawrence! I hope you've had a great week. Any chance you can join me at the QSO show I told you about last week?*

He could not. Something about getting ready for the work-week. His loss.

TEXT 3: *Nat buddy! It's the Queer Songbook Pride show Sunday night. Can you join me?*

Third time lucky, as they say.

It seemed only fitting that Nat was going to be my date. He and I had been hooking up for over a year at this point and we had shared many concerts and records during that time—including the last QSO Pride show where both of us were gobsmacked at the level of talent and queer magic in the room. If I were being honest with myself, I was kind of glad the two other gents turned me down and I got to take Nat to another night of great music. Sometimes, the goddesses do intervene. So much for dating men my own age. Not that I was trying all that hard anymore.

Nat was finishing up some final work on his PhD so didn't have time to join me for beer at my place before the show, and with my *molluscum* still present, that was probably for the best— Nat and I were never good at keeping our hands off each other! Alternately, we agreed to meet at the Black Eagle and enjoy a pint or two on the patio closer to show time.

At the Eagle, Nat arrived a few minutes late looking incredible, as per usual. He was wearing a brand new form-fitting Fred Perry polo with a pair of tight shorts and black Vans, and I wasn't the only one who noticed how good he looked. The men at the Black Eagle sat up as he walked in and I was delighted to watch their eyes follow him as he walked over to me and gave me a big hug and kiss. This one was mine tonight, boys, move along.

It had been a while since we had seen each other, so we spent some time catching up on what was happening in our respective lives. The big news was that Nat was leaving Toronto. He would finish his PhD thesis at the end of the summer and had secured himself a gig at a university in Spokane, starting in the fall. Fantastic news for Nat, but selfishly, I was a little sad. This had always been his plan—to start a career in academia—but I'd sort of hoped Nat's time in Toronto would be extended by a gig at U of T or somewhere nearby. Sadly, nope. First Preston, now Nat— it seemed like all the good ones were leaving Toronto.

We arrived a bit late to Buddies and the place was packed, but somehow, someway, the two front-row centre seats were sitting empty. It seemed impossible, but on inquiry we were told no, they were not reserved. I guess everyone else just assumed they were too.

June 17, 2018, was a special night. Not only was it the annual Pride show, but it marked the release of the first QSO album, *Anthems & Icons*, a collection of eight songs of special meaning to the queer community. The Queer Songbook Orchestra was founded in 2014 by artistic director Shaun Brodie and is an ever-evolving ensemble of incredible musicians who have banded together to celebrate queer artists, queer voices and queer stories. In their own words, they are a "professional chamber pop ensemble dedicated to utilizing story and song to express, honour and elevate 2SLGBTQ+ experience, while providing opportunities for mentorship and other supports to queer, trans, questioning and allied youth." But to anyone who attends a show, they are so much more. Their performances are unlike anything I've seen, and at every one I've attended, it felt like mainlining queer joy directly into my veins.

At a QSO show almost every song is accompanied by someone in the community sharing a story about their own lived queer experience. The audience that night was treated to many beautiful tales of queerness along with songs arranged for a massive band and orchestra. That night, Nat and I both discovered the works of a queer artist from the seventies and eighties named Arthur Russell, through a fantastic song "Let's Go Swimming." We were both stunned that we had never heard of him before. Further investigation was required. Thanks, QSO!

The most surprising moment of the night for me was when a fantastic vocalist, Leah, told her story of Janet Jackson's version of Rod Stewart's "Tonight's the Night," from Janet's 1997 album *The Velvet Rope*. Hearing Janet sing about a same-sex partnership and tryst gave Leah the courage to believe one was possible. She then led the band in a heartfelt and tear-filled (for the audience) version of the slow and sexy song, completely transforming it from the kind of creepy version Stewart is known for. Reclaiming "Tonight's the Night" for the queers! Thanks, Janet. Thanks, Leah.

The climax of the show, though, brought the house down. "Rise Up" by Toronto's own Parachute Club was released in the summer of 1983. Celebrating peace and tolerance with the instruction "rise and show your power," it was a top ten hit in Canada from coast to coast. The band was a big collective of musicians with strong female membership and was fronted by a queer woman, Lorraine Segato. They were an eclectic mix of funk, reggae, pop and more. "Rise Up" was quickly adopted as a protest song, and it is rumoured that the first public performance of the song was at Toronto's 1983 Pride Parade. Produced by a young Daniel Lanois, "Rise Up" went on to win a Juno in 1984 for single of the year, beating out a pretty stacked CanCon field including Men Without Hats, Bryan Adams and Corey Hart.

I first heard the song while watching after-school music video programming. All my friends went home from school, turned on the TV and watched CBC's *Video Hits* to see the latest and greatest of all sorts of genres. We were blessed to live in a time when pop, rock, alternative, metal, ska and more could all live on one channel, oftentimes within the same half-hour.

As the years passed, "Rise Up" took on a different meaning for me. One of the friends with whom I had watched the video on television was the daughter of Dr. Henry Morgentaler's lawyer. Morgentaler was a health care practitioner who provided safe abortions to women at a time when doing so was illegal in

Canada. Providing a valuable and much-needed service got him in a heap of legal trouble, but it was his defence that ultimately went to the Supreme Court and struck down the anti-abortion law in Canada . . . but that was still several years away. In 1983 the fight was very much on.

As a result of this friendship, I got pulled into a variety of causes and conversations well over the head of a fourteen-year-old boy. But somehow, I knew this one was right. I think I had already recognized myself as an outsider and realized that all of us had to band together to fight for what was right. That the rights of all people matter. In September 1983 a group of my young friends and I decided to attend a pro-choice rally at Queen's Park to support Morgentaler and add to the voices demanding change in Canada, advocating for a woman's right to choose. There I was pictured in the *Globe and Mail* holding a placard that stated: *Every Child A Wanted Child*. As an adopted kid, the weight of the message seemed appropriate. Here I was, surrounded by protesters of every kind—feminists, queers, friends . . . humanists all.

The odd thing was, I never questioned it. I was terrified of my attraction to other boys. I was terrified of being identified as an outsider. I was terrified of showering after gym class. I was terrified of everything. But here, among this crowd, I felt at home and I wasn't the least bit terrified of being pictured in a national newspaper at a pro-choice rally. A budding feminist queer was born. I was ready to rise up.

Before the protest began, a familiar tune started up to get everyone into marching mood. It was "Rise Up." The song didn't really grab my attention on after-school TV; I felt it was too poppy, aimed at a mainstream audience. But in this context, it all made sense. This massive group of lefties and weirdos all started dancing and singing the lyrics, demanding social change.

Rise up now. Show your power.

I had started to find my tribe.

To hear an orchestra of queer musicians and a choir of singers and friends belt out "Rise Up" at the start of a Pride celebration in 2018, thirty-five years later, was an incredibly moving moment. I was bawling my eyes out as I danced in the front row. Nat could only guess that I was right when I shouted at him, "This song is so important . . . SO IMPORTANT," with tears streaming down my face.

Having grown up a few decades later and south of the border, Nat had never heard the song, let alone the names Henry Morgentaler and Morris Manning, his lawyer. We sat outside the theatre after the show in the June evening air and I was able to recount all the history to him as we snuggled on a park bench. He was a keen listener and loved hearing about my experiences with that song, with the Manning family and with Morgentaler himself. Knowing Nat would be heading back down south of the border soon made the night even sweeter. He'd be heading back with new-found knowledge of Canadian artists, aided by me and the QSO. Queer stories passed on to a new generation through music. That's something to be proud of.

Sex would have been great that night, but sharing something this special with Nat was even better.

HERE YOU COME AGAIN

Newly emboldened by my decision to leave my job, I wanted to finally figure out how to join the Dolly Choir, the Tennessee Mountain Homos, the ragtag queer choir I had fallen in love with during my first Steers & Queers Pride event in 2015. Without the stress of a job, I figured I could find the energy to learn some Dolly songs and maybe connect with a few new friends. The one major problem: I can't sing.

Singing has always been tough for me. Like most of us, I hate the sound of my own voice. Speaking or singing. Maybe it was all the times I was mistaken for my mother when I answered the phone? Maybe it was the boys teasing me for sounding gay? How does that sound exactly? Seems the straight boys have it figured out.

One memorable experience was being scorned by a friend's sister while singing along to Fleetwood Mac as a very young kid, still in single digits. The older sibling scowled and told me I was singing off-key. I didn't even know what she meant, but I knew it was bad and I was embarrassed. There were no further sing-alongs to *Rumours* that day. I've been nervous to sing ever since.

With the main Steers & Queers organizer, Lauren, on my dodgeball team, it didn't take long to figure out whom to contact. The Tennessee Mountain Homo Choir is an inclusive bunch. I was terrified I would have to audition or that there was a waiting list a mile long to join, but it turned out all I had to do was ask. Best of all, I was told skill was not required. Only heart. That's the choir for me.

Rehearsals for the show had already started and it was mandatory I attend the next one, learn my lyrics and catch up. I could do that. I entered the rehearsal room in the Artscape building on Shaw Street for the first time and the place was full of Dolly-Choristers from years past. Now here I was. One of them. Queer community. Queer magic.

It came as no surprise to me that the choir was run and led by two queer women. Heroes both. Sonya, the intrepid leader, robe supplier and wig wrangler for those of us who needed one, and Linda, the choirmaster. And master she was. A few of the members were trained singers, but Linda took the whole mess of us and helped create a joyous noise. Plus, she sang like a goddess and led us through the tougher parts of the repertoire by example. It's not until a trained vocalist and teacher takes you through Dolly Parton's songs that you realize how fucking hard they are to sing. Dolly tricks you by making her songs sound simple and easy, but they are anything but. During that first rehearsal my immense respect for her artistry grew.

I was thrilled to discover that among the tracks chosen for the choir that year was one of my favourites, "Here You Come Again." It was Dolly's first big breakthrough single outside the country charts, and it was ubiquitous after its release in 1977. Seared into my memory is hearing it at a curling club my parents had dragged me to as a kid. Kids weren't really welcome there, or anywhere in the seventies, in fact. Best seen and not heard. Once in a while it was inevitable that a few parents had to bring their kids to the rink, and when it did happen, there would be a few of us left alone to roam and explore a massive building while our parents were occupied on the ice. On one of those days, killing time and waiting for my parents to finish a game and take me home, I found myself in the men's change room with a boy a few years older than me, *ergo*, cooler than me. It felt special having this one-on-one time with an older boy. I don't know if I was crushing on him, but I knew something felt different. The lockers. The showers. The towels. The smell. I didn't understand it, but I knew I liked being there with him. Alone with him. There was no one else around, and as we idly chatted, "Here You Come Again" came on the radio. I wanted to squeal. I wanted to sing along. But my inner voice kicked in: "Pipe down, faggot."

The access to this boy, in this sexually charged atmosphere, was too rich. I didn't want to fuck it up. My job was to just be cool. Be a man. But in my heart, I wanted to sing. I knew that to open my mouth was to lose access to this space, though, to this boy. So I kept quiet.

Finally, forty years later, it was my time to sing.

On the night of the show, the Dolly Choir was ready to take the stage at the Gladstone Hotel and perform. I knew the lyrics inside and out, but I had a cheat sheet tucked into my short-shorts just in case. Holy shit, I was nervous. As the choir members prepped in the green room, my buddy Marcilyn and I started in on the Jameson's. Most of the Dollys were getting as glamorously trashy as they could, but we were fighting a case of the jitters, big time.

You've never seen a dressing room until you've seen twenty queers getting ready for a Dolly Choir performance. Wigs were modelled. Bras were stuffed. Makeup was traded. Drinks were had. It was joyous queer chaos. And while I loved being part of it, I was terrified.

After about a hundred swigs of Jameson's and at least as many beers, I donned my trashy blond mullet wig and white robe. It was showtime. As we filed onto the stage one by one and found our marks, the applause started in earnest. The audience was ready for the choir. The nerves quickly dissipated when a crowd of several hundred Dolly fans and queers hailed our arrival. I looked to my left, I looked to my right, and all I could see were blond wigs and white robes. And friends. A posse of new queer weirdos dedicated to raising our voices in unison to spread the gospel of Dolly. What a trip. With their support, I could do anything.

The backing track started, and upon hearing the first few notes, the crowd went positively wild. I was clearly not the only one who loved "Here You Come Again." I was terrified of getting up there onstage in front of so many people, but it was instantly clear to me that it didn't matter how well or how badly I sang. We were all there for the joy of it. Nobody here wanted to see me fail. No one was going to tell me I was singing off-key.

My dear friend Andrea took a video of me performing that first number, and I looked hilarious. Equal parts terror and joy, it was like that long-ago photo of me at the Tears for Fears concert. I was a man truly experiencing something for the first time. I'd faced a fear. I'd fulfilled a life goal. I had a blast.

Can I get a GAY-MEN?

HIGH AND DRY

On June 16, 2012, a tragic stage accident in Toronto killed one of Radiohead's drum technicians, Scott Johnson, during set-up for the final show of their North American *King of Limbs* tour that year. Several others were injured in a stage collapse that also destroyed a pile of their rigging and equipment. The show was immediately cancelled, and whether it was legal complications, bad blood or just the emotional trauma of the accident, Radiohead skipped Toronto on several tours afterwards. It seemed they were never coming back. So when Toronto was announced as part of the band's summer of 2018 tour, Dustin and I made a pact: we knew the shows would sell out instantly, so we would work in tandem to get tickets and attend the show together, since neither of us had seen them before.

Dustin and I had finally settled into a nice friendship after a few weeks and months of awkward friend dates. I was still a little confused—part of me still loved him, a big part of me still wanted to fuck him—but I'd secured the perfect concert buddy and record-swapping pal. I didn't want to let that go.

Radiohead was a favourite of ours when we were dating, and we spent a lot of our time listening to them together. As expected, the concerts sold out almost immediately, but somehow the goddesses beamed down their light on us and we secured two pretty good seats for the July 19, 2018, show at the [Insert Corporate Name Here] venue. We could not believe our good luck.

Not paying attention to my calendar, I also booked a trip to Halifax Pride with Carolyn and some friends that coincided with the Radiohead concert date. My flight was the morning of July 19. Fuck. Fuck, fuck, fuck. It wasn't an easy decision, but I couldn't miss the opportunity to travel with a group of some of my favourite people. It broke my heart to do it, but I asked Dustin to find a new date for the show. Radiohead was going to have to wait for me.

The day before the show and my trip, Dustin and I agreed to meet for a couple of beers in Trinity Bellwoods Park, the site of our first kiss. We hadn't seen each other in a couple of months and a friend date was long overdue. The morning of our date I finished a novel I had been enthralled with for several weeks: Andrew Sean Greer's *Less*. The book was published in 2017 and won the Pulitzer Prize the following year. It's a beautiful and funny story about an aging gay writer struggling with his creative life, his romantic life and what will come next in his story. It hit home for me for all those reasons, but more so because of its honest look at a romantic relationship between two men—one older, the other significantly younger. The book reflected my life almost too closely. When Dustin and I were dating, I never considered we had a real shot at a relationship because of our age difference, and it was only after he broke up with me that I realized how much I liked him, how much I cared about him, how much I wanted to give the relationship a real shot. I may have fallen in love with Dustin without admitting it to myself, or to him. But I was afraid to say anything, so I kept my mouth shut. I vowed to never let that happen again.

After reading the last word of *Less*, I cried. Not just a little sniffle, but real tears rolling down my face. I stared at the ceiling and thought, "Wow." Mr. Greer shot an arrow straight to my heart. I was stunned by his artistry.

Toronto is never better than on a hot July night. The park was jammed with people making the most of our short summer.

Groups of friends and lovers packed the place with blankets and takeout beers, so it took Dustin and me a while to find our spot on the lawn near a bunch of circus performers practising their craft. One acrobat in particular caught both our eyes. As we sipped our first beer and chatted, we ogled this beautiful guy together as he walked his tightrope stretched a few feet off the ground between two trees. I not only had a great concert buddy, but now I had a fun cruising buddy, too!

I couldn't help but ask how things were going with his boyfriend of the last several months. This boyfriend was not someone I liked. I had connected with him on Scruff and had gone on one date with him a year prior and was immediately put off. He was a great-looking guy, but obsessed with status and social climbing. I was shocked when I discovered that Dustin was interested in him and that they were actually dating. Admittedly, I was jealous, but more importantly, I was worried for him.

Things weren't going so well, it seemed. Based on what Dustin told me, the relationship was not much longer for this world and, admittedly, a little spark of hope glimmered in my heart. It was foolhardy—I knew we were never getting back together, but I couldn't help myself. He still held some power over me. I think he always will. Adding salt to the wound, Dustin was taking his boyfriend to Radiohead with my ticket. On my dime, no less. Grrrr.

During our second beer, I started to tell him about finishing *Less* earlier that day and how much I loved it. In almost no time I was crying in front of Dustin again, and not just a little bit this time. I was on the verge of sobbing but managed to pull back and control myself. It was clear to me that this time the reaction was not about the book but about my current circumstances— about Dustin, about me. I hoped he was not making the same connection, but I wasn't so sure. As I laid my head in his lap and sheepishly apologized for the outburst, he assured me again that my emotional responses to art and music were a big part of why he liked me so much. I gazed up at his handsome face, at the darkening blue sky, the night slowly creeping in, and thought how lucky I was to have Dustin in my life.

As we packed up our stuff and hugged each other good-bye, I asked if he was free on July 31. I had a spare ticket to see St. Vincent and as a *mea culpa* I wanted him to join me. Thankfully, he was available, so we had our next friend date scheduled, only a few weeks away. If we couldn't share Radiohead, we at least had St. Vincent, another mutual love, to look forward to.

I rode my bike home, sad that I was missing Radiohead with my buddy but excited for the upcoming trip to Halifax with my friends. Please, for the love of Yoko, come back to Toronto, Radiohead. Dustin and I need to complete that dream together. Nothing less will do.

I HAVE NOTHING

As a recently unemployed fellow, I had planned to spend as little money as possible that summer, but Carolyn's proposal of a group trip to Halifax Pride was too tempting. I tried to resist, but she can be incredibly persuasive. She and our friend Mae had been hired to headline the opening night's comedy festival to kick off Halifax Pride, and Carolyn dreamt up a coven of eight special people to make the trek out east to support them: the Magic 8-Ball. Somehow, I made the cut. In quick succession Carolyn, Mae, Christina, Sarena, Bernie, Lana, Cece and I all made our travel plans. It was me, three-quarters of Mintz, one member of the influential Montreal band Lesbians on Ecstasy, one comedian on the cusp of a major breakthrough and two more queer women in our circle all piled into an Airbnb with two suites. And everyone got their own bed. My version of heaven.

A few days before the flight out, I finally got the all-clear on my *molluscum* nightmare. Hallelujah. I wasted no time in planning a hookup with a cute guy I had connected with online earlier in the summer but had to keep putting off until I was healthy. The pause on my sex life made me realize that I hadn't just been "sowing my oats" the past few years; I loved sex, and I loved the connection with new men, new friends, even more. I wanted to hop back up on that horse . . . and FAST!

Jonny was a big cutie with giant blue eyes. He was taller, broader and thicker than many of the men I'd been with recently, but I was learning that size and shape don't matter so much. Connection does. We definitely had a good connection.

Jonny brought over a bag full of harnesses and jocks, dressed me in one of each and then proceeded to pound me on the kitchen floor. It was entirely what the doctor ordered after a few months of no sexual activity. I still hadn't experimented with dress-up and role play all that much, so I was particularly excited to explore it with Jonny after months of pent-up desire. He proved the perfect guide.

With that out of the way, it was witching time.

Our Magic 8-Ball were all travelling at different times, but Christina and I ended up on the same flight so planned to meet at the airport. I'm an obsessively early traveller, I show up everywhere early. But on that occasion, for some unknown reason, I rolled into the airport at the very last minute—barely enough time to hear the final boarding call and my name called, as a last effort to get the remaining idiot on the plane. Oh fuck. I made the flight with seconds to spare and shuffled down the aisle to see Christina beaming from her seat, mostly from relief at seeing me, I'm sure. I settled in next to her with a "Holy shit" and buckled up for takeoff.

That flight was the start of something magical for us. We'd been friends for several years by that point but never had any time by ourselves; we were always together as part of a larger gathering, or me fawning over her and Mintz. From that point on, Christina and I were almost inseparable the entire trip. The P&C Dream Team was born.

In Halifax, we rented bikes. We toured together. We got up first every day and took coffees to Point Pleasant Park while the rest of our team slept and arose slowly. We walked to the ocean and put our hands and feet in the cold water of the Atlantic. We dreamt. We talked. We stared at the water. The trees. She wanted to make another movie, I wanted to write.

During those walks we talked about Yoko Ono and a project Christina was working on, researching Yoko's contributions to the art and music world. We talked about legacy and what we wanted to leave behind. How we wanted to spend what time we had left in the world. Neither of us figured we'd leave a legacy as large as Yoko's, but why not try? We connected in a way I had never dreamt possible. She was one of those people I had long admired but never figured would have much interest in me. Christina made a lesbian romantic comedy feature film that I adored, *Portrait of a Serial Monogamist*. She was in several awesome bands beyond Mintz and was also a visual artist, a writer and a major thinker. Oh, and she also ran the coolest hotel and queer space in Toronto. Christina was a visionary and a community builder.

I was thrilled we bonded so intensely and was surprised she found my ideas worth listening to. We talked a lot about the writing I was doing, and my attempts to make connections between music, sex and my life experiences. She challenged me to keep pushing, to keep trying. Make mistakes, get messy, but do the work. And have fun doing the work.

Christina wasn't the only one who got my artistic impulses racing on that trip, though. Watching Mae and Carolyn together during their comedy show was incredible. Their chemistry is unmatched and seeing them play off each other was perfection. For me, it was watching two friends be goofballs, but for the audience of several hundred, it was watching two performers at the top of their game. We all won.

Carolyn closed the show with a new stand-up comedy routine she had recently been working on that I had seen her perform once or twice. The premise was about a dream she had that she could choreograph the greatest pairs figure skating routine to Whitney Houston's "I Have Nothing" despite not knowing how to figure-skate or how to choreograph anything. Carolyn built a hilarious and inspiring set around this insane idea and explained exactly how she would execute it. She killed the audience that night. It was certainly not the last of *I Have Nothing*. She managed to spin that idea into a six-part series that debuted on Canada's streaming service Crave in the fall of 2023.

Aimlessly walking the streets of Halifax the morning after the comedy show, Mae and I broke away from the pack. They told me in some detail about the TV show they were about to film in partnership with Netflix—Mae was using their life as inspiration for the story and content. Crazy that my friend was about to star in their own show while using their queer experience as inspiration? That was allowed? I never really believed that my story was worth telling. Talking with Mae made me realize that real-life queer experiences are worth talking about it, and that our mistakes and our triumphs can be used as fuel for art. They should be fuel for art. Maybe my real-life queer experience was worth something?

I told Mae that I had been writing about my dating and sex life and using music as a framework to tell those stories. By exploring my record collection and the events of my life, I was starting to make some connections about the person I was and the person I was looking forward to becoming. They immediately understood the idea, asked me a bunch of questions about the stories and how I was structuring them. Mae encouraged me to keep writing and to share some of my work with them. Mae was a great ally that day and continues to be an inspiration. To see their show *Feel Good* come to life on Netflix a few years later was wild. I was so happy for my friend.

The Halifax trip was perfection. Summer on the east coast— roaming around in a pack, singing, eating oysters, drinking wine, dancing, playing games . . . and laughing. Always laughing. Non-stop laughing.

While Christina and I waited for our flight home, I bumped into a gorgeous guy I'd gone on a few dates with and made out with one memorable evening on a street corner. He was a total babe and we laughed about the chances of meeting a hookup at the Halifax airport. We laughed even harder when one of the flight attendants on our route home was Jonny, whom I'd fucked a few days before our flight out east. True story. You can't make that shit up.

When we hugged at the airport back in Toronto—Christina ready to ride her bike with her ukulele strapped to her back, me ready to hail a cab—neither of us wanted to let go. A new bond had been forged.

My world shifted that weekend. After spending five days with seven queer folks, artists, witches, writers, singers, musicians, comedians, actors . . . was there a way back to where I was before? Watching and talking with Carolyn and Mae that weekend made me realize that all our queer stories were worth sharing, that we can all learn by sharing our histories and experiences. I was heading home newly emboldened to write my own story.

Was old Pete dead? Was I finally finding a path forward, carried along by these inspiring artists? I sincerely hoped so. If nothing else, I came away from Halifax with a very close friend. The P&C Dream Team was just getting started.

LOS AGELESS

Coming down from the highs of Halifax wasn't easy, but having a date with Dustin and St. Vincent sure helped me get back into normal life—one not surrounded by a superstar queer team.

My love for St. Vincent had started years earlier. I bought a CD copy of her 2009 album *Actor* and was immediately a convert. It came out the month after I turned forty, which was a particularly challenging time in my adult life. One of my greatest life mentors died the week before my birthday, my father died several weeks later, and my first long-term relationship was on life support.

Trish was a friend of my parents but quickly became a good friend and mentor to me. She was one of the first people I knew of an older generation who really embraced life and had a good time with people of all ages. She danced, she laughed, she drank red wine and loved being at the centre of every party—living proof that life doesn't end at middle age and that friendships don't have an age limit. Cancer claimed her life way too early. My father's death seven or eight weeks later from a variety of health issues was far less of a surprise than Trish's, but it still rocked me.

Actor was an escape to another world for me. It's a rich, multi-layered work with beautiful instrumentation. Strings, woodwinds and brass all add to the core sound of vocals, guitar, bass, keyboards (all of which Annie Clark, a.k.a. St. Vincent, plays!) and drums. A woman who writes her own music, plays most of it on her record and is willing to take the kind of creative risks that she does is my kind of artist. To later discover she was also queer was just icing on the proverbial cake.

The first time I saw St. Vincent perform live was with David Byrne in support of their collaboration *Love This Giant*, released in 2012. She had released her third solo album, *Strange Mercy*, the prior year, and while her reputation was growing, she was still far from the mainstream. September 20, 2012, at the Queen Elizabeth Theatre in Toronto helped change that. The entire crowd was there to see David Byrne, and admittedly, he was the bigger draw for me too. A lifelong fan of Talking Heads, I had bought their debut album soon after my first B-52s record and played "Psycho Killer" and "Pulled Up" until the grooves were almost worn out. I had never seen Talking Heads, or Byrne, perform live and I decided it was time. I was happy to see St. Vincent and witness their collaboration, but like everyone else, I was way more invested in Mr. Byrne.

The show was loosely structured around a huge brass band that would support Byrne and St. Vincent doing songs from the new album, and then each artist was afforded a chance to play some of their own work. Whenever St. Vincent took centre stage by herself, the place turned electric. You could feel the energy in the room shift, and with each and every song she pulled the audience in closer and closer.

"Surgeon" from *Strange Mercy* was the game changer. As she stood spotlit at the lip of the stage in a gorgeous black cocktail dress, guitar slung across her chest and shuffling back and forth on her preposterously high heels, the place was rapt. St. Vincent's voice was mesmerizing, her guitar playing out of this world, and her movement and choreography completely wild. She gained an entire audience of new fans that night, and it was awesome to watch it. To hear it. To *feel* it.

I have always posited that if she were a cis-gendered guy, St. Vincent would be heralded as one of the greatest guitar players of our time. Alas, rock 'n' roll media is slow to recognize women's contributions to the art form. Finally, in 2023, *Rolling Stone* named her in their "Greatest Guitarists of All Time" list. She deserved those flowers a lot sooner.

The entire show was jaw-dropping. How many times do you get to watch two brilliant artists of different generations along with a tuba, a trombone, saxophones, a trumpet, a French horn and a theremin onstage? Never before, never since. It was heartening to see Byrne allow this young upstart to own the show. He had to know it was happening, and he seemed more than happy to stand back and let her shine. I swore at the end of the show that I would never pass up an opportunity to see St. Vincent again live, and I've been true to my word so far.

Dustin and I met at the end of his workday for a beer and a burger at an outdoor market before the show, and I was crushed to hear that Radiohead were transcendent. One of the best shows he had ever seen. I was less crushed to hear that he was officially single again.

As we got settled into our seats, I told him about the infamous Clash show here at the same venue (then the O'Keefe Centre) back on September 26, 1979. A few riled-up fans ripped out a handful of the plush red velvety seats—fuelled by punk anger and anarchy, I guess. I remember Citytv's *The New Music* program report on the show, as it caused quite a scandal in conservative Toronto at the time. He could hardly believe that the Clash played such a small venue or that I had the chance to see them a few years later at Maple Leaf Gardens.

St. Vincent kicked off the show with "Sugarboy," off her most recent album, *Masseduction*, and the crowd roared its approval. Dustin and I got up with the rest of the audience to dance and move, and we couldn't help but bump into each other. With each touch, each bump, I felt that familiar shock of excitement run through me.

The second song was one of my favourites, with a deep, funky groove—"Los Ageless," also from the new album. The lyrics were not lost on me as I danced and moved with my friend and ex-lover. My interpretation of the chorus is St. Vincent wondering how she can lose a particularly hot lover and not completely lose her mind. There simply weren't better lyrics to describe my state of mind in that moment with Dustin.

A few tears fell as I watched the show, as they are wont to do with me. Here I was with one of my favourite performers and recording artists and one of my favourite ex-boyfriends, whom I sort of wished was my current boyfriend. I was forty-nine years old and crushing on a twenty-five-year-old. Oh, what a world. I wouldn't have had it any other way.

The rest of the show was breathtaking. St. Vincent's artistry was sublime; she had thought through every detail and was at the top of her performance game, and she knew it. Everything from her singing and playing to the stage set-up, choreography, costuming and lighting—all combined to create a living work of art. She sang her last song before the encore, "New York," unaccompanied at the front of the stage to remind us what an incredible voice she has and what a great songwriter she is. Stripped of any instrumentation, filter or production, her voice was spectacular all on its own.

The show wrapped up with three more blistering tracks and we soon found ourselves spilling out onto Front Street with the rest of the crowd. We were speechless. We were also a little high, which contributed to our speechless state, but after a show like that it was nice to just walk, breathe in the warm summer air and digest the artistry we had just witnessed. We found our bikes nearby and rode home through the quiet streets of Toronto while we talked and laughed and felt the warm air against our faces. Life could go on like this forever.

After we pedalled along to King and Sudbury streets, it was time to say goodbye. Not so long ago, Dustin would have invited me back home to fuck, but tonight we shared a chaste kiss astride our bikes and said goodbye. He rode west, I rode north. Both alone.

YOUNG, GIFTED AND BLACK

On August 16, 2018, the goddesses made us all weep. At 10:08 a.m., I got the news by text from one of my early music listening buddies, Chris:

Aretha is dead. [crying emoji]

Three words, one symbol, and just like that . . . blunt force trauma to my heart. I was gutted.

The news wasn't exactly a shock, as the press had been reporting her demise for years. The media had caught wind that Aretha was ailing in the few weeks before she died, and boy, did they dine out on it. The "Aretha death watch" in the media was gruesome, but it was hard to tune out. We knew the end was coming. Surprised or not, the Queen was dead. And there will never be another like her.

In the early 1980s, my friend Michele introduced me to some of Aretha's early songs like "Respect" and "Do Right Woman, Do Right Man." I was immediately smitten. You know when you know you want dick but you really like a girl, and you're fifteen and so a girl is the right choice and you kind of even have a crush on her but you actually yearn for her gorgeous boyfriend who drives a blue pickup truck and plays Bob Marley records? Remember that feeling? That was Michele for me.

One afternoon while the two of us were record shopping on Yonge Street, the golden mile of record stores in 1980s Toronto, I picked up my first Aretha album on Michele's recommendation: *Aretha's Gold.* We went back to my parents' house and peeled off the shrink wrap, one of my favourite rituals still, and plopped on side one.

Gold is right. Song after song after song, Aretha hits it out of the park. Her early years at Atlantic Records yielded some of the greatest songs of the modern era and captured quite possibly the greatest singer in the history of recorded music at her absolute best. The music is jaw-dropping, but her voice is superlative. It pierced my heart that day, and every day since.

Proudly Black, she didn't try to commercialize her music or image for a white audience, or for anyone. Aretha waited for the people to come to her. She wore turbans and afros on her head. She wore caftans and revealing outfits that highlighted her ample cleavage and full figure in equal measure. She released an album titled *Young, Gifted and Black* with the titular Nina Simone song as its centrepiece. At her commercial peak Aretha forced her label to release a live gospel album, much to their horror (*Amazing Grace* stands as the biggest-selling gospel record of all time). She sang at Martin Luther King's funeral. She was a feminist and civil rights crusader, and she did it all her way. An absolute fucking legend.

Younger gay men seem to be drawn to a certain type of diva, attracted to over-the-top behaviour or outfits more than actual talent (see: Britney, pick-a-Spice-Girl, Kylie—I know, come at me), or those with outsize talent coasting on past glories (see: Mariah, Christina) or who were happy to release album after album of overproduced easy listening in the interest of massive record sales (see: Celine, Barbra). For gay men of a certain age, though, Aretha is the diva of all divas with talent to spare. If the young boys want to see antics, I suggest they watch the YouTube video of her performing at the Kennedy Center Honors in 2015, only a few years before she died. Ever the show-woman, she walked out onstage in a massive fur coat with a bedazzled clutch and then proceeded to sing Carole King's "(You Make Me Feel Like) A Natural Woman" and tear it to shreds, with a fur coat drop near the end for the ages. Bonus content is watching Carole completely freak out, exploding with joy at watching Aretha sing one of her best-known songs, and also witnessing President Barack Obama be moved to tears and get a pretty sweet groove on. That's how a diva does it, boys.

August 16, 2018, was also the day I planned to meet David for the first time. He was a twenty-nine-year-old medical school graduate, newly back in Toronto after finishing his studies, and had landed only a few blocks away. His profile indicated he was a budding vinyl collector, so we agreed to a date at my place so he could "check out my record collection." Mmmm-hmmm, I'd heard that one before.

I texted him that afternoon in warning: *I hope you like listening to Aretha Franklin . . . and seeing grown men cry . . . both are likely tonight.* He was still game. Maybe there would be sex alongside our mourning Aretha's loss?

When David arrived, the first surprise was how damned good-looking he was. A guy who presented much better in real life than he did in photos was always a treat. I also hadn't converted the metric height statistic on his profile into terms I understood, so was pleased to discover he was over six feet tall—another great surprise.

We fell into an easy rapport over some red wine and cheese. David was a very smart guy and a great conversationalist. I discovered he was a cyclist, which helped explain his great legs and butt (he was wearing rather tight-fitting shorts, I'd have been a fool not to notice!). He was also incredibly well-travelled, including many countries in Asia, South America, Europe and beyond. A past resident of several cities, including Toronto, Montreal and Los Angeles, young David had a lot to offer, it seemed. Best of all, he was a professed music fan and had been an avid concert-goer for most of his life.

Out came *Aretha's Gold.* There is nothing I like better than pulling out an album I bought thirty-five years prior and sharing it with a new friend. David was an Aretha fan too and we interspersed our conversation about travel and music with comments on some of Aretha's greatest songs. While talking with him, it occurred to me for the first time that I had been exploring Aretha's classic soul and R & B recordings when in high school, while the rest of the world, and all my peers, were listening to some of her worst offerings. She had massive success in 1984 with the album *Who's Zoomin' Who?*, containing the still-cheesy hit song "Freeway of Love." Give me classic Aretha any day, any time.

It was time for more wine. While I fetched our drinks, David moved over to the couch to see the concert tickets I had framed on the wall behind it. The collection included ticket stubs from some of the first live music I had ever seen. I knelt beside him on the couch with our refreshed wine and joined him in the trip down memory lane. He was impressed that Adam Ant at Massey Hall was my very first concert, in 1983. As we talked, my hand found his ass and damn, it felt good. "Fleetwood Mac," he proclaimed! My hand moved its way down his thigh. "Wait, how many times did you see Simple Minds? . . . I love them." Instead of answering, I finally kissed him, and damn, that felt nice too.

Time for a new Aretha record . . . Hmm, which one? Out came 1975's *You*, which starts with the Aretha-penned classic "Mr. D.J. (5 for the D.J.)" and features a brilliant shot of her in all her 1975 glory on the cover. As Aretha sang, I took off David's shirt. Kissed his chest. Bit his nipples and felt his cock respond through his shorts. I bit down harder and it was like a lightning rod shot through his body. Catching his breath, David confessed he was expecting a more chaste kind of date as I had come across as a real gentleman in my communications on Scruff! Chaste? I removed his shorts to show him who was chaste. As I stood to remove my own shorts, he asked with a sly grin if I was "feeling overdressed." I most certainly was, but not for long.

We continued to make out and play with our erections through our underwear, David in his black Uniqlo boxer briefs, me in my white Bikkembergs briefs. It was quite a sight. I think we were both surprised at how much fun the other was and how sexy we found each other. A beautiful queer surprise on a dark day filled with loss.

As side one concluded and we listened to the click of the album stuck in its final groove, I suggested we go downstairs to my bedroom. We kicked off our underwear as we crossed the living room floor.

Finally naked, him between my legs on the bed, I suggested he fuck me, as I was incredibly turned on by this point. He told me, "I'd love to, but before we do, you need to know I'm undetectable . . . positive but undetectable."

Oh fuck. Oh fuck. Oh fuckety-fuck-fuck-fuck.

Breathe, Pete. Breathe. Just fucking breathe.

He was still on top of me with his dick between my legs when I heard this news. His dick was going a bit soft with his admission, but fuck, it still felt like a loaded gun down there. What a fucking surprise. Okay, intellectually I knew that undetectable = untransmittable. There is science behind this, proven science that is accepted by the medical community and the queer population at large. I should have been enlightened on this issue, but I was still not quite on board. And I was sort of embarrassed that I wasn't yet.

The AIDS panic I felt as a teenage boy was still alive inside me. It never left. I never dealt with it. Hearing David tell me that he was HIV positive struck terror in my heart. It was as if all the pent-up fear, rage and frustration I had been carrying with me for decades suddenly surged in my veins and raced to my brain.

As David lay on top of me, I admitted that the news terrified me. I tried to explain some of my baggage to him as he patiently listened and answered my many questions. How long have you had it? Do you know how? What's your medicine regimen? We slowly shifted positions. Talking, not fucking, became our primary activity for a bit. We discussed U=U and that making sense of it and having sex with an HIV-positive person was all very new to me. I didn't recoil; I still kissed him, still stroked his body. I knew these activities carried no risk. But I was still scared. More than scared.

I guess not everyone takes the news so well . . . and believe me, I didn't think I was handling it so fucking well. He recounted tales of being scorned, of being immediately thrown out of people's homes, of being shunned upon disclosure of his status. Without discussion. Without conversation. Just . . . "Go."

I learned that David had been positive for five years, was in perfect health, and that his doctors had told him to expect to enjoy a perfectly normal lifespan and sex life. I also discovered that he hadn't told his parents yet. Nor all his friends. Stigma? Hell yes, it still exists around this disease. I knew that my ignorance and irrational fear were still part of the problem.

We continued to play with each other's dick during our conversation, and it wasn't long before we were handling two boners in need of release. And release we did. Our come blended on our bodies, on the sheets, on the pillow behind my head.

Interesting that my fear did not get in the way of desire. There's a first time for everything. Rationally, I knew that our sexual activity carried no risk, but there was still a voice in the back of my mind saying, "Holy shit, what have you done?" Decades of panic and fear do not disappear after one sexual encounter.

It was time for more Aretha. Back upstairs on the couch, I put on her strange and wonderful 1973 record *Hey Now Hey (The Other Side of the Sky)* and continued to be dumbfounded by her mastery. Dressed only in our underwear, David and I spent several more hours listening to records, kissing, fondling each other's balls through our underwear, and chatting. It was one of the nicest dates I'd had in months.

It wasn't until I put on Aretha's 1970 masterpiece *Spirit in the Dark*, her finest artistic statement in my estimation, that the first tears came. *Spirit* was the first record she made after leaving her husband, Ted White, and in every song, every note, you can hear how free she feels. How renewed. It's a statement of not just a great singer but a true artist. Aretha had it all.

My tears were mostly for Aretha that night, no doubt about it. But I think I was shedding some for me too. Maybe it was time for me to feel free. To stop living in fear, and allowing that fear to guide my decision making.

Close to midnight, we agreed to call it a night. David put on the rest of his clothes and we kissed by the door. There was no question that a second date would be arranged soon. The Queen was dead, and maybe some of my baggage around HIV was dying too.

CENTERFOLD

David and I started hanging out together a fair bit after our night with Aretha, and we decided to spend one of the late August days at Hanlan's, Toronto's clothing-optional queer beach on Toronto Island. We discovered that we both had a few friends heading over to the island that afternoon and figured we would roam around and connect with folks during the day. Never in a million years would I have expected to find myself standing naked in the thigh-high water enjoying cold beers with my current fuck buddy and two of my recent exes, William and Dustin. I knew they'd both be over there but did not think we would all be enjoying each other's company as a group. The four of us stood in a small circle assessing handsome men, tragic bathing suits and the terrible music emanating from the massive speaker someone had carted to the beach. The most surprising part of the situation for me was that no one was uncomfortable in each other's company. Each knew I'd had a relationship of sorts with the others and we were all happy to just hang out, mostly naked.

Finally, a song broke through that wasn't from one of the divas: Everything but the Girl's 1994 smash song "Missing." I was shocked to discover all the boys starting to move their hips and sing along even though they were all barely born when it came out. It's one of those songs with staying power, I guess, and for good reason—it's still a great jam.

Back on the beach, both David and I had to pee, so we headed to the infamous cruising grounds, a patch of tall grasses with well-worn footpaths twisting throughout, for a bit of relief. We found a relatively private spot and, standing side by side, our piss hitting the sun-warmed sand, we made eye contact and started to kiss while we crossed swords. My stream hit his leg and we both laughed as he retaliated by aiming his stream at me. With our Speedos pulled down, connected at the lips, we both had each other's piss dripping down our legs. Only at Hanlan's.

On our way back to the beach, we stumbled across a scene that stopped us dead in our tracks: an insanely sexy twenty-something bottom with an enormous erection jerking off while getting fucked by a giant, bearded muscle-daddy. David and I couldn't turn away and it was clear that this couple was looking to show off. We started to kiss again and pulled our dicks out as we watched. More and more guys—some couples, some sin-gles—also stumbled upon this epic scene. Dicks came out and glances were shared, but almost no one made a sound. It was queer desire in the late-day sun, and both David and I loved participating in it in our way. The big-dicked bottom took the load of his top, and with that the show was over. The group dispersed—some for more cruising and fucking, and some, like David and me, to find our friends again and wash the pee off our legs in the lake.

A few more hours of swimming, another beer or two, and making out naked on the beach with a baseball cap covering my hard-on, and it was time to go home.

Back at my place, David and I immediately jumped into my shower to rinse off the sunscreen and sand. Our first shower together. Hmmm. David spent a great deal of time soaping me up from head to toe, focusing considerable attention on my hard-on. Now it was his turn. I did the same but turned him to face the wall and finger-fucked him with my soapy fingers. He writhed and moaned against the wall as I had complete power over him via my fingers in his ass. Just as I was thinking it was time for a long-overdue release, he suggested we hold off so we could have another go at each other later in the evening. Brilliant idea, young man.

Our dressing for dinner meant putting on fresh underwear, and when he donned a pair of teeny blue cotton bikini briefs, my mind reeled! They reminded me of the old Jockey ads I used to drool over in the 1980s. Gymnast Bart Conner won a pair of gold medals in the 1984 Olympic Games and was one of Jockey's spokesmen in the latter part of the decade. He was cute, he was blond, and he had a killer gymnast's body. In his own words (or at least some very clever copywriter's words) from the ad: "Men don't have to be tall, dark and handsome to enjoy the comforts of Jockey underwear. They can also be short, blond and suave. I wear Jockey brand. Just Jockey."

Bart and Jim Palmer—a Hall of Fame baseball player I really had no knowledge of except for his sexy, hairy chest, who also posed in similar Jockey ads of the same era—fuelled hundreds of teenaged Pete's orgasms. This was how masturbation worked back in the eighties, kids. No internet. No Google search. No access to guys getting gangbanged and fisted with the click of a mouse. We had straight guys in underwear ads that we kept hidden in plain sight. And those ads are seared into my memory.

I can remember back in August 1987, I had recently turned eighteen and screwed up the courage to buy my very first porn-lite magazine. Greg Louganis, double Olympic gold-medal winner in diving at the 1984 Los Angeles games, had posed for *Playgirl*. This was a very big deal and it somehow hit my closeted radar. He was one of the most famous and beloved athletes at the time (and still closeted himself), and I guess Greg posing naked was irresistible to the mainstream press.

I recall being terrified that someone would spot me at the convenience store I normally went to, so I biked to an unfamiliar neighbourhood in hopes that no one I knew would see me buying the magazine. I was almost sick to my stomach when I put the copy of *Playgirl* up on the counter. It was the first public acknowledgement I had ever made that explicitly said, "I'm gay." As any eighties kid can attest, you could pretend that your parents sent you to the store for cigarettes, but nobody was going to believe that your mom sent you for the latest copy of *Playgirl* . . . and really, had a woman ever bought a copy of *Playgirl* in the history of its publishing? The store proprietor probably didn't give a shit, but to me, buying the magazine felt like a bold, subversive and absolutely terrifying act. Thank god for the little brown paper bag. I stuffed my purchase into my knapsack as fast as I could and got the hell out of the store even faster. Undetected. Phew.

I still remember the pink-toned lighting and Louganis's beautiful body shot in front of a parachute, of all things. While we never saw his dick, a towel always strategically placed to hide the thing I most wanted to see, I stared at those photos of Greg in a variety of beefcake poses on a pedestal for hours. I traced my fingers along his abs, biceps and thighs. And boy, did that man have some Speedo tan lines. We were, thankfully, treated to the sight of his spectacular butt in all its glory! I've never looked at any tan lines the same way again! I knew it was wrong, but I also knew it was right. I dreamt of Greg while my right hand worked up and down for hours.

To be frank, it was most certainly not the last porn magazine I would buy. Not by a long shot. Once I saw real porn, and real erections, I didn't have much use for *Playgirl* anymore. I kept Greg's issue for years but lost it somewhere between moves. If anyone still has a copy, please DM me. Seeing David there in his little blue briefs reminded me of all this teenage foolery and put a smile on my face.

But we weren't done with Olympians just yet. Netflix had just added *I, Tonya* to its roster of films and neither of us had seen it. We poured some wine and curled up into each other on the couch as we watched the train wreck that was poor Tonya Harding's early life. So sad. We watched her win championships. We watched her break records. We watched her come fourth at the 1992 Albertville Olympics, just off the podium. By the time of "the incident"—when rival skater Nancy Kerrigan was beaten with a club on the back of one knee, paving Tonya's way for victory at the national championships, just before the Olympic Games in 1994—it was time to pause the film. We both had to pee again—too much beer, too much wine.

On the way to the washroom we chatted about how unbelievable Tonya and Nancy's story was. David was barely born, so had no conscious memory of the event, and it was hard for me to impart how much of a phenomenon "the incident" was in a pre-internet world. It caught everyone's attention. It was a news story with real staying power.

As we peed, we crossed swords again and smiled playfully at each other as we did. A playful smile turned into a playful kiss, and before we knew it we were naked again and climbing on top of each other on my bed. Almost immediately he asked if I'd like to fuck him, and yes, I most certainly would.

And it was fucking great. Our first fuck and the first time I fucked someone I knew was HIV positive. I knew his viral load was undetectable, and yes, we still used a condom, but still, there was a slight nagging in the back of mind saying, "Holy shit." I knew in my brain there was no risk of transmission, but it still wasn't easy to completely shut off thirty years of baggage in an instant. My mind was quieting, though, ever so slowly.

Sated by the sex, we put our underwear back on, poured a bit more wine and resumed the movie. After about five minutes we both realized we were done. Sun. Swimming. Beer. Sex. More sex. Wine. There was only so much stimulation two men could take. We both hit the sheets and fell asleep almost instantly. Or we passed out. Tomato/tomato.

The next morning we made a pact to save the rest of the film for our next date, which wouldn't be easy. We were both charmed by Tonya Harding and her insane and incredible story. While we didn't know how the film ended, we knew that in real life Tonya didn't come out a winner. On went David's blue briefs and off he went to enjoy the rest of his Sunday. I wasn't just charmed by Tonya, I was also pretty charmed by young David.

ONLY LOVE CAN BREAK YOUR HEART

On September 12, 2018, I found myself heading out to see Saint Etienne. I was never a fan—not of any of their albums, not even a song. In fact, I couldn't have named a song if I had to. Why was I going? Young David, of course.

When we first connected online, his profile mentioned that he was looking for new friends in a new city and hoping to find a date for the Saint Etienne show in September. "Check" on the first request, and I could satisfy the second need quite easily. With a ticket price of only twenty-five bucks and a venue that was a mere

ten-minute bike ride away from home, I'd pretty much go see anything. Throw in a cute boy to boot and I was easily sold.

It was curious to me that a twenty-nine-year-old was introducing me to a band whose first album was released in 1991. He
was two, maybe three years old when Saint Etienne released
Foxbase Alpha, while I was twenty-two, arguably at the peak of
my music consumption years. Their next couple of albums came
out in '93 (*So Tough*) then '94 (*Tiger Bay*). David would still have
been a toddler, while I would have been in my mid-twenties.

Saint Etienne is a trio of musicians with nods to sixties soul
and seventies disco but with feet firmly planted in the early nineties
dance and electronic music scene. They seemed tailor-made for me,
or for any young gay man in the nineties for that matter. Herein
lies the problem. During this exact era I was practising what some
in the psychiatric community might have called "avoidance."

Avoidance, according to Merriam-Webster
    Avoidance (AVOID´ANCE, *n.*)
    1 (obsolete)
        a : an action of emptying, vacating, or clearing away
        b : outlet
    2 : annulment
    3 : an act or practice of avoiding or withdrawing from
        something

Number 3! That's the one for me. Avoiding or withdrawing from
something. That about sums me up in the early nineties. I spent
1991 through 1995 living in a house with a group of friends near
Toronto's Queen Street West neighbourhood. Straight friends.
Each and every one. One drunken evening out with my old
friend Michele (she who introduced me to Aretha Franklin), we
agreed that I would move in with her, her boyfriend and her
boyfriend's sister. I don't know if it was the many pitchers of

beer, the psilocybin or a simple trust that Michele would be aligned with good people, but I agreed to move in without even meeting two of my three new roommates.

My time with them was a blast. Greg, the boyfriend, played bass in a killer blues band called the Sidemen. Michele, Vanessa (the sister) and I spent countless nights out in bars around Toronto dancing, drinking and smoking dope with the group of friends that all surrounded the Sidemen. Great music. Great dancing. Great friends. All straight.

We threw epic parties that are still talked about today. Countless parties. Sometimes small, sometimes large, but almost all involving dressing up in vintage seventies outfits, blasting disco and funk of that polyester era while dancing and singing the night away. Some of the people were close friends, while many were drop-ins at Stafford Street just for the night. The one thing they had in common? You guessed it . . . all straight. I had just come out of the closet in 1991, and I wasn't ready to live any kind of authentic gay life. I was able to say "I'm gay" to my friends, if not my family yet, but I was still terrified. Many men my age pushed aside their AIDS panic and fear and embraced their queerness, their otherness. But not me. I just wasn't ready.

The Saint Etienne tour was to celebrate the twentieth anniversary of their fourth album, 1998's *Good Humor*. The show was advertised as a set devoted to playing the entire album in sequence followed by a second set of the band's greatest hits. While I don't love a reunion or anniversary tour, I completely understood the band's reasoning for doing one. Thanks to streaming, it is not easy to make money from music these days, and for a band that had only a modest level of success the first time around, Saint Etienne weren't likely pulling in a ton of royalties anymore. Or any royalties anymore. So, touring was the thing.

Just before the show at Toronto's Mod Club (now known as the Axis Club) started, I took a look around. It was packed with gay men my age. Positively packed. Some I knew, some I didn't. Some were with partners, some were with friends, some were alone. It was one of the gayest audiences I had ever seen at a live music show in Toronto—Cher, Madonna and Bette Midler (don't ask) excepted. It seemed that while I was out at blues shows in Toronto in the nineties, there were a ton of out gay men dancing to Saint Etienne.

Expecting the core trio of Bob Stanley, Pete Wiggs and Sarah Cracknell, I was thrilled to see that the band was accompanied by a full complement of musicians, including drums, guitar, bass and even a flute! The first part of the night the band was good. Not great, but good. David had warned me that *Good Humor* wasn't their best work, but given the anniversary date, they were giving the album its full due. Still, we danced, and we watched as the crowd warmed up to the band and started moving and singing along. We leaned into each other, we smiled at each other, and we held hands as we listened and swayed.

Back when I was living at the house on Stafford Street with my straight friends, I found the closest thing I had to a boyfriend in the early nineties quite by accident. I met Stephen at a friend's pool party one summer afternoon. He was beautiful. With his short blond hair and sparkling blue eyes paired with his gorgeous gymnast's body, he was hard to miss. We started talking and soon found ourselves in a makeshift diving competition in the backyard pool and swapping stories while we drank cold beer.

Stephen and I slowly felt each other out all day long. No Grindr. No Scruff. No markers. No signs. We patiently dropped clues before we finally started making out twelve hours later under a canopy of fireworks on a naval base. A kiss never felt so good.

Stephen and I dated for several weeks—mostly furtive humping, kissing and trying to figure out how to suck each other's dick in my bedroom. But we did go out too. With my straight friends. Stephen suggested we go to Woody's and other local gay spaces to meet other gay men, to have gay experiences, to explore a gay life. I was still not ready. I was ready to suck a gorgeous boy's dick, it seemed, but I still wasn't ready to be gay.

He went off on a planned trip overseas and, like a chickenshit, I used the opportunity to end the relationship. Not like an adult, by telling him, but simply by avoiding him when he returned.

Avoidance. I was great at it.

When Stephen returned from Europe, I just shut down. I ghosted him before ghosting was really a thing. I was an asshole and I've never forgiven myself. The worst part was, I really liked him. Really, really liked him. I just wasn't ready. I denied myself the possibility of a deep connection with Stephen due to my fear of sex and the gay community. The choice broke my heart as much as I likely broke his.

The second set of Saint Etienne was a whole different show! The band were clearly in their element playing their more well-known, upbeat songs, and it showed. The energy in the room increased tenfold, and as David and I moved closer to the stage, we became more and more engrossed in the music and the energy of the crowd. With David's hands on me I remember thinking, "Shit, this is what it's all about." Life. Love. Music. Celebration. Up close to the stage it was like a reunion of gay men from the nineties, and they were loving it. I was loving it. David was clearly loving it. And we were all loving it together.

As the set was nearing its close, David leaned over to me as a new song started and whispered, "This is it." He was hoping they would play one of their more popular songs, a cover of Neil Young's "Only Love Can Break Your Heart." I puzzled over how this nineties electronic-influenced, soul/disco hybrid of a band could make Neil's classic tune work. But boy, did they ever.

It's not the first of Neil's songs to benefit from a reworking with a female voice. k.d. lang's "Helpless," Nicolette Larson's "Lotta Love," Emmylou Harris's "Wrecking Ball," the trio of

Emmylou Harris, Dolly Parton and Linda Ronstadt doing "After the Gold Rush," and the Cowboy Junkies' reworking of "Powderfinger" are all arguably better than Neil's original versions. He's a brilliant songwriter, but let's be honest, he's never been the best singer.

Only love can break your heart, huh, Neil? Is love really the only thing that can do that? What about avoidance? Denial? Regret? Missed chances? Those all definitely did a number on my young heart. It took over forty years of my life before Dave well and truly broke my heart by withdrawing love after I'd left my boyfriend for him . . . but by then I'd already done a number on myself.

Did I break young Stephen's heart in my twenties back on Stafford Street? Probably. Have I done it again with someone else since? Probably. Will it happen again? I truly hope not. It was time to stop living in denial of what I wanted. At forty-nine I was finally ready to fully embrace a queer life. Some of us take a little longer to get there than others.

(YOUR LOVE KEEPS LIFTING ME) HIGHER AND HIGHER

When Preston left for his theatre gig in northern Ontario, I truly thought I'd never see him again. He was on the cusp of turning twenty-four and would be surrounded by other like-minded, and like-aged, creative folks and I was sure he'd fall in love and forget all about me. As the summer progressed, the frequency of our contact grew sparser until it all but stopped. I wasn't happy to be right, but I was sure that I had been slowly and definitively ghosted.

A couple of months after our last communication, though, Preston reached out again—he was home and wanted to set up a dinner date. Dolly-lujah! It wasn't a permanent ghosting! Just a temporary haunting. I was having a blast with David, but Preston's effect on me was incomparable. I hadn't connected with anyone as intensely, sexually or emotionally, since Preston had left town, and I was ready for more.

At the appointed time, on the appointed date, I was douched, dressed in Preston's favourite jockstrap and ready to go. The jock was in rough shape, with one of the straps literally hanging by a thread—the last time we had fucked, he confessed he wanted to tear the thing off me with his teeth but stopped himself before doing so. I begged him not to self-edit next time. Here's to second chances.

We shared a sweaty late-August hug when Preston arrived and it felt amazing to have his body pressed against mine again. I made the move to kiss him, but he deflected with a peck on the cheek. Uh-oh, something was up.

I was mixing our first cocktail when he dropped the bombshell: Preston had a boyfriend. My heart sank. The summer had played out exactly as I predicted. His new fella was a summer theatre friend and they decided to continue their romance, monogamously and long distance-ly. Fuck. My heart broke a little, again.

We agreed to remain friends, but I knew it was going to be hard. I admitted that I was still very sexually attracted to him and Preston confessed that he felt the same way. My ego was soothed, but it was worse knowing he wanted to fuck me but was holding back. Argh. Dolly, give me strength.

At the next available opportunity, I scurried downstairs, peeled off my jockstrap and slipped on a comfy pair of granny panties. I tucked the jock away in a corner of my underwear drawer and made a promise to it: "You and Preston will have your time, friend. Just you wait and see."

Despite the elephant in the room, we quickly fell back into our ease and comfort with each other. The cocktails helped. We shared stories of our summers and talked about our successes and struggles with creating art over the time we had been apart. Preston was one of my favourite people to talk with about creative inspiration with and I was relishing the opportunity to go deep with him again.

Preston had more news to share: he had been hired by the National Ballet of Canada to work on their November presentation of *Anna Karenina*. Holy shit. I was floored. Less than a year out of dance school, he had just finished a great summer theatre gig and had now landed a job with one of the most prestigious dance companies in the world. He reiterated that he was not a ballet dancer and it wasn't technically a dancing role, but he would be onstage throughout the entire show and be witness to the entire creative process. Weeks and weeks of rehearsal for a ten-day run. No matter how much he tried to underplay it, I knew it was a monumental achievement. Mental note: I'd be going to the ballet in a few months.

The rest of our night was delightful. Preston treated me to a delicious Vietnamese dinner at a cute local spot near my place on Bloor Street and we chatted, laughed and scoped out cute boys who passed by our window seat. Our legs constantly brushed up against each other and that electric shock still shot through my entire body. Ugh, being just friends was not going to be easy.

We parted ways with another sweaty hug in front of the restaurant and went our separate directions along Bloor. Sex or no sex, I was pretty damn happy to have Preston back in my life.

It had been years since I attended a ballet. My ex, Brad, worked for one of the primary sponsors of the Toronto Four Seasons Centre and for a while we were the lucky recipients of free tickets. Good ones. The ceremony and the pretentiousness of the ballet always annoyed me, but damn, I loved the artistry. More often than not, when I attended the ballet with my ex, I had to smile and shake hands with some straight, white, rich couple in the box we sat in, but I played my role as required (shut up, smile and look pretty), much like the dancers onstage. I would sit beside my ex and watch a parade of gorgeous men do astonishingly beautiful things onstage. Back then, I wouldn't be surprised if I had drool running down my chin as I ogled those young men and wondered what they were hiding behind those dance belts. I would gaze in wonder and fantasize not just about sex with them—any of them, all of them—but about running away with one of those gorgeous young men and starting, and having, a different life from the one I was living at the time.

Ten years later, I was actually living in a different fantasy world of my own creation. I was now at the ballet precisely because I had been fucking one of the men onstage for the better part of a year. Sure, he was untouchable at that moment, but I had created a life for myself where being with one of those performers wasn't just a distant dream but a reality.

During his rehearsals for the show, Preston asked if we could meet for a breakfast date. Of course. It was over eggs at Aunties & Uncles (RIP) that he told me his summer romance was officially over. Long distance wasn't working for them. Monogamy wasn't working for them. End of story. I experienced a mix of wildly oscillating emotions—sad for my friend, but hope sprang eternal for me. He was still heartbroken and tending to his wounded spirit, and it was clear that Preston needed to focus on that and his upcoming show right now. Message received: cool it, Pete.

On the night of the ballet I smoked a bit of dope just outside the illustrious Four Seasons Centre, at Preston's suggestion, and then began my very long climb to Ring 5—the location of my seat was as high as I was! I heard the orchestra for the first time as I sat down. They were warming up before the show, as orchestras do, and my heart and body were warmed. Somehow, in the excitement of seeing Preston onstage, I had forgotten that ballet is performed to a full bloody orchestra.

Act One started, and it was a massive number. Dozens of performers were staging a political rally to the music of Tchaikovsky—it was positively breathtaking. I knew I should be swept away by the beauty of the music and the dancing, but all I could focus on was, "Where's Preston? Is that him . . . oh, wait . . . is *that* him?" Finally, during the third scene, I spotted him. It was as though no one else was onstage, no one else was in the entire theatre. Preston, all six foot three of him, on one of the most prestigious stages in Toronto, hell, the world. It was amazing to witness, and I felt a surge of pride for my friend.

Once I had spotted him, I could finally relax and enjoy the show. I used to dread coming to the ballet with my partner ten years prior, but I was overjoyed to be having this experience all by myself, way up in the cheap seats. Preston was untouchable from where I sat, but I had a hunch he wouldn't stay that way for long.

THE DARK ROOM

The Saint Etienne show was the high-water mark for David and me. We were intensely compatible sexually, but the cracks in our friendship didn't take long to appear. He very much wanted to be boyfriends who spent all our time together, and the more I wanted to have time alone, the more frustrated he got. Things went from great at Saint Etienne to mediocre at Christine and the Queens (a killer show at the Danforth Music Hall) and finally to pretty dismal by Destroyer (a terrible acoustic set at the Great Hall). It was becoming clear that David and I weren't destined for any more concerts together. It was either all in or all out for David. I opted for all out. My choice or not, it still hurt.

What I needed was some nursing from Carolyn and my witch circle, and as luck would have it, Carolyn was hosting Mintz and a few other friends at her place the weekend after David and I pulled the plug on our brief romance.

Christina and I were sitting in a corner at the party watching our friend Celina across the room. We both admired her many talents so much. It was during this conversation at Carolyn's party that I discovered my friend Celina, from Mintz, had written and recorded a song with the incomparable Mary Margaret O'Hara. What the ever-loving fuck? For real? Christina and I were side by side on the couch, sipping some wine, when she dropped the MMO bomb. I was telling her how much I admired Celina's natural ability for playing and singing when her recording credit with Mary Margaret came up. How did I not know this? How did Celina forget to ever mention this?

Mary Margaret never made a follow-up to her incredible *Miss America* record, but she did record some new music for a film she appeared in called *Apartment Hunting*, which was released in 2000. The following year the soundtrack to the film was released with several new Mary Margaret O'Hara songs. Christina and I found the soundtrack credits online, and there it was, track three—"Rain." Celina's name, clear as day, on the songwriting credits. When we played the song on my phone, there was our friend's voice harmonizing with Mary Margaret herself. I was gobsmacked. There really was no end to Celina's talents, I thought. It's a gorgeous song.

Later that night, when I was still trying to process this information, Celina asked me if I wanted to jam sometime, just the two of us. Holy shit. Emboldened by the many glasses of wine consumed, I leapt at the chance and she and I set up a date for the following week.

While the idea of jamming with Celina sounded like a good idea after thirty-seven glasses of red wine, when the actual day approached, sober, it seemed somewhat more daunting. What had I gotten myself into? I can't reiterate enough: I don't play music. I had told her this a thousand times.

"You have instincts, I've seen it." Celina's confidence in me was unshakable. I didn't understand her ill-placed faith, but hell, if she saw something in me, maybe it was there. Even if it wasn't, we'd have some Scotch, share some laughs and play some records together.

Learning how to play music was something I had always wanted to tackle in a more serious way, but I always put it off. I killed the recorder in grade school, and in high school I was pretty good on the clarinet. I had wanted desperately to play saxophone, but so did just about every other kid in my class, so I was arbitrarily assigned the clarinet. Sigh. Another arrow to my queer heart from the quiver of the high school administration.

Sadly, Malvern Collegiate didn't make it easy to pursue my love of music and learning how to play it. Some asshole in the school music program decided that if a kid wanted to continue with music education after grade ten, they had to join the school marching band. No fucking way. I was trying to hide, to disappear, and there was no way in hell I was dressing up in a kilt and marching around the football field blowing into a clarinet.

I had dreamt about learning guitar since I was in grade school but didn't act on it until the few weeks leading up to my fortieth birthday. I was determined I was going to get over my fear, buy a guitar and learn to play. A gift to myself. Days after I bought my guitar was when I got the news that my life mentor Trish had died, followed by my father a few weeks later. I went into a pretty deep funk, mourning them both. The grief over both overlapping in my head and my heart made me a very sad and confused middle-aged gay man. Adding to my depression was the recognition that my long-term relationship with Brad was dead. No longer dying, but dead. I was stuck. Nothing like major personal catastrophes to make you reassess where you are in your life.

I was paralyzed by grief and fear. The last thing I wanted to do was put my ego aside and try to learn how to play guitar. The instrument became this strange albatross, sitting unused across the room from me. The longer I waited to pick it up, the more daunting the idea of learning to play it became. For years, I never touched that guitar. It survived the end of two relationships and four different house moves, collecting dust.

Inspired by the first Audience of One living room concert with Mintz, I finally made some peace with my guitar. I would grab it while I was watching TV or waiting for dinner to cook and pick at it here and there, idly strumming away. I found it relaxing to just noodle around. Outside of a few chords my friend Christine taught me so that I could strum along with David Bowie's "Five Years," I just did my own thing.

On the night of the jam session, Celina arrived weighed down with a pile of instruments. Amongst her guitar and a few percussion instruments was the kalimba and her one-of-a-kind berimbau—the instruments we jammed together on at my birthday party. As we sipped some Scotch and caught up with each other, my nervousness was palpable. I was fidgety and distracted. "So, how do we start?" I asked.

"Just do what you usually do when you play. Just play anything. It doesn't matter." She passed me my guitar.

Easy for you to say, Celina. I felt like a deer in the headlights sitting in the armchair across from her, my guitar resting on my knee. *Goddesses, please give me strength. Albatross, be gone.*

I plucked away and after a few minutes started repeating a run of three or four notes in a pattern I found. Celina sat up straighter, leaned towards me and just said, "Yes, keep doing that." I played the riff again and again while she watched and studied it. Once she had it memorized, I was told we were going to record it and use it as the basis to write a song.

"What the ever-loving fuck? I can't do that!" were the first words out of my mouth.

"Sure you can." Her confidence was absolute.

Okay, trust your friend, Pete. Just keep going and don't listen to that voice of doubt that always wins. Keep your foot on the neck of that albatross.

Celina pulled out her phone and told me it was time for me to record the pattern to a click track, a timed beat, so that we could add other layers on top of it. I flubbed my guitar part a few times, but she patiently stopped recording and we would start again. No drama. No frustrations. After a couple of tries I nailed it. Three or four bars of a guitar line on a constant loop. That served as the foundation for the music.

Celina found a pre-recorded beat and added it to my guitar part. Damn, we were on our way. Working with her made the process seem easy. We played the track back while she strummed some complementary parts on her guitar. She found a great groove and we recorded her guitar part next.

The kalimba would be the secret weapon. I had demonstrated a knack for playing it at my birthday the year before, but I really had no idea what I was doing. We needed a real complementary part—Celina's job. After a few different options she played a gorgeous pattern that we agreed was perfect. How could she coax the most beautiful sound out of such a primitive-looking instrument? There seemed no end to Celina's genius.

Layer by layer. Part by part. We kept at it! I loved watching the song come together in front of my very own eyes and ears. Lyrics were not going to be easy, but we looked to the name of the drumbeat and used it for inspiration. "The Dark Room" was born. Celina and I shared ideas and jotted down phrases. Slowly we shaped the lyrics into several verses and a chorus. An actual song. Thankfully, by the time we had to record the vocals, my fear was suppressed by Scotch. There was method to Celina's madness!

Singing into her phone to our pre-recorded track was a gas. We laughed and encouraged each other, and we kept going until our song was sounding pretty damn good. After several hours and putting a pretty healthy dent in the bottle of Scotch, we had a rough track. A song about queerness, finding the courage to follow the light, finding support from your friends, your community. A mini coming-out story in two and a half minutes.

We're all just here in the dark room
Standing side by side
We are all together
Somehow we'll survive
Reach for me, reach for me
Pull me to the light
Reach for me, reach for me
Push me back outside

The song's never going to see the light of day, but for the first time in my life I wrote a song. I wrote a song with a woman who had sung and written with Mary Margaret O'Hara, for fuck's sake. Put that on my gravestone, please.

Celina made it easy for me. She created a safe environment for me to explore and work with her on a shared project. The experience wasn't so dissimilar to sex—two people coming together to share some time, share some space and create something magical together. I'm never going to be a songwriter, but damn, that night felt good. I was so happy to have made a little queer baby with my good friend. I could only hope it was the first of many.

AERIAL

Soon after David and I parted ways in the fall of 2018, I noticed a friend of mine posting on social media with increasing frequency about how she was still struggling with shame for being gay. Kelly was in her late thirties, out as a queer person for almost twenty years and still trying to make sense of growing up gay. A kindred spirit.

Find a queer person and you will almost certainly find shame there. We have all experienced it. A lot of it. Some of it's buried, some of it's more obvious, and for some of us, like me, we think we've dealt with it. The more folks I talk to, though, the more I recognize that shame is ever-present in queer culture. Some of us just learn how to deal with it better. Or hide it.

Preston had finished his performances with the ballet and we had planned to catch up over a bottle of wine late on a December Monday afternoon. Our plan was to simply share space while we each worked on a creative project—me on writing, him . . . I'm actually not sure what he had planned to do, but we both had good intentions.

He arrived at five thirty and I asked him to pour some wine while I put on Kate Bush's 2005 double LP *Aerial*. It seemed a perfect choice for a dark, depressing December afternoon. Sides one and two played in the background while we caught up and shared news.

When I dropped the needle on the second album, everything changed. Preston's whole physicality morphed within a few notes of the first song on side three, "Prelude," with its simple piano intro. He bolted upright, eyes alert, and asked, "What is this?" At my answer, his body relaxed and he responded, "Of course." Our conversation stopped almost immediately. As the album progressed, he pulled a blanket over both of us and we moved closer

and closer together. I poured more wine and we were only interrupted by me getting up to flip side three to side four.

The album ends with the epic eight-minute song "Aerial,"
and by that time we were a two-man pretzel—my knees were
drawn up into his torso, his left arm came across our bodies to
stroke my left leg with his head resting against my right shoulder while I rubbed his neck. We were an intergenerational queer
pile of limbs and bodies pressed together. Twister was never this
much fun.

It was the closest I'd been with Preston physically since this
new idea of "friends" was introduced to our relationship. When
Ian, my Billy Bragg date, and I shifted from lovers to friends, it
was very natural and smooth. With Dustin it was far from easy,
but we were making good strides. With Preston, I was still
really struggling. The close physical contact was beautiful, but
I wanted more.

We took a few minutes to breathe and digest the prior forty-
two minutes. *Aerial* is a masterwork and Preston had lapped it
up; Kate Bush had done it again. He used words like *virtuoso* and
magical to describe what he'd just heard, as we both pondered
why Kate wasn't heralded as one of the all-time great musicians
in the history of recorded music.

I would argue that it's because (1) she's a woman, and (2)
she's a woman who has released some of her best music in her
forties and fifties. *Aerial* came out on November 7, 2005, and it
was the first album of original Kate Bush material in twelve
years, since her somewhat lacklustre *The Red Shoes* in 1993. Most
of us had given up hope that there would be new music from
Kate, and to hear that she had completed another record was
most welcome news to her starved fan base. To learn it was a
double album was just icing on the cake. But would it be good?
Her fans waited in breathless anticipation.

It would be good.

I went to the old HMV superstore at 333 Yonge Street (RIP), picked up my CD copy on the day of its release and raced home to listen to it. The first CD, subtitled "A Sea of Honey," is 37 minutes and 58 seconds of classic Kate, but with a distinctly more adult voice—both in actual sound and also in the songwriting and songcraft. Songs about her son, her washing machine and even pi (yup, the mathematical figure) are built slowly and effortlessly. It was good, but it didn't move me like some of her earlier work.

The second CD, "A Sky of Honey," is when shit gets real, an interconnected set of songs describing a twenty-four-hour period starting with sunrise, moving through the day to sunset, and back to sunrise again. It's a journey unto itself. It was some of Kate's best work to date, and it was so great to have her back in the cultural conversation. Critics and fans all agreed: *Aerial* was very, very, very good.

Trying to find a copy of *Aerial* on vinyl was a long and fruitless quest. It was the last of Kate's records with a major label and EMI only pressed a few vinyl copies upon release; they now cost a small fortune. Thankfully, in the fall of 2018, Kate re-released her entire catalogue on vinyl on her own label, *Aerial* included. Praise the goddesses.

To be able to give Preston his first experience of Kate Bush with *50 Words for Snow* felt like a privilege to bestow on a fellow queer. To be able to do it again, side by side on the same couch, almost a year later, with *Aerial* was a rare gift. With that double-header, I was pretty sure Preston was never going to forget me.

Once we had caught our breath, Preston asked if he could share some video footage of his dancing, as both a performer and a choreographer. Who would say no? I was thrilled. The next forty minutes we spent watching several clips of his student shows at Ryerson, and I was blown away. I always had the sense he was pretty good, but I was wrong: he was brilliant. I knew nothing about dance, but I could tell he was special. Preston moved so gracefully and effortlessly, and for better or worse, his immense beauty added to the overall effect. He was simply gorgeous up on stage, in every sense of the word.

The last piece Preston shared was one he had choreographed, featuring a cast of twelve dancers. He was nervous to share it, I could sense his unease, but he drummed up the courage and hit Play. It was spectacular. He cried a teeny bit during the viewing, and in response to his emotional openness I cried too. He explained that it was very difficult for him to share his work and to be as vulnerable as it takes to do so. It was something I understood all too well; sharing art and creative ideas can be paralyzing for me. That he was able to allow me into this part of his world felt very intimate. It was clear he was going to have to get used to it, but in that moment we celebrated the small steps.

All through the viewing and the conversation that followed we continued to be in each other's physical space. The computer sat across from the two of us, and as I stroked his neck, he stroked my knee. Finally, I mustered up the courage to ask out loud, "Do you think we'll ever have sex again?"

He laughed and thanked me for asking what we were both obviously thinking about. The response was a surprise, though: "I don't know, but I'm not having sex right now."

Goddess, what a waste. It felt as though Kate Bush's twelve-year dry spell had descended upon my couch. After the end of Preston's summer romance he had been taking a lot of time to think about his relationship to sex and intimacy. He needed the time and space to just think about it and sort it out for himself, he told me. I didn't expect a twenty-four-year-old to have that kind of self-awareness, and it inspired a very lengthy conversation about sex, intimacy and vulnerability for both of us. These are issues a lot of gay folks struggle with, regardless of age.

As my friend Kelly had laid bare on Instagram, as gay people grow up, we are all subjected to taunting and homophobia—oftentimes before we even understand what being gay is. We internalize every schoolyard use of the word *fag* or *lez* that we hear. The hatred and vitriol does not wash off our backs, as we often tell people it does. It collects in a giant pool somewhere deep down within us. By the time we realize that we are a "fag" or a "lez," we are made to believe it's the worst possible thing a person can be. Shame.

The common narrative is that, upon coming out, we realize our true selves and we erase our shame. We even have a yearly festival, called Pride, to celebrate our otherness. I think Pride and Shame can easily coexist. For so many of us, they sit side by side in our psyche.

Like Preston, many young gay people, especially men, start having sex at an early age these days. Early and almost always in secret. As a teenager, still in the closet, Preston would have clandestine meetings with men and then head back home to try to process the sex, often anonymous hookup sex, with no one to talk to about what he'd experienced and help make sense of it. It's a recipe for fucking disaster. Not a great foundation for a healthy relationship with sex and intimacy.

It was a story I had heard from many of my young lovers over the past several years. So many of them have snuck out of their parents' suburban houses at fifteen or sixteen to have sex with a stranger they had met on an app, almost always fifteen to twenty years older than them. Most of those men were kind, but not all of them. The internet and apps have made sex easily available, which is great on so many levels, but we can't be blind to how some of those hookups affect younger folks. A lot of those meetings just result in more shame for the younger boys. I think sneaking around behind their parents' backs and feeling unable to tell their friends about these encounters results in a sense of emptiness and guilt for many of these boys. It's not the sex itself, but the inability to acknowledge it.

For the first time but not the last, Preston used that same word, *shame*, to describe his feelings about sex when he was younger. He is not alone. By allowing ourselves to be vulnerable, Preston and I shared real and deep intimacy that night. It's sort of funny that we began our relationship with a fuck, and now a year and a half later we were finally exploring something even more intimate. Maybe it was a start to erasing shame for both of us.

How do we put a stop to the cycle of ignorance and shame? We need a huge cultural shift in government, education and parenting. Kids are immensely vulnerable, and despite what the right-wing idiots of the world say, teaching kids about the many sexual identities that exist in the world does not equal recruitment. Kids need to understand that sexuality and gender take all kinds of forms, and the expression of them should be encouraged, not hidden, not shamed.

Teachers and parents need to squash the taunting and the shaming. I was called a faggot by classmates hundreds of times, from as early as grade two until I faded away from high school. Many of those taunts were overheard by teachers and just ignored—condoned by their silence.

Preston felt shame. Kelly felt shame. Pete felt shame. We were all unique individuals representing queer folks in their twenties, thirties and forties, and yet we all still carried shame. Maybe shame is the queer norm, not pride.

Maybe we need to pull our heads out of our Grindr screens and start having *that* conversation more regularly, and add a little more reflection on shame to Pride.

CAREER OPPORTUNITIES

Carolyn's birthday party was an annual highlight, one of few, early in the calendar year. In February 2019, she wanted to keep things intimate and enjoy the company of her closest friends—the best way to spend a cold winter's evening, in my estimation.

The week leading up to the party, I had been interviewing for a job I wasn't sure I wanted. It was another corporate marketing gig at a local television production company. It was a great job on paper, but it was exactly the kind of role I had run away from the prior summer. My last interview felt like a formality, and I was almost certain I was going to be offered the position. On one hand, I was relieved: I needed to find a job and start making some money—my "just say no" to corporate life was starting to really hurt my bank account. On the other hand, it felt as though I was breaking a promise to myself to be free from that world and forge a new path. A party with my friends was just the distraction I needed.

When I arrived at Carolyn's apartment, all the usual suspects were there, including the full complement of Mintz. The big buzz that night was the upcoming album residency that Carolyn was hosting. She had rented a recording studio two hours east of Toronto for eighteen days to make a record of entirely new music under her name. She framed it as an "artists' retreat" and invited a few non-musicians to participate, including me. Everyone cleared their schedules to support our friend but also to take part in this amazing creative opportunity.

I was incredibly honoured. To be included felt like a gift. I planned to write and document some of the action, but I was welcome to contribute in any way I saw fit. The residency was only a few weeks away and everyone was beyond excited. We were positively giddy.

During the festivities, I spotted Christina off in a corner working on a massive India ink drawing and enjoying her own little space in the party. I filled my wineglass and crossed the room to connect with her for a chat. I knew she would be the perfect person to talk to about my potential job offer.

During our Halifax trip I had reiterated to her again and again that I was done with corporate marketing. I wanted to put my energy into something that had more meaning. Something queer. Something arts-driven. All these months later, I still didn't want to trade money for happiness. I didn't want to have to compromise myself to fit into a corporate mould again. But damn, I needed to earn some cash.

I watched Christina draw with envy and awe. Her movements on the paper were so confident, so assured. I could only dream of that kind of confidence when it came to making art. I told her about the new job opportunity and my inner conflict surrounding it. Beyond the ethical and moral quandary, I was worried it was going to interfere with my plans to go be a Mintz groupie and write at Carolyn's residency.

Christina was in a pretty meditative state between the drawing and the wine, but on hearing the news she went very, very quiet. Dead still. I sipped my wine and let her digest the news and thoughts I had just shared. I had great respect for this woman and was willing to wait for whatever pearls of wisdom she would offer.

The energy in her body all of a sudden shifted, her hand lifted off the page, her head jerked up, and she practically shouted, "Come work for me!"

Those were the last words I expected to hear. "What are you talking about?" I was completely flabbergasted.

She told me that the person who did all the entertainment programming at the Gladstone, the hotel Christina was still managing, had resigned that afternoon. I'd be the perfect person to replace her.

"You can't be serious." My inner doubt was raging. I had never done that kind of work. Surely she couldn't actually be serious?

Christina's mind was made up and she was not taking no for an answer. It was all clicking for her, I could almost see it falling into place in her mind. "You know all the bands I need you to know about, all of the tastemakers in the city, what's happening culturally, and you know how to connect people."

She wasn't wrong. When I wasn't working and meeting people in the marketing and communications world, I spent all my free time consuming arts and culture. Mostly music.

"Look around you," she instructed. "Everyone in your social circle is a musician or a comedian or an actor." It was true. Carolyn's place was packed with artists, I was the outlier, and not just because I was the only cis-gendered dude at the party. "Plus you have decades of relationship building, and practical work skills that will make my life easier. You're actually perfect."

With a few more sips of wine I was starting to come around to Christina's way of thinking. What if she was right? I never imagined that my love of going to see live music in Toronto, tracking what bands and venues were doing, going to see friends' comedy shows, attending book launches, and generally knowing what was going on culturally in my city would turn into marketable knowledge and skills. But here we were.

We kept drinking and talking about how perfect it all was while she drew. By the end of the night I was completely drunk on wine and totally intoxicated by the idea of this job opportunity. There would be no more pretending about who I was for the sake of a job. My entire career I had edited myself and my behaviour for the folks I worked with. I dulled my edges and hid my queerness to try to fit in. I could truly be myself at the Gladstone, a queer space. And "myself" was exactly what Christina wanted. I was scared shitless, but most of the good things in life terrify me at first. This would be no different.

The next day, fighting a doozy of a hangover, I texted Christina to say:

if you were serious last night, let's talk, this could be fun.

A new job in arts and culture programming in a queer space, with a queer visionary and artist as my boss—was I dreaming? I had always felt as though I faked my way into every job I got, suffering from imposter syndrome writ large. This opportunity made sense, though. With a little guidance, I could do this.

I met Christina later that day and we finalized the details. I would start in a week. My only concern was that I didn't want it to interfere with my time at Carolyn's album residency. Thankfully, Christina didn't want to get in the way of that either, and we figured out a way to work my start date around it. I couldn't wait to get started on the new job, but more importantly, I had a recording studio to get to.

IF NOT NOW . . .

I was bundled up on the evening of March 8, 2019, and squinting into the constant glare of oncoming headlights as Sarena drove us along Highway 401. We were headed to the famed recording studio the Bathouse, a few hours due east of Toronto near Kingston. It had been the Tragically Hip's recording studio and clubhouse for most of their career, and it's also famous for hosting Canadian musicians like Broken Social Scene, Bruce Cockburn, Feist, July Talk and many, many more for recording sessions. Some of the best Canadian albums in recent history have been recorded there. Carolyn had booked the studio for eighteen days, and Sarena and I were headed for day one.

The *Untitled Carolyn Taylor Project* was going to be a full album made almost entirely by queer women, and I had been granted entry to the coven for as long as I wanted to participate. I felt like the luckiest queer man in the world. With my new job at the Gladstone about to begin, I wasn't going to be able to stay for the full eighteen days, and quite frankly, it would have been weird if I had. I'm not a musician, so I wouldn't be contributing to very much of the music creation, but I would have been an idiot to pass up an invitation like this one. I planned for two separate stays, one at the beginning of the residency and another for the final few days.

During the first night at the Bathouse we were like a pack of wild teenagers let loose on spring break. Queer spring break; one where we had an entire recording studio set up with every instrument you could imagine, including a grand piano, all wired and miked for our use, with one of the best engineers in the country, Nyles Spencer, recording our every move. Not to mention eighteen days' worth of booze in the kitchen.

It was impossible to resist the energy in the space that first night, and despite having no experience, I was able to put aside my self-doubt and ended up playing drums, guitar and some keyboards. I even sang some group chants. The energy of the coven was so powerful that I was able to let go of all my many inhibitions and got swept away in the magic of it. No easy feat.

No one in the room could believe how lucky we were to be part of this group of people with seemingly endless days to create, to write, to sing, to play, to eat . . . to be with a group of folks with unending creative energy and love for each other. Not to mention the laughter. There was so, so, so much laughter. At the end of night one, Sarena and I went upstairs to the room we were sharing and crashed out on our side-by-side double beds, exhausted with joy.

As the days passed, the recording was getting done and the songs, some only half-formed, were sounding great! Heading into the project, the plan was to capture the magic as it happened. Most bands come to a studio with a cache of songs written and/or arranged, ready to bring them to life. Not this project. It was to be entirely improvised and created during those eighteen days. Ambitious.

Most of my time was spent in a corner attempting to be as innocuous as possible. I had my notebooks and my laptop and sat quietly, both documenting the action and trying to absorb the creative energy that might inspire my own writing practice. I wrote new pieces, read some of the more recent writing I had done, and wondered if it could all come together in some way to create a long-form work. But how? I still hadn't figured that big question out.

As I watched and listened, I finally started to understand why it takes so long to make records. The set-up process can feel endless at times, tuning and retuning instruments was often exhausting, and replaying and revising parts to capture the right take can be maddening. Again and again and again. But I loved it all.

I quickly discovered that playback was my favourite part of the process—hearing what had just been recorded through the studio's outrageously good sound system. Everything sounds great through a set-up as well-built as the Bathouse's.

After my first few days it was almost time for me to leave the creative nest for a short spell and go home. I had a new job to get settled into, but more importantly, Dustin and I had tickets to see Robyn. We had bought them ages before, and while I had to skip Radiohead with him for my trip to Halifax—with most of these same women—I wasn't going to miss Robyn. I still felt like a chump about the Radiohead situation. Plus, it was Robyn. Gay Christmas awaited.

Carolyn had introduced me to Robyn shortly after the 2010 release of *Body Talk*, when we were driving home from a cottage weekend together. I was hooked instantly when I heard

"Dancing On My Own" and "Call Your Girlfriend." Those songs have become so ubiquitous, it's easy to forget how good they are. While I was in my monogamous bubble with Brad, I didn't realize that Robyn had been adopted by the queer community as a hero and beacon of shared queer joy. Dustin and I were both major fans, and when we were lovers, we listened, danced and sang along to her many anthems. It would be a true treat to be able to go and experience her live show together. My plan was to return to the Bathouse in about a week, post Robyn, so I wasn't terribly crushed to go home. But it still felt as if I was leaving something so special, something I would never forget.

I almost escaped without putting my voice to tape, but during the final hours of my first stay Carolyn finally pushed me into the studio to record. I had never been recorded in a professional studio. I had used a mic before during work presentations, but this was a whole different thing and the thought of it made me nauseous. I was utterly terrified.

The Pete of a few years prior would have taken a pass. I would have tried to convince Carolyn to move on to a different track, or re-record something else. Yet the trust and joy of creation I had watched and been a very small part of gave me the courage to try. With only a few weeks to go before my fiftieth birthday, what the hell did I have to lose?

Knowing that this might happen, and to challenge myself, I had chosen the Kate Bush *50 Words for Snow* piece about Preston and our intense sexual connection. The explicit content in that story made me uncomfortable, and I wanted to confront my own shame about discussing my sexuality and desire. Something about "50 Words" before my fiftieth birthday also had a nice symmetry to it. What better way to confront my fear than at a studio surrounded by my favourite queer women?

Sarena came into the room with me for reassurance, and at Nyles's instruction I went for it. No second takes. No second chances. I made a few flubs, but all in all it felt pretty good. I had no idea if it would ever be used in the final album mix, but that wasn't really the point. Trying, trusting and speaking the truth, my truth, were the points of the exercise.

In the blink of an eye I was out of the studio and sitting in a car on my way back to Toronto, my nerves still rattling my body.

Despite my exciting new job and the Robyn gig with a favourite friend, my time in the city passed slowly. Painfully so. I simply could not wait to get back to the Bathouse.

March 20, 2019, was the day of my return to the famed recording studio. The spring equinox—an auspicious omen if ever there was one. The morning of my trip I also learned that Adam Ant would be returning to Toronto to celebrate the anniversary of his album *Friend or Foe* later in the year, another great sign. While I was away from the Bathouse, I was told, the numbers had swelled to bursting and I had missed several amazingly talented women who came through and contributed to the project. Some awesome songs were created during that time, but I was thrilled the personnel were back to the core team when I returned.

To honour the equinox, we set up a bonfire outside on the snow-covered lawn, at the lip of a forest, in the dying light of day. We sipped pink champagne to toast the transition from winter to spring as darkness fell. Last day of the winter, first day of the spring. As the night really took hold, a gorgeous full supermoon rose to bless us and we walked trancelike to the lake to worship the glowing orb. We stood at the water's edge, gazing up into the night sky, listening for cracks in the ice. When we were able to stop laughing, we could hear the low rumbles, a quiet and intermittent thunder. A sure sign that winter was receding and we were on the brink of renewal season.

I don't know if it was the supermoon, the champagne or maybe a bit of dope, but we all found ourselves back in the studio for a jam session for the ages. Nothing planned. Nothing preordained. Carolyn, Sarena, Christina and Celina all planted themselves at whatever station felt right, and Kristy and I found cozy spots on the floor surrounded by percussion instruments, wires and cords criss-crossing between us. Almost instantly we hit liftoff. The yes point.

For over eighty minutes we found another place, another level. Was this the "Hidden Place" that Björk sang about? Wherever it was, it was fertile as hell. Every time the energy lagged or a piece found an organic end, someone else took up the lead with a new line or a new rhythm and the band followed suit. While I wasn't miked, I sang, I chanted, I pounded the floor and felt as though I was contributing a small piece of the music created that night. It was otherworldly. I have never felt anything like it.

Listening to the playback, we were all shocked. It was incredible. There were easily three or four sections that would work on the album as separate songs. Talk about divine inspiration. Thank you, goddesses. Thank you, supermoon.

The next day was a bit more low-key, but we had planned a celebratory night in the loft above the barn. It was another tricked-out space filled with instruments ready for playing, and off in the corner there was Gord Downie's mic from the final Tragically Hip show. That evening was just for us, no recording, no pressure. Celina and I collaborated on beats using a drum kit and only our hands, and I swallowed my inhibitions again to step up to the mic and sing a few improvised verses of "Toodle-Pip," a Mintz classic. The creative energy was impossible to resist.

The music continued, as did the laughter—I wish that sound had been recorded. Queer joy. March 22 was a transition day. Time for Kristy to go home. Time for Christina to leave for a few days to celebrate her partner's birthday. Time for Samara, someone I had never met, to arrive. The days at the studio were dwindling and real life was creeping back in.

Late in the afternoon, while listening to some playback of the day's work in the sound room, Carolyn turned to me and instructed more than asked, "Let's do one of your pieces, right now." Everyone jumped on the idea, and with both Adam Ant and Dustin fresh on my mind, I decided that would be the piece. We filed into the studio, and as I stood there, Carolyn asked, "Where do you want us?" Four queer musicians and friends looked at me expectantly. No time to think, no time to doubt. If I had learned anything these past few days and weeks at the Bathouse, it was to just go for it, the music would follow.

"Sarena, you on bass. Celina, beats please. Carolyn, vox and any keyboards you feel. Samara, hmmm . . ." I had no idea what Samara even played, so, at Sarena and Celina's suggestion, I asked her to play harmonium and any other percussion nearby.

As the musicians moved to their corners, they asked for some guidance on what the feel of the piece was and what the sounds should be. I gave a brief rundown on the highlights of the written work and played about thirty seconds of "Kings of the Wild Frontier" from my phone so they could hear the drums I'd been obsessed with all my life. They all nodded, that seemed like enough information to get started.

It was time. I looked around the room as I stood at my mic, my computer propped up on the music stand. I almost shit myself. I was terrified. These women were there for me, though, to lift me up, to support me both musically and emotionally as I was about to read and perform a vulnerable piece. They all knew I was nervous and felt far outside my comfort zone, so they stood at the ready. Carolyn smiled at me from her seat to my left and nodded.

"Okay," I said into the mic, and away we went.

The music and Carolyn's chanting started as if it was exactly as it was supposed to be. I was dumbstruck at what was happening musically. I trusted my instincts to let the song build, and it wasn't until the thirty-second mark that I began telling my story about meeting Dustin and introducing him to Adam Ant. I wanted to just let the band jam, but I forced myself in.

Once I started, there was no turning back. I took my time and let the music have room to breathe. The witches watched me and gave each other subtle cues based on my reading. The music swelled at peaks in the text and pulled back for the quieter moments. For over sixteen minutes we played and listened and chanted, all improvising off each other. I felt as though I had left my body—sixteen of the most fulfilling minutes of my entire lifetime to date.

Queer magic. Witch magic.

I finished my reading and nodded to let the group know "that's it," stepped back from the mic, and the quartet took another thirty seconds to slowly fade out. After the final couple of notes faded away, we left a few seconds of silence in the room. I could hardly breathe. As soon as Nyles confirmed he got the take, we all let out a collective cry of astonishment. It was perfect! It was special, and we all knew it. A sixteen-minute magical baby.

I made a record. I made a song. With musicians and artists I not only admired but also loved. There had been many shocking discoveries in my late forties, but none would eclipse this one. While we listened to some of the playback, we laughed, we congratulated each other, and we all thought, "How on earth do we get this to Adam Ant?"

I will never be able to communicate to Carolyn, to all these women, how much those sixteen minutes meant to me. It has always been the women in my life who have inspired and guided me. Always. Every one of those women at the Bathouse changed my life in the most magnificent way.

FUCK THE PAIN AWAY

I had only been home from the Bathouse a few days when I woke up on March 30 with a wicked, wicked hangover. How did that happen? I had had such good intentions to spend a nice quiet Friday night at home by myself, but the goddesses had other plans.

Late in the afternoon on the twenty-ninth, Carolyn stopped by my new job at the Gladstone for a quick visit and a coffee. She was going to be meeting Andrea for a Friday night glass of wine later at the hotel and asked me to join them to do some party planning. Andrea and I were both turning fifty within a week of each other and had plans to commemorate our one hundred years on Earth with a joint party. As it happened, my birthday was on a Friday that year, so we had a date: April 5, 2019.

I waffled over the idea of throwing a party, but thankfully, Andrea came to the rescue. Neither of us felt comfortable with all the attention of a big bash, but if we held hands and jumped into our fifties together, we each figured we could enjoy ourselves by deflecting attention onto the other. We were the perfect pair of extroverted introvert birthday twins.

We had a low-key spot at a local legion hall on Dovercourt Road all sorted out . . . until we didn't. They had double-booked the venue and left us hanging in the lurch with only a few weeks' notice before the big day. Christina and the Gladstone came to the rescue, offering up the hotel's much-coveted ballroom to host our little party. Phew. Crisis averted.

Before I could enjoy "fun time" with my friends, though, I had a few more hours of my new job to do: book a band, plan a comedy night, and do some legwork on a burlesque show in the coming weeks and months at the hotel. But before I knew it, Carolyn, Andrea and I were sharing a bottle of red wine in the hotel's café bar.

Sarena and Christina joined us in due order. More wine was ordered, and the talk was so quick, it was hard to keep up. We were all still high from the album residency and were full of stories and reminiscences from only a week earlier. While we were all excited about the music created at the Bathouse, we also had a birthday party to plan, and each of these women would be playing a role. How did I end up at the cool kids' table? It took me about forty-nine years and 359 days, but I finally made it.

As our impromptu party at the Gladstone was breaking up, I got a text from dear old Dustin. He was having some friends over for a drink at his place before going to the Beaver (RIP), a legendary queer bar only a few doors down from the Gladstone on Queen Street. Did I want to join? Well, d'uh. I hopped on my bike and headed to Dustin's.

I was already pretty tipsy, but I had a couple more drinks when I arrived and smoked a little bit of dope. Both probably not great choices after my earlier wine consumption, but I was having fun, damn it! I was going to be fifty in a week, and life was short, right?

At the Beaver, I made out with a cute young ginger on the dance floor. I flirted like mad with a handsome bespectacled fellow in a one-piece flight suit who I had seen at the Gladstone earlier that day. I watched the sexy DJ get a blow job while he played music for the crowd. Very late, I drunkenly pedalled my very intoxicated ass home through the impossibly quiet streets of Toronto. All of which explains how I ended up in a horrifically hungover state.

While I was wasting the day away, recovering from the previous evening, I got a text from Justin. A text from Justin usually meant only one thing, and I was right, he was sniffing around for a sex date. I'm always horny when I'm hungover, but I wasn't sure I had the energy for a date with Justin and explained my pathetic state.

His reply: *You need a Caesar and you need to get laid.*

Who could argue with that logic?

Justin had a dinner party to get to, so he had no expectations of hanging out beyond sex. Perfect.

After a short nap and an Advil, I heard the knock at my door. Justin looked incredible. Wearing an oversized white cotton shirt with the buttons wide open, proudly displaying his hairy chest, he greeted me with a deep kiss and a squeeze of my dick. Hello to you too!

Out of his knapsack he pulled a bottle of Clamato and a Tupperware container of spice mix to rim the glasses. Something else needed rimming first. He took my hand and led me downstairs and sat me down on the bed. He undid the one button of his shirt that was clasped and let it drop to the floor. His pants and his underwear followed. I was happy to watch and admire his beautiful body and his gorgeous uncut dick from my position on the bed.

He pushed me backwards and lay on top of me as he started to kiss and grind against me. He knew my energy was lagging, so he totally took control. Justin turned me over, stripped off my pants and underwear, spread my legs, and dove in. It sounded as if he was thoroughly enjoying himself as he worked away behind me with his constant moans and gasps. His obvious pleasure took me out of my own head and my own pain.

When Justin started teasing me with that beautiful dick, it was time to turn over on my back. He put on a condom, lubed up his dick, pushed my legs over my head and plunged in. It hurt like hell, so he stopped for a second to let me adjust. I took a few breaths and then I nodded to indicate I was ready, and he started the thrusting again. He pushed in and out, taking his time. Justin told me he wanted to see me come while he was fucking me, so I did, and I could see his pleasure. He pulled out of me, ripped off the condom and jerked himself to a frenzied orgasm on top of me, and everywhere else. Justin was a hell of a sprayer.

We lay there for a minute to catch our breath, but he soon bounced up and gleefully proclaimed, "Caesar time!" I heard him puttering around in the kitchen, and after only a couple of minutes he returned to bed with a gin Caesar for each of us. It was strong, but the salted and herbed rim definitely helped in the flavour department.

Once our drinks were drained, Justin got up and prepared to split. He had places to be, people to see. If there is a better remedy for a hangover than getting rimmed and fucked by a man less than half your age, I would love to hear about it. The gin didn't hurt either.

This would be the last time I'd get laid in my forties. Getting fucked by an insanely cute twenty-two-year-old was not the worst way to see out my fifth decade on the planet. Hangover cured.

MISSING U

The Queer Songbook Orchestra was celebrating its fifth anniversary at the Longboat Hall on March 31, 2019. I was turning fifty only five days later, so it was destined to be the last show of my fifth decade, the last show of my first half century. Who better to take to the show than my buddy Dustin. We'd been fuck buddies, maybe even boyfriends, and we'd come out the other side of that as friends. Good friends. When I turned fifty, I'd be twice his age and I loved that we could share this friendship across decades. Despite my constant urging and several invitations to join me at a QSO show, he had never seen one until that night.

Dustin lived only a few blocks from the venue and it was an unusually cold late-March night. Sub-zero, ice-cold, middle-of-February temperatures. So, after parking my bike and waiting for him outside the venue, I started to get more and more annoyed with every passing minute he was late. Dustin was always late, and while I had learned to accept it, as my feet and digits started to freeze, I was less forgiving.

I was about to pull out my phone to text him when who did I see turn the corner and head towards the entrance? No, not Dustin. Jeremy Dutcher! If you don't know Jeremy, take a break from these pages this instant and do some homework. He's a two-spirit Canadian Indigenous witch genius. His first record had come out in 2018 and was a unique combination of his own classically trained voice and piano playing mixed with recordings from his Wəlastəkwiyik ancestors, a dying language with only a few speakers left alive. He won the prestigious Polaris Music Prize for that work, and while I loved the album, it wasn't until I saw him perform at the Danforth Music Hall that I really witnessed his genius come alive. He's all witch, coming from the same orbit as Yoko, Björk and Joni. Incomparable. And he hadn't even turned thirty yet.

Of course, I couldn't help but stop him to gush. Jeremy was absolutely gracious. I was certain he was there to perform that night, but when I asked, he admitted he too was only there as a fan. He asked me to hold his handbag while he smoked a joint, and I couldn't believe my good luck to be hanging outside this storied venue shooting the shit with such an amazing artist. In a flash, Jeremy took his bag back from me and went inside. No time to even suggest an alleyway or toilet blow job. Sigh.

Before my impatience could return, I looked down the street and there was Dustin. I had never been so happy for him to be late for something, and when he arrived, I excitedly told him about my chance meeting. A quick haul or two on my vape pen for a wee hit of THC and we followed Jeremy inside. The place was packed and Dustin offered to grab us a couple of beers while I found us seats.

While he was buying us a drink, I looked around and was a little starstruck. Beyond the usual QSO roster of musicians, there were a few amazing artists in attendance. There was Mary Margaret O'Hara, oh please be singing (she didn't). Oh shit, there's Oscar nominee Owen Pallett, please be performing (he didn't). Oh yay, there's my buddy Casey Mecija, solo artist, leader of Ohbijou, and dodgeball player extraordinaire . . . and she did perform. It seemed the QSO were growing their fan base, and their reputation.

There was a palpable buzz, and as Dustin sat beside me, he commented that he could feel the energy in the room. We all could. We were in for a treat.

As the show started, I put my hand on his knee and we looked at each other and smiled. It wasn't a sexual gesture, nor did it set my hand on fire the way it used to. It was just one friend acknowledging the closeness and comfort of another. I still thought Dustin was gorgeous, one of the finest-looking boys I've ever had the pleasure of having sex with, but I loved having him as my friend. It took me a while to lose the romantic attachments I had in my mind about Dustin, but I got there. And he was patient with me while I took the time to figure it out.

It was only a few songs into the show that I started to cry. Alex Samaras is a Toronto-based vocalist, queer angel and QSO mainstay; he blessed the audience with "Easy to Be Hard" from *Hair*. That song and that film have always had a special place in my heart. The song is kind of an allegory for finding your queer family—the one that supports you and loves you beyond the one that raised you, and I think a lot of queer folks in the audience connected with it.

Alex's version was so exquisite. My sniffling tears almost turned to unhinged sobs. I tried to control myself, but it wasn't easy. Dustin felt the energy and put his hand on my back to support me. I tried to convey to him what the song meant to me, but words failed me. Dustin was used to my outbursts by this point in our relationship, so we were all good. No embarrassment. No discomfort.

Dustin's turn for tears was not far behind. Thom Gill, a brilliant guitarist and singer, another queer angel and QSO regular, pulled a Robyn cover out of his hat with "Missing U." Thom's was a slowed-down, sexy and sad version of a favourite song for both Dustin and me. The lyrics detail the end of a relationship, and Robyn mourning the space that a lover, or a friend, has left behind. Whoever Robyn was missing, they were gone. Having just seen her perform the song a few weeks prior only added to the poignancy of the moment for Dustin and me. It was gorgeous. It further cemented how glad I was that I *wasn't* missing Dustin—not missing what we could have had, because what we did have was pretty fucking great.

The tears came and went as each new song was introduced with amazing stories from queer folks—some musicians, some not, some practised storytellers, most not, all sharing pieces of their own queer identity and experience with the crowd, with the world. It was like nothing else I'd ever experienced. Finally witnessing the QSO for himself, Dustin leaned over and told me, "This is incredible, I think I finally get it." I suspected he would never miss the opportunity to see these folks again.

Near the end of the show, we were treated to a celebration of the impossible-to-define Jackie Shane. A queer Black trans woman who made Toronto her home in the 1960s, she was a bona fide star of the club circuit of the time and even broke through to the mainstream with her only radio hit, "Any Other Way," in 1962. The QSO have played a small part in shining a light on Jackie's incredible legacy, and it was the phenomenal singer Lydia Persaud's job to bring the song to life that night. And she killed it. An R & B / soul classic with a horn line to die for, the band and Lydia filled the place with celebratory queer joy. It was a hell of a moment.

At the end of the show we said a few hellos to some friends and to some of the band members before Dustin and I filtered out with the rest of the audience into the cold night. We both had to work the following day, so we shared a hug and a chaste kiss at my bike as we headed off in our separate directions.

Both of us left that night changed. It happens at every QSO show I go to. Our hearts were warmed at the shared experience, at the stories, at the songs. Neither of us would ever forget it. Finally, I felt secure and solid in my friendship with Dustin. We didn't need anything from each other, we didn't desire sex from each other. We were friends. Just friends. And that was glorious. We came together thanks to a sex app and we ended up as queer family. That is something to celebrate.

A CASE OF YOU

Preston and I planned a dinner date at my place a few days before my fiftieth birthday. We both knew my birthday party would not be the time for a proper catch-up, so we made time to see each other before the big event. We hadn't seen each other for a while and he was anxious to hear about my time at the recording studio with Carolyn. And I was eager to see him.

Upon his arrival at my place, I noticed he had let his beard grow in a little bit and when I told him how good I thought it looked, he gave me a devilish grin and replied: "I'm glad you like it." Oh boy, here we go again. We just couldn't help but flirt and tease each other.

We snuggled up on the couch, arms and legs entwined as per usual, catching up and enjoying a glass of wine. We still hadn't had sex since Preston's return to Toronto and who knew if we ever would again. I told Preston it was his turn to pick a record while I started dinner. He laughed and told me I had never asked him to do that before. That seemed impossible after dozens of visits, but I guess I did like to play the tutor. He was stumped, so while he dug into my collection, I played some songs from albums I was too cool to buy in high school that I had recently picked up: "Take on Me," a-ha. "Freedom," Wham! "Walking on Sunshine," Katrina and the Waves. All great pop songs, and all songs I thought might mark me as a homo.

From his position on the floor in front of my albums he asked, "Do you have 'Human' by the Human League?"

Rarely have I been so delighted to simply reply, "Yes." I had recently picked up a copy of the album from a dollar bin and hadn't had a chance to really listen to it. But to have spent that dollar to be able to please Preston was a bargain of epic proportions.

The song is from *Crash*, the Human League's fifth full-length album. Like everyone else in 1981, I adored "Don't You Want Me" from their third, and best, album, *Dare*, but the Human League weren't my favourite band. *Dare* has a few killer tracks on it and the band were always on my radar, but I still think of them as a singles band.

The needle dropped on track three and we snuggled up on the couch for a proper listen. "Human" is a damn fine song and Preston was completely taken away, transported back to a time when he was a kid and his parents would play "Human" in the car. When he mentioned how much he loved the Jimmy Jam and Terry Lewis production sound, I was amazed by the reference. Jam & Lewis started their career as members of the Time, a Minneapolis-based band that toured and worked with Prince, but it was their production work on Janet Jackson's smash albums *Control* and *Rhythm Nation 1814* that really cemented their names in the music business. They went on to work with Janet on several other albums, as well as legendary artists like Mary J. Blige, Chaka Khan, Michael Jackson and dozens more. Not to mention Pia Zadora; no one has a flawless resumé.

Preston was right about the album sounding like a Jam &
Lewis production, and I told him how much the Human League
were stealing from those records the duo had produced.

"No, it's them," I was told.

As I grabbed the album and read the liner notes, I was
shocked. In an effort to cross over to a more mainstream pop
audience, the Human League turned to Jam & Lewis to produce
the whole damned record. I discovered that Preston was a Jam &
Lewis expert! It seemed that, in addition to the Human League,
Janet Jackson's *Velvet Rope* and *All For You* records (both produced by Jam & Lewis) were car trip soundtracks for his family
in the 1990s and early 2000s. Nothing like Janet's sexual esca-
pades for a parents' road trip with the kids.

I still don't think *Crash* is a very good record, but damn,
"Human" kills. Chalk one up to the twenty-six-year-old telling
me a thing or two. I loved that Preston had turned the tables on
me again, just as he had on our first date.

Over dinner, I shared all the stories I could remember from
my time at the Bathouse. Preston was an eager listener and
interrupted with dozens of questions about the process: How
many instruments did each woman play? What time did we
record to in the night? How did everyone improvise so many
songs in such a short time? What did we eat? His enthusiasm
was palpable; he was trying to live the experience through me
and my stories.

As Preston automatically started doing the dishes while I
tidied and put things away, I was amazed at the ease and effi-
ciency with which we worked together. Our sex had always been
marked by an easy flow of movement and silent communication,
and it was fun to discover that vibe working in the domestic
arena too. Though, let's be honest, I would rather have been
fucking Preston on the kitchen island than doing dishes, but
still, our connection was obvious.

As the candles burned down to nubs, it was time for the moment of truth. I promised him I would play the track I had recorded with the band at the Bathouse. I was so nervous, but I was ready to share it with someone. Ready to share it with him.

Wine was refreshed. The sixteen-minute song was cued up. After one final breath, I hit Play.

Sharing my writing with Preston was getting easier, but the sound of my own voice . . . agony. Part of the artist's journey is sharing the work, though, right? Preston was mostly silent throughout the track, but active. He smiled in all the right spots. He laughed when I meant for the listener to laugh. He sighed when something hit him emotionally—and apparently my words hit him often.

His judgment was quick: he loved it. And I believed him. For the first time, I had the ability to listen to the recording objectively, and I recognized that it was pretty damn good. Preston wanted to know everything about my track and I was all too happy to have him quiz me about the process that day. How many takes? Who played what? Who were these people, and when could he meet them?

Next, it was his turn. He showed me some video clips of the Cirque du Soleil show he had just been cast in. He would be playing the main character, naturally—he was the perfect fit as the host and emcee. Preston is effortlessly charming and hand-some, and I could see how that would play out in the role he was showing me. Before long I would be losing Preston to his bur-geoning performance career again.

It seemed only fitting to play some k.d. before he headed off into the night. I pulled out *Hymns of the 49th Parallel*. Released in 2004, it's an album of songs from some of her favourite Canadian songwriters. It's heady territory: Neil Young, Joni Mitchell, Leonard Cohen, Jane Siberry and more. She's a spectacular singer, k.d., and maybe even better as an interpreter of others' work than her own. No slight to her own songwriting, but she seems more at home in the words of others, her peers.

It's a beautiful record, and with the aid of the wine consumed and our dialogue about creation and performance we were immediately transported by it. We sat and listened and let k.d. wash over us. By song two, k.d.'s own "Simple" (I love her hubris and confidence at including one of her own songs with some of the best songs and songwriters Canada has ever produced), I was snuggled up beside Preston on the couch with my head resting on his chest. We just listened as my head rose and fell almost imperceptibly with his breathing.

While Joni's "A Case of You" was playing, I made a spontaneous decision. I thought I'd heard him say "I love you" to me a few weeks ago in passing but was too chickenshit to ask if I'd heard him correctly. It was an awkward moment and I wasn't sure I was ready to hear the answer, so I didn't ask for clarification. Now, I propped myself up on one elbow, inches from his face, and screwed up more courage than it took to play the track from the residency.

"I love you. In some weird and wonderful way, I love you."

My heart was bare. It was out there. Ready to be crushed. I hadn't used that word with another lover since the end of my last long-term relationship, many years before. It was a word I had used very carelessly in the past. Sometimes I meant it, often I didn't. I swore to myself I would never use that word lightly again. And there it was, hanging in the air.

"I said it first," he laughed. "I love you too."

We smiled at each other. I kissed Preston lightly on the lips and put my head back on his chest and hugged him as tightly as I could. Oddly, I felt safe; I knew Preston loved me for exactly who I was. I guess that's what love should feel like. I wasn't sure what this meant for us in the future, but it felt wonderful. A twenty-six-year-old and a days-away-from-fifty-year-old finding comfort in a real and connected love.

People often ask me what I could possibly gain from dating younger men, some young enough to be my child. Nobody expects my answer: love. Somehow, after fucking dozens of men, I had learned the difference between infatuation and love. Between sex and love. This was love. Two men of different generations who had had sex countless times, baring their souls to each other. No stated future, no hold on the other. Just love. Free-floating love.

I loved Preston. We weren't going to skip off into the sunset together forever and ever. In fact, I had no idea what the future of Pete & Preston was going to be. But I knew I loved him. And he loved me.

If this was fifty, bring it on.

(JUST LIKE) STARTING OVER

Turning fifty always seemed like an event in the far, far distant future. When I was a kid, and later a teenager, the idea of being fifty years of age was incomprehensible. Life was over. There were no new experiences. There was no fun. If my parents were anything to go by, life at fifty was mostly filled with daily drudgery and counting down the months and years until retirement—a goal that has been marketed to all of us as the golden years of golf and "freedom."

No thanks. I'd rather take "freedom" now.

When I approached Christina about Andrea and me needing a last-minute venue for our joint birthday party, her response was quick. "Oh, absolutely we're doing that here!" she replied. "No question." The only stipulation was that if it was going to be at the Gladstone, Christina was determined it would be a bash and not the intimate gathering Andrea and I had originally planned. And no party was complete without a full-on cabaret!

So be it. Andrea and I agreed to let whatever would be, be. If someone wanted to do something and perform, or make a gesture, we would let it happen. It made us both uncomfortable, neither one of us was good at asking for favours, but what the hell, you only turn fifty once. Luckily, we had a very talented group of friends, and in no time we had a stacked group of performers and several DJs, and our delightful friend Adrien volunteered to oversee sound and lights. Our little, casual drop-by party was turning into a massive event.

Through the kindness of our friends, we also had the infamous "Tower Suite" at the hotel for our use—a two-floor apartment with a kitchen, a huge living room, and a bedroom with a private deck on the rooftop of the hotel. This same room has hosted many artists and musicians over the years, including the one and only k.d.-fucking-lang. Could the goddesses provide and let me have sex in the same bed in which k.d. hopefully banged some hot piece of ass? A boy can dream.

After we checked into our room on the day of the event and enjoyed a couple of drinks with our close circle of friends, I put on my new one-piece party outfit—a navy work coverall from Mark's unzipped to the waist (no shirt required, thank you) with a turquoise bandana around my neck that Andrea lent me. Now it was time to face the music.

When Andrea and I made our way downstairs to the hotel ballroom, the place was already jammed. I didn't invite my biological family. I didn't invite the friends I grew up with. I didn't invite anyone from high school. This was queer family. My. Queer. Family.

Family, plus a pile of my recent lovers.

Ian, my Billy Bragg date, and his boyfriend were there, looking hot as hell.

Preston came solo and charmed the hell out of all who met him.

Dustin was there with his new boyfriend and a couple of other pals of his I knew. I barely saw him, but was so happy to know he was there.

William, my B-52s and Fleetwood Mac tutee, came solo, but it seemed he was more interested in Preston, Ian and Ian's boyfriend than he was with me. I could hardly blame him.

Matthew, and his tusk, came with his new live-in boyfriend, and they looked beautiful together.

I had learned so much about myself with each and every one of these men. Here were my poets, mentors, dreamers, DJs, tech nerds, teachers, writers and more—the men I had dreamt of possibly being. I saw different pieces of myself reflected in each of them. Regardless of their age, they each gave me a glimpse of the man I could be. These men accepted me exactly as I was, which helped build my confidence and maybe even gave me a tiny bit of swagger. But of equal importance, they helped me celebrate an id that I had always been too terrified to liberate. Their energies, their sex and their friendship changed me. I loved them all for it.

When it came time for the cabaret, I was having so much fun I almost forgot I had to get up onstage. Mintz agreed to play a song or two on one condition, and it was a doozy: they would only play if I agreed to perform the Adam Ant story we recorded at the Bathouse. They'd improvise and I would storytell.

Fuck. What a Catch-22. I had to do it. There was no way I wanted to turn fifty without the incredible women of Mintz performing. It was time to put aside my self-doubt about artistic expression and do it. Time to stand up and be heard. With these women supporting me, I didn't need to be afraid.

Andrea's partner, and my dear friend, Elvira kicked things off as host and emcee. As per usual, she was her funny, perfect and charming self. The room was putty in her hands.

Christina and Celina's musical project Ina unt Ina were the first performers. Every birthday party should get kicked into high gear with two unicorn-headed, purple, sparkling magical creatures singing "Sexy Bitch." They treated us to a couple of amazing tracks and the party swooned alongside me.

Our friend Jamie performed as a Stevie Nicks impersonator, Crystal Visions, and sang a gorgeous rendition of "Landslide," live. No lip-synching for this queen! Andrea and I stood arm in arm, gobsmacked, crying at our friend's talent and devotion to his muse.

Mintz treated the crowd to a great improvised set, but they had a special surprise in store. They wrapped up their performance with a new track, "Pet-Andria," a magical place and track inspired by the two guests of honour. Honestly, who has friends like this? Somehow, I do.

Without being told, I knew what the end of "Pet-Andria" meant. I was up next. Gulp. I couldn't believe it. I was standing at the lip of the stage, my dear friends behind me ready to back me up. I'd had a few drinks but was still shaking. I wasn't anywhere near ready. But if not at fifty, when would I be? My nerves were not eased by the fact that Dustin was in the audience, about to watch and listen to a story about him. Yikes.

Celina counted us in and we were off to the races. The performance had all the heft of the recorded version, but I'd whittled the text down to five or six minutes instead of the sixteen from the original track—I wasn't sure the party was ready for the entire opus. All of us onstage fell into sync almost immediately and found a sweet groove of music and storytelling. Right in the pocket.

When we were done and Mintz faded out, the place erupted. The audience, Andrea and all our friends went wild. Mintz came forward for a final bow and I was in tears. Christina and Celina to my right, Carolyn and Sarena to my left. Andrea jumped up with Elvira and we basked in the love of our friends.

This was me. Finally.

This was the life I'd always dreamt of. Standing on the stage, not quietly in the corner. A writer. A performer. Surrounded by family. My hard-earned queer family. When Mintz dubbed me "the audience of one" a few years earlier, it was the perfect moniker. I liked to keep to myself. Observe. Hide. Decide what to share. What not to share. Now, I was finally ready to let it all out and have people see me, warts and all. I had taken the long road, but I wouldn't have had it any other way.

It was a completely overwhelming moment, but thankfully, our friend Lauren was the next DJ on deck and she dropped Pete Shelley's "Homosapien" (at my request) to get us off the stage. The rest of the night I danced, flirted, sang, drank and laughed with my friends. It was a little slice of queer heaven on earth.

My birthday wish was to sneak away with Preston and have sex in my deluxe suite, but no, we were to be friends only that night. A couple of clandestine kisses on the dance floor was as far as that dream got. Having him there on this occasion and having him tell me he loved me was enough. I fell into bed that night, not with a new or old lover, but with two of my favourite queer women, Andrea and Elvira, at my side. k.d. lang should be so lucky. Lovers come and go, but your friends are always there.

I don't think I'll ever fully appreciate how lucky I was to find these women. My queer women. My witches. My coven. I truly believe it's always women who bring out the best in us, especially us queer men.

Good night, Elvira. Good night, Andrea. Good night, Carolyn. Good night, Mintz. For maybe the first time in my life, I could not wait to see what tomorrow would bring. I'd been told that life was pretty much over at fifty, but it felt as though mine was just getting started.

LOVERS IN A DANGEROUS TIME

Fifty turned out to be a fantastic year for me. I excelled at my new job at the Gladstone, delighting in work that matched my own values and moral compass for the first time in my life. I saw countless live bands that I either had booked for the hotel or went to see at other venues. I deepened my friendships with Mintz and my queer women coven. I saw many of the men I had befriended through my dating and sex life, and I met many new sexual partners. I recorded a few of my stories accompanied by a soundtrack created by Sarena and our friend Susan. I started taking PrEP. I kept writing new stories. I was fearless.

But best of all, I met the love of my life, Christopher.

Christopher is one of Canada's most renowned choreographers and dancers, and I was lucky enough to connect with him at a reception after one of his shows, *Marienbad*, in May 2019. After we eyed each other across the room of fans, he finally approached and, following a brief conversation, asked if we could go out sometime. Yes, please.

We both had busy lives and Christopher was travelling regularly, so it took several months for us to set up a date. During that first date, in November 2019, we each shared, amongst other things, that we weren't interested in monogamy within a relationship. Similar to me, Christopher had been down that road with a few partners and it hadn't worked for him either. Perfect. A sexy, smart, successful artist who had learned a few of the same lessons I had. Was he the unicorn I had been searching for?

After that first date, it was on. We fell for each other . . . and FAST! We had brilliant sex chemistry, we shared many interests, including a love of art, reading and performance, and, maybe most importantly, we made each other laugh. Every day. All the time. I had tried monogamous relationships, I had tried playing house, just like the straight folks. It didn't work. This was new. This was good. Fifty was awesome.

But, as the old saying goes, all good things must come to an end. It was during the last few weeks of my existence as a fifty-year-old, in March 2020, that Christopher and I debated the oncoming pandemic with a group of friends on the eve of the first lockdown, at Lipstick & Dynamite (RIP). Only a few weeks later I turned fifty-one, on April 5, 2020—just after the world shut down thanks to the coronavirus. For someone who liked celebrating his birthday, spending my fifty-first with a very small number of people in my backyard, visiting one or two at a time for scheduled appointments, was not the ideal. Where was Mintz? Why did my friends have to pee against the sad, withering pear tree?

Fucking COVID. I never imagined I would be so grateful to have taken the opportunity to celebrate my milestone fiftieth birthday when I had the chance. The whole world was suddenly stuck in a strange liminal place. Travel restrictions were imposed internationally and locally. Borders between countries and Canadian provinces were closed. Even travel within Ontario was frowned upon. Bars, restaurants, live music venues and record stores were all shut down. There were warnings to only leave your house for necessities. Grocery store shelves were picked clean of many of those same necessities—toilet paper, canned goods and more. People were freaked out, and I was one of them. Thank the goddesses that the Ontario and Canadian governments decreed that liquor and cannabis fell into the "necessities" category. That supply chain seemed blessedly unaffected.

On the plus side, I was newly in love, which proved a delightful distraction from the world's collapse. On the minus side, well . . . everything else. I was newly unemployed from my dream job at the Gladstone, technically furloughed, and I was terrified and unsure of what was happening in the world.

Like many at the onset of the pandemic, Christopher and I assumed the lockdown would be temporary, a few weeks at most. We decided to treat the time as a respite from the everyday routine of work, social commitments and overextending ourselves constantly. "Every night is New Year's Eve" was our new mantra, even if we didn't truly believe it. In the throes of new love, Christopher and I were still thrilled to see each other, and sex was a panacea for the craziness outside. We found comfort in our fucking but also in just being there for each other. We lived on opposite sides of town, and while everyone was mandated to stay within a close radius of their home, we broke the rules and travelled to see each other. Christopher on the east side, me on the west; I never would have predicted what a luxury biking ten kilometres across town to my boyfriend's place would come to be.

My bike rides to and fro felt like trips through a war zone. The streets were deserted, and the few people I encountered were as likely to be screaming at each other to stay away as they were to be crossing the street to avoid conflict.

Strange days.

At Christopher's loft we would open Spotify on his phone and play "pass the phone"—choosing influential songs from our youth to share with each other over his wireless speaker. Him: Jefferson Airplane. Patti Smith. Jimi Hendrix. The Beatles. Janis. He indulged me with stories of racing down to the local shop for the new 45 release of songs from all those artists. I ate it up. Sadly, those records and those stores are long gone.

Me: Depeche Mode. Kate Bush. Talk Talk. Tears for Fears. Aretha Franklin.

While the world was watching *Tiger King* on Netflix early in the lockdown, Christopher and I were diving into my record collection and having dance parties for two in my living room. Out came so many of my classic LPs: Tom Tom Club. Talking Heads. Grace Jones. The B-52s. Twelve-inch singles I hadn't played in decades became salve for our lagging spirits. We danced and dreamt of easier times, of an end to this pandemic so life could resume. Both of us found comfort in the music we identified with. We told each other what we knew about the artists we loved and what they meant to us at different times in our lives. It was a joy to share these stories and experiences with each other, to learn from each other.

Dancing in front of Christopher was no easy task, though. Having seen his brilliance onstage in front of an audience of admirers, to dance in front of him was intimidating as hell. But I was aided by copious amounts of wine and edibles and threw myself into the task with as much gusto as I could muster.

We were having great sex, but, irony of ironies, we found ourselves "COVID monogamous" in the spring of 2020 whether we liked it or not. All of a sudden meeting men for sex, strangers or not, felt like a massive risk. And that risk felt all too familiar. The language public health agencies used around mounting COVID case counts and "testing positive" further triggered my deep-seated fear of the HIV virus. Hearing those two words, *testing positive*, mainlined fear and panic into my brain again. I was newly terrified of meeting men for sex. The response to COVID was nothing like the AIDS crisis, though. It took years and countless deaths before governments and health agencies reacted to HIV/AIDS in the 1980s.

Despite our best efforts to have fun and enjoy our COVID spring, a new fear was setting in: this pandemic was here to stay. How long would the epidemic and the lockdown last? Only time would tell, but I was definitely wrong about it ending after a few weeks or months. Way wrong. Shit was getting real. All of a sudden a massive social circle didn't seem so important; having a few close friends was.

With endless days and weeks to do nothing but think, I was going deep into my psyche. All the things that were dear to me were falling away; there was no live music, there were no parties with friends, there was no job to go to, and Carolyn and Christina had both left the city, leaving me feeling a bit rudderless. Other friendships were fading away as it seemed everyone was going through a friendship cull, leaving less-rewarding relationships to wither on the vine.

Christopher and I had the luxury of having friends with beautiful cottages to stay in throughout the summer of 2020. Again, we were the lucky ones. Getting outside the city, the war zone, never felt so good. We knew many people who created COVID bubbles, small circles of friends with whom to socialize and spend time. Christopher and I were too scared for that, so we kept to a bubble of two.

I had never been so fascinated with birds and squirrels and anything else that might be happening in the natural world as I was during the summer of 2020. The feeling of grass under my feet. The reflection of light on water. A fish cresting the surface of a lake. All these things took on new-found resonance for me. We would sit by the lake in the morning with coffee, or on a porch overlooking grass and trees, and talk about our dreams, what our subconscious minds were trying to tell us. During our REM sleep, both of us were having vivid dreams and reliving formative life events, good and bad, trying to make sense of our lives up to that point. We were living in very confusing times. Who else to help us make sense of it all but the incomparable Joni Mitchell? During that summer of 2020, there was no other artist I listened to more. Thank the goddesses for Joni.

Christopher helped me take a much closer look at 1972's *For the Roses*, one of his favourite Joni records. I had sort of overlooked it as a lesser *Blue*, but upon closer inspection her development as an artist from *Blue* to *Court and Spark* is so beautifully mapped out on this record. The use of more instrumentation beyond her voice, guitar and piano. The hints of jazz. It's breath-taking. I played the holy trifecta of *Court and Spark*, *The Hissing of Summer Lawns* and *Hejira* for Christopher. Has there been a better run of five consecutive albums in the history of recorded music than *Blue* to *Hejira*? Quite simply, no. It's unlikely we'll ever see it happen again. We'd lie back in the late afternoon or early evening and marvel at Joni's wordplay, her musical sophistication, her voice. They broke the mould when Joni Mitchell was born. Truly a one-of-a-kind artist.

All the introspection came back to one thing for me: gratitude that I met Christopher when I did. While some folks were left grasping for connection at the outset of the pandemic, we had a head start of several months to decide that we loved each other. For me, our time in lockdown only strengthened what we had and helped confirm for me that I really liked spending time with this fellow—every minute, every hour. Christopher and I had no idea where our paths would lead us, but we were definitely making a life together. Dreaming of a future together.

Miraculously, as the summer progressed, the infection rates were waning, along with the summer light. After many long conversations and an evaluation of risks (real and imagined), Christopher and I decided to open up our relationship again—it was time to call a few old friends. Our relationship went from COVID monogamous to COVID very-cautiously-and-selectively-non-monogamous. Stepping out never felt so good. It wasn't without some trepidation, though. Was human connection, sex, going to result in me acquiring a potentially deadly virus? Ugh. Here we were again.

Christopher and I hardly went wild, but we each had a few dates with old and trusted friends. We even collaborated on the first threesome of my life. It was thrilling. The few times we did connect with other men, we made sure to keep our distance from other friends or relatives—creating our own post-sex quarantine guidelines. We didn't want to endanger any of our close circle based on our sexual proclivities. Truth be told, I'd have traded in those sexual adventures for a few good hugs from a few of my closest friends—give me Mintz, give me Andrea and Elvira! But everyone was working on their own schedule, their own timetable.

When I look back on the summer of 2020, those halcyon days of Joni and reintroducing some casual sex back into my life seem so innocent. As the days began to get colder and darker, a stark new reality was setting in: this fucking pandemic was just getting started. By the fall of 2020, COVID case counts were climbing, restrictions were getting tighter again, and my job prospects were still pretty grim. Christopher and I were back to COVID monogamy. The COVID dance parties for two were fewer and farther between, but we were still taking great joy in each other's company. In each other's body. Our connection was truly deepening while the world was going insane around us.

I turned to some of the masters for wisdom during those dark days. Like Yoko, a handful of my favourite artists put out records in the latter parts of their careers that seemed tailor-made for the days we were living in. It was time to listen to what Leonard, Marianne and Bob had to say.

Leonard Cohen, Marianne Faithfull and Bob Dylan, all in their seventies and eighties, had recently released records of new material. Cohen's *You Want It Darker* was released in 2016, Faithfull's *Negative Capability* came out in 2018, and finally Dylan's *Rough and Rowdy Ways* was launched smack dab in the middle of the pandemic, in June 2020. Each work is about making connections—with friends, lovers, collaborators and sometimes with audiences. Leonard, Marianne and Bob weren't fools; none of them wished they had worked harder, made more money, bought more expensive cars. These incomparable artists were exploring death, lives lived and how it feels to stare down the end. These themes were definitely the kind of work I was interested in exploring during those dark times.

Christopher and I were doing the same thing. We weren't prepping for death per se, but we were questioning everything: our work prospects and goals, whether we wanted to live in the city any longer, if we had the energy and ideas to create. We were two people irreversibly changed by the COVID pandemic.

As Mr. Dylan sang on *Rough and Rowdy Ways*, I like to think that I too contain multitudes. I can be many things. I tried for so long to define myself by other people's rules and expectations, and always failed myself. Fuck that. I was finally figuring out who I wanted to be. Listening to these three troubadours sing about their lives and dreams only helped me feel more strongly about pursuing my own life path.

My next birthday landed on a very cold April 5, 2021. With Andrea, Elvira and Christopher all at my side in the backyard, we celebrated my fifty-second birthday with the best gift I could possibly have hoped for: a confirmation for my first dose of a COVID vaccine, scheduled in only a few days. Hope, packaged up in a little vial of clear fluid. Amazingly, a vaccine was created, tested and ready for distribution within twelve and a half months of the first lockdown in 2020. Blindingly fast, it seemed. And for free—no cost at all. Now, how about one for HIV? I guess it's all about resources and who holds those purse strings. PrEP is brilliant, but prohibitively expensive for many. How about we eradicate HIV for good by investing in a vaccine and making PrEP available at no cost immediately? Oh, right, capitalism.

The vaccine didn't spell the end of the pandemic as quickly as we all hoped, but it did signal the start of something new. A rebirth of sorts. I spent the next year relearning how to engage with the world. It was not easy. Parties and bigger social gatherings still scared the shit out of me, but I forced myself to go to a few. After every outing I monitored my health like a man possessed; with every headache or tickle in my throat I was convinced I had acquired COVID.

The vaccine gave Christopher and me the confidence to open up our relationship yet again. COVID monogamy was a thing of the past, even if I didn't jump into the hookup pool as gleefully as I once did. But it sure felt good to be touched and desired by new friends again.

My greatest of birthday gifts was yet to come.

As we approached my fifty-third birthday, Christopher received a grant to create a new solo dance piece and quietly started going to rehearsals to work on his project at the Citadel, a rehearsal and performance space devoted to dance on Parliament Street. I wanted to know all about it, but he was incredibly tight-lipped about the work. I chalked up his reluctance to his artistic process, and at Christopher's request I would have to wait until the premiere to see what he was working on. All he told me was that Thom Gill, our friend from the Queer Songbook Orchestra, was recording all the music that would be used. The two artists had collaborated many times during Christopher's career, and we both knew Thom would bring his particular brand of genius to the project in the most beautiful way.

The premiere of *New Tricks*, Christopher's new work, was scheduled a few days before my birthday. On opening night I sat in the Citadel, with many of our friends in attendance saying hello and giving tentative hugs; hugs were handed out so freely before the pandemic and now had to be negotiated each and every time. The pre-show playlist Christopher had curated was loaded with a few favourites from our pandemic dance parties: Pete Shelley's "Homosapien," Depeche Mode's "Strangelove," Talk Talk's "It's My Life" and several more. It felt like a party and the show hadn't even started yet.

A few minutes past the posted start time, the lights dimmed, the energy in the room shifted. Showtime. My beautiful boyfriend walked out onstage and the entire room hushed in anticipation; I was clearly not Christopher's only fan.

The first piece started to a rendition of a Blossom Dearie song that Christopher had introduced me to during our many days and nights together during COVID lockdowns, and I watched him move across the stage with a curious combination of awe and pride. His movements were so unexpected and striking. The second song started, and it too was a familiar one: a Nina Simone track that we had listened to repeatedly during the pandemic. It dawned on me that this was more than a coincidence, and my emotions started to get the better of me by this point. My eyes were watery, my heart was pounding.

When I heard "Deeper Well" by Emmylou Harris start, my suspicions were confirmed. Christopher had created a dance piece to a soundtrack of the songs we had shared over the course of the pandemic. I started crying in earnest and barely stopped for the remainder of the show. For me, the next sixty minutes were like those long-ago nights on his couch passing the phone back and forth and playing our favourite songs for each other. I know Christopher's motivations and inspirations for *New Tricks* went far wider and deeper than just our relationship, but I saw and heard what I wanted to. Isn't interpreting art up to the viewer, after all?

A solo dance piece created and performed by my boyfriend to a playlist of music recorded by the Queer Songbook Orchestra's Thom Gill with vocal contributions by QSO mainstays Alex Samaras and Lydia Persaud. Queers making art together was the best way out of a pandemic, in my opinion. The best path forward for my life.

New Tricks was a document of our love during the pandemic. A thing of beauty. It was a birthday gift far beyond my own imagination. The soundtrack to my queer joy is almost impossible to define, but the one Christopher created for *New Tricks* comes pretty damned close.

In the aftermath of his show I marvelled at how lucky
Christopher and I were to be able to share our story, and the art
he created to our favourite music during such a dark time. How
many soundtracks were lost, or never got made, during the AIDS
pandemic? The stories of men who didn't make it, whose lives
were cut short long before their fifty-third birthdays, before the
second pandemic in my lifetime. Christopher and I were definitely the lucky ones.

I still needed to find a job that made me happy, do some
writing and figure out what I wanted to be when I grew up, but
even so, I approached fifty-three with renewed optimism; more
muted than at fifty, but I had hope, I had my coven, and I now
had a beautiful partner by my side.

It had taken me over fifty years, but I was finally able to find
love on my own terms, completely outside the heteronormative
paradigm. I had a deep love for my partner but was also free to
explore my sexuality and connect with other men whenever I
wanted to. This was the relationship I had always wanted, but
I needed to invent it entirely on my own, with Christopher's
help, of course. A truly queer partnership.

On the other side of COVID, it was time for a new start yet
again. How many new starts do we get in this life? Never believe
you can't just lift the needle and start the record all over again.

How do we begin anew? Day by day. Track by track. Album
by album.

I needed to call Preston, text Dustin. Boot up Scruff, turn
on Grindr. Buy a few new records. I had a life to live and new
stories to write.

It was time to start curating a new soundtrack.

THANKS & ACKNOWLEDGEMENTS

To the entire Penguin Random House Canada team, but most of all Sue Kuruvilla, Evan Klein and Scott Sellers—thank you for letting me cry in your boardroom and believing in this project. In particular, thanks to Scott for taking care of me with such tender kid gloves and making this first-time writer feel so valued. Additionally, thanks to Geffen Semach for your editorial eye and Lisa Jager for the incredible cover design.

Christopher House—thanks for putting up with me; I know it's not easy. I love you and thank you for listening to me and helping to puzzle out this book with me. Your artistry continues to be an inspiration.

All the readers and people I talked with ad nauseam regarding this project—Cecilia Berkovic, Nick Breyfogle, Kristin Briggs, Aurora Browne, Simon Carpenter, Keith Cole, David Demchuk, Anne DesBrisay, David DesBrisay, Ali Eisner, Susan Gale, Rachel Giese, Ian Gilchrist, Kate Glover, Samantha Hodder, Christopher House, Elvira Kurt, Mae Martin, Rachel Matlow, Marcus McCann, Christopher Miller, Mintz, the Nyhuus family (Erik, Ken, Pete, Sam and Thom), Andrea Ridgley, Colin Salter, Shannon Smith, Jordan Tannahill, Jenn Whalen, Zoe Whittall, Preston Wilder, Storey Wilkins, Ashley Wilson, Jeff Wilson and Marnie Woodrow—your ideas, advice and creative energies helped make this book real.

Mintz: Celina Carroll, Sarena Sairan, Carolyn Taylor and Christina Zeidler. What more can I say that isn't in this book? But thank you for nurturing my creative voice, for being kind and for never laughing at me, just with me. Each of you continues to be an inspiration.

Jen Moroz and Hilary Doyle—you two were the best writing group I could have asked for. Thank you for making me a "Woostie" and for pushing my ideas and voice forward.

FADO Performance Art Centre and the "Performance Club 2: Valley of the Dolls with Keith Cole." Shannon Cochrane and Keith—you made book club so much fun! The homework you assigned during Performance Club 2 truly informed this book and my writing. Thank you both, and to all the participants.

Sake of Sound: Susan Gale and Sarena Sairan. Your creative energies helping me soundtrack my stories helped give me confidence in this project. Let's make more musical stories!

Gibraltar Point Centre for the Arts—allowing me to complete a residency on Toronto Island was a game changer for me as a writer and for the content of this book. I loved being there and was amazingly prolific that week. Please continue to do the important work that you do.

The Queer Songbook Orchestra—thanks for setting such a high bar and introducing me to such a beautiful way to tell queer stories. Performing with you will forever be an artistic highlight of my life.

The Gladstone still stands but the ownership changed during the COVID pandemic. It's no longer queer managed, nor does the cultural programming reflect the utopia that was built briefly there. Thank you to all who made it so great in its heyday. Another queer space gone from Toronto's landscape.

To all the men—the ones in the book, the ones who didn't make the final cut and all the ones I hope to meet—thanks for sharing your stories and your energies with me.

Mom and Dad, thanks for always supporting my vinyl habit and love of recorded music.

For the sake of expediency, and privacy, a few of the men and situations described in this book are composites of multiple people and events.

Since I completed this book, the music community has lost Shane MacGowan, Christine McVie, Sinéad O'Connor and many others not featured in my storytelling. Thank you for sharing your artistry, and peace be with your families and fans.

Like many cities, Toronto has lost countless queer spaces since the writing of this book and in the aftermath of the COVID pandemic. The community is a lesser place in the absence of each of them.

PETE CRIGHTON has worked as a marketing executive in the arts for many years. He has also studied comedy at Second City, graduating from their Conservatory Program in improv, scene writing and performance and still sings (badly) in the Dolly Parton choir "the Tennessee Mountain Homos." He lives in Toronto.